Political Science: In New World Order

Political Science: In New World Order

Amir Ansari

2008

CYBER TECH PUBLICATIONS
4264/3, Ansari Road, Daryaganj, New Delhi-110002 (India)
Ph.: 011-23244078. Fax: 011-23280028
E-Mail: cyberpublicationsdelhi@yahoo.com

POLITICAL SCIENCE: IN NEW WORLD ORDER

Amir Ansari

First Edition 2008

Published by :

G.S. Rawat for **Cyber Tech Publications**
4264/3, Ansari Road, Daryaganj, New Delhi-110002 (India)
Ph.: 011-23244078. Fax: 011-23280028
E-Mail: cyberpublicationsdelhi@yahoo.com

Printed at : **Amit Enterprises**, Maujpur, Delhi, (9810878184)

Preface

There is a respectable impulse-indeed an honoured tradition-in political science that urges political scientists to stay "relevant" to contemporary problems. I am prepared to guess that fully half the research agenda of the discipline-maybe more-is generated in response to various current events: wars, elections, laws, crime rates, scandals, press releases, those sorts of things. In this volume I have presented at least one example of a review of literature that follows the news pretty closely. Attentiveness to current affairs is of course only one of the stigmata of our particular scholarly community.

Our other distinctive features include broad agreement on standards of discourse, mutual attentiveness to the substance of one another's work, and the reasonable chance that through the consideration of that work by many minds, and its passage through many hands, over time a consensus can be established about what we believe, at least for the time being, to be true or useful on topics covered by our studies. This of course does not mean that our community is always shielded from mistakes. Valuable and truthful contributions can be ignored and even winnowed out of the contemporary consensus of political scientists, and foolish ideas are on occasion carried along in the main stream. It happens. Obviously, we hope it does not happen too frequently or for too long. Such a hope is given concrete embodiment in customs widely shared among academic disciplines that permit the entry of voices expressing disagreement or criticism, or offering new ways of approaching old subjects.

Here in this book I have tried to bring all the aspects of political science viz. ancient and contemporary but it is quite impossible to bring whole subject in a nutshell. Still I hope readers will find it interesting to go through the book. Your feedback boost us to do something more better so keep giving feedback.

—Author

Contents

Preface

1. Antecedents of Political Science 1
2. History of Political Science 20
3. Political Philosophy 45
4. Essentials of Political Science 99
5. Politics 174
6. Democracy 194
7. Constitutional Structure 224

Bibliography 266

Index 270

1

Antecedents of Political Science

While the study of politics in the Western tradition is first found in ancient Greece, political science is a late arrival in terms of social sciences. However, the discipline has a clear set of antecedents such as moral philosophy, political philosophy, political economy, history, and other fields concerned with normative determinations of what ought to be and with deducing the characteristics and functions of the ideal state. In each historic period and in almost every geographic area, we can find someone studying politics and increasing political understanding.

In ancient India, the antecedents of politics can be traced back to the Rig-Veda, Samhitas, Brahmanas, and Buddhist Pali Canon. Chanakya (c. 350-275 BC) was a professor of political science at Takshashila University, and later the Prime Minister of Mauryan emperor Chandragupta Maurya. Chanakya is regarded as one of the earliest political thinkers, and is also known as the Indian Machiavelli. He wrote the Arthashastra, which was one of the earliest treatises on political thought, economics and social order, and can be considered a precursor to Machiavelli's The Prince. It discusses monetary and fiscal policies, welfare, international relations, and war strategies in detail, among other topics on political science.

The antecedents of Western politics can also trace their roots back even earlier than Plato and Aristotle, particularly in the works of Homer, Hesiod, Thucydides, Xenophon, and Euripides. Later, Plato analyzed political systems, abstracted their analysis from more literary-and history-oriented studies and applied an approach we would understand as closer to philosophy. Similarly, Aristotle built upon Plato's analysis to include historical empirical evidence in his analysis.

STUDIES

The advent of political science as a university discipline is evidenced by the naming of university departments and chairs with the title of political science arising in the 1860s. Integrating political studies of the past into a unified discipline is ongoing, and the history of political science has provided a rich field for the growth of both normative and positive political science, with each part of the discipline sharing some historical predecessors. The American Political Science Association was founded in 1903 in an effort to distinguish the study of politics from economics and other social phenomena.

In the 1950s and the 1960s, a behavioral revolution stressing the systematic and rigorously scientific study of individual and group behavior swept the discipline. At the same time that political science moved toward greater depth of analysis and more sophistication, it also moved toward a closer working relationship with other disciplines, especially sociology, economics, history, anthropology, psychology, and statistics. Increasingly, students of political behavior have used the scientific method to create an intellectual discipline based on the postulating of hypotheses followed by empirical verification and the inference of political trends, and of generalizations that explain individual and group political actions. Over the past generation, the discipline placed an increasing emphasis on relevance, or the use of new approaches and methodologies to solve political and social problems.

The national honor society for college and university students of government and politics in the United States is Pi Sigma Alpha.

CONTEMPORARY STUDIES

Political scientists study the allocation and transfer of power in decision-making, the roles and systems of governance including governments and international organizations, political behavior and public policies. They measure the success of governance and specific policies by examining many factors, including stability, justice, material wealth, and peace. Some political scientists seek to advance positive theses by analyzing politics. Others advance normative theses, by making specific policy recommendations.

The study of politics is complicated by the frequent involvement of political scientists in the political process, since their teachings often provide the frameworks within which other commentators, such as journalists, special interest groups, politicians, and the electorate analyze issues and select options. Political scientists may serve as advisors to specific politicians, or even run for office as politicians themselves. Political scientists can be found working in governments, in political parties or as civil servants. They may be involved with non-governmental organizations (NGOs) or political movements. In a variety of capacities, people educated and trained in political science can add value and expertise to corporations. Private enterprises such as think tanks, research institutes, polling and public relations firms often employ political scientists. In the United States, political scientists known as "Americanists" look at a variety of data including elections, public opinion and public policy such as Social Security reform, foreign policy, U.S. congressional power, and the Supreme Court-to name only a few issues.

ALTERNATIVE TERMS

Alternative terms for the academic study of politics are political studies, or even politics. While political science implies use of the scientific method, political studies implies a broader approach. The term politics is used at the University of California, Santa Cruz, New York University, and Princeton University while the term government is used by Smith College, Dartmouth College, Harvard University, Cornell University, Georgetown University, University of Sydney, University of Ulster, Victoria University of Wellington (which has both a School of Government and a separate Political Science and International Relations Programme) and the London School of Economics and Political Science to describe the field, but the choice of a label for a department often has little to do with how the subject is studied.

POLITICS

Politics is the process by which groups make decisions. Although the term is generally applied to behavior within governments, politics is observed in all human (and many non-human) group interactions, including corporate, academic, and religious institutions. In general, politics can be considered the art of navigating through tensions among multiple "I"s and the "we" to achieve collectively desired ends. For the Greek philosophers, politics was the means by which philosophy came into practicality. Political Philosophy is the study of what politics is and what the best regime is. Political philosophy is the study of the polis (Greek roughly meaning City). This is the mother field in the study of politics. Political science (also political studies) is the study of political behavior and examines the acquisition and application of power. Government Properly speaking, Government is study of one's political regime. It is the lesser of all study of politics.

DEFINITIONS

- Power Max Weber defined power as the ability to impose one's will upon another, while Hannah Arendt states that "political power corresponds to the human ability not just to act but to act in concert."
- Authority is the ability to enforce laws, to exact obedience, to command, to determine, or to judge.
- A government is the body that has the authority to make and enforce rules or laws.
- Legitimacy is an attribute of government gained through the acquisition and application of power in accordance with recognized or accepted standards or principles.
- Sovereignty is the ability of a government to exert control over its territory free from outside influence.

POLITICAL IDEOLOGIES

Left-Right Politics

Most political analysts and politicians divide politics into left wing and right wing politics, often also using the idea of center politics as a middle path of policy between the right and left. The meaning of left-wing and right-wing varies considerably between different countries and at different times, but broadly speaking, it can be said that the right wing is linked to moral and social conservatism, law and order, and religion, while the left wing is linked with redistribution of wealth and resources towards the poorer and disadvantaged sections of society and secularism. The right wing is more often linked to the idea of social equity, and the left wing to the idea of social equality. The right wing also tends to be more traditional, while the left wing is generally more likely to experiment with new ideas.

Certain politicians have tried to transcend the left-right divide, such as Manuel Gómez Morín, De Gaulle, Juan Peron, and Jean-Pierre Chevènement. Christian Democracy is notable for its claim to combine left and right wing politics. Manuel Gómez Morín is particularly notable for developing his idea of "national action" in rejection of left-right politics.

Authoritarian-Libertarian

While left and right refer to different methods of developing an economically stable and just society, authoritarianism and libertarianism refer to the amount of freedom, liberty and sovereignty each person possesses in that society relative to the state.

THEORETICAL VIEW OF POLITICAL POWER

Many questions surround the political notion of power with both positive and negative aspects attached to it. Generally, power is considered integral to politics and is the subject of a great deal of debate. Many academics define political power by referring to various academic disciplines including politics, sociology, group psychology, economics, and other facets of society. The multiple notions of political power that are put forth range from conventional views that simply revolve around the actions of politicians to those who view political power as an insidious form of institutionalized social control-most notably "anarchists" and "radical capitalists". The main views of political power revolve around normative, post-modern, and sociological perspectives.

NORMATIVE FACES OF POWER DEBATE

The faces of power debate has coalesced into a viable conception of three dimensions of power including decision-making, agenda-setting, and preference-shaping. The decision-making dimension was first put forth by Robert Dahl, who advocated the notion that political power is based in the formal political arena and is measured through voting patterns and the decisions made by politicians.

This view was seen by many as simplistic and a second dimension to the notion of political power was added by academics Peter Bachrach and Morton Baratz involving agenda-setting. Bachrach and Baratz viewed power as involving both the formal political arena and behind the scenes agenda-setting by elite groups who could be either politicians and/or others (such as industrialists, campaign contributors, special interest groups and so on), often with a hidden agenda that most of the public may not be aware of. The third dimension of power was added by British academic Steven Lukes who felt that even with this second dimension, some other traits of political power needed to be addressed through the concept of 'preference-shaping'.

This third dimension is inspired by many Neo-Gramscian views such as cultural hegemony and deals with how civil society and the general public have their preferences shaped for them by those in power through the use of propaganda or the media. Ultimately, this third dimension holds that the general public may not be aware of what decisions are actually in their interest due to the invisible power of elites who work to distort their perceptions. Critics of this view claim that such notions are themselves elitist, which Lukes then clearly admits as one problem of this view and yet clarifies that as long as those who make claims that preferences are being shaped explain their own interests etc., there is room for more transparency.

Postmodern Challenge of Normative Views of Power

Some within the postmodern and post-structuralist field claim that power is something that is not in the hands of the few and is rather dispersed throughout society in various ways.

AUTHORITY AND LEGITIMACY

Max Weber identified three sources of legitimacy for authority, known as the tripartite classification of authority. He proposed three reasons why people follow the orders of those who give them:

Traditional

Traditional authorities receive loyalty because they continue and support the preservation of existing values, the status quo. Traditional authority has the longest history. Patriarchal (and more rarely matriarchal) societies gave rise to hereditary monarchies where authority was given to descendants of previous leaders. Followers submit to this authority because "we've always done it that way." Examples of traditional authoritarians include absolute monarchs.

Charismatic

Charismatic authority grows out of the personal charm or the strength of an individual personality. Charismatic regimes are often short-lived, seldom outliving the charismatic figure that leads them.

Examples of Charismatic regimes include: Julius Caesar, Augustus, Hitler, Napoleon, Mao Zedong, and Fidel Castro.

For a charismatic regime to survive the rule of the individual personality, it must transform its legitimacy into a different form of authority. An example of this would be Augustus' efforts to create the position of the Roman principate and establish a ruling dynasty, which could be viewed as a shift to a traditional form of authority, in the form of the principate that would exist in Rome for more than 400 years after his death.

Legal-rational

Legal-rational authorities receive their ability to compel behavior by virtue of the office that they hold. It is the authority that demands obedience to the office rather than the office holder. Modern democracies are examples of legal-rational regimes. People also abide by legal-rational authority because it makes sense to do so for their own good, as well as for the greater good of society.

Other Considerations

Often hybrid forms of the above will be found, especially in transition from one form to another, such as in the transition from the Weimar Republic to the Nazi domination of Germany, in which the Nazi party gradually suspended many laws regarding various civil rights for an indefinite period.

INTERNATIONAL RELATIONS

International relations (IR), a branch of political science, is the study of foreign affairs of and relations among states within the international system, including the roles of states, inter-governmental organizations (IGOs), non-governmental organizations (NGOs), and multinational corporations (MNCs). It is both an academic and public policy field, and can be either positive or normative as it both seeks to analyze as well as formulate foreign policy. Apart from political science, IR draws upon such diverse fields as economics, history, law, philosophy, geography, sociology, anthropology, psychology, and cultural studies. It involves a diverse range of issues, from globalization and its impacts on societies and state sovereignty to ecological sustainability, nuclear proliferation, nationalism, economic development, terrorism, organized crime, human security, and human rights.

The history of international relations is often traced back to the Peace of Westphalia of 1648, where the modern state system was developed. Prior to this, the European medieval organization of political authority was based on a vaguely hierarchical religious order. Westphalia instituted the notion of sovereignty, which essentially meant that rulers, or sovereigns, would recognize no internal equals within a defined territory, and no external superiors. Classical Greek and Roman authority at times resembled the Westphalian system, but both lacked the notion of sovereignty. Westphalia encouraged the rise of the nation-state and the institutionalization of diplomacy and armies. This particular European system was exported to the Americas, Africa, and Asia via colonialism and the "standards of civilization". The contemporary international system was finally established through decolonization during the Cold War. However, this is somewhat over-simplified. While the nation-state system is considered "modern", many states have not incorporated the system and are termed "pre-modern". Further, a handful of states have moved beyond the nation-state system and can be considered "post-modern". The ability of contemporary IR discourse to explain the relations of these different types of states is disputed.

INTERNATIONAL RELATIONS THEORY

What is explicitly recognized as international relations theory was not developed until after World War I, and is dealt. IR theory, however, has a long tradition of drawing on the work of other social sciences. The use of capitalizations of the 'I' and 'R' in International Relations aims to distinguish the academic discipline of International Relations from the phenomena of international relations. Many cite Thucydides' History of the Peloponnesian War as the inspiration for realist theory, with Hobbes' Leviathan and Machiavelli's The Prince providing further elaboration. Similarly, liberalism draws upon the work of Kant and Rousseau, with the work of the former often being cited as the first elaboration of Democratic Peace Theory. Though contemporary human rights is considerably different than the type of rights envisioned under natural law, Francisco de Vitoria, Hugo Grotius and John Locke offered the first accounts of universal entitlement to certain rights on the basis of common humanity. In the twentieth century, in addition to contemporary theories of liberal internationalism, Marxism has been a foundation of international relations.

THE STUDY OF IR

Initially, international relations as a distinct field of study was almost entirely British-centred. In 1919, the first Chair in International Politics established at the University of Wales, Aberystwyth, from an endowment given by David Davies, became the first academic position dedicated to IR. In the early 1920s, the London School of Economics' department of International Relations was founded at the behest of Nobel Peace Prize winner Phillip Noel-Baker. In 1927 the first university institution entirely dedicated to the study of IR, the Graduate Institute of International Studies (Institut universitaire de hautes études internationales), was founded in Geneva, Switzerland; it sought to supply a pool of specialized personel for the League of Nations. While schools dedicated to the study of IR have been founded in Asia and South America, IR as a discipline remains to be studied chiefly in Europe and North America.

EPISTEMOLOGY AND IR THEORY

IR theories can be roughly divided into one of two epistemological camps: "positivist" and "post-positivist". Positivist theories aim to replicate the methods of the natural sciences by analysing the impact of material forces. They typically focus on features of international relations such as state interactions, size of military forces, balance of powers etc. Post-positivist epistemology rejects the idea that the social world can be studied in an objective and value-free way. It rejects the central ideas of neo-realism/liberalism, such as rational choice theory, on the grounds that the scientific method cannot be applied to the social world and that a 'science' of IR is impossible. A key difference between the two positions is that while positivist theories, such as neo-realism, offer causal explanations (such as why and how power is exercised) post-positivist theories focus instead on constitutive questions, for instance what is meant by 'power'; what makes it up, how it is experienced and how it is reproduced. Often, post-positivist theories explicitly promote a normative approach to IR, by considering ethics. This is something which has often been ignored under 'traditional' IR as positivist theories make a distinction between 'facts' and normative judgments, or 'values'.

During the late 1980s/1990 debate between positivists and post-positivists became the dominant debate and has been described as constituting the Third "Great Debate" (Lapid 1989).

Positivist Theories

Liberalism/idealism/Liberal Internationalism

Liberalism arose after World War I in response to the inability of states to control and limit war in their international relations. Early adherents include Woodrow Wilson and Norman Angell, who argued variously that states mutually gained from cooperation and that war was so destructive to be essentially futile. Liberalism was not recognized as a coherent theory as such until it was collectively and derisively termed idealism by E. H. Carr.

Realism

Realism was a response to liberalism that chiefly denies that states seek to cooperate. Early realists such as E.H. Carr and Hans Morgenthau argued that states are self-interested, power-seeking rational actors. Any cooperation between states is explained as purely incidental. Realists saw World War II as the vindication of their theory. It should be noted that classical writers such as Thucydides, Machiavelli, and Hobbes are often cited as the "founding fathers" of realism by contemporary self-described realists. However, while their work may support realist doctrine, it is not likely that they would have classified themselves as realists (in this sense of the term).

Neorealism

Neorealism is largely the work of Kenneth Waltz (who actually called his theory "structural realism"). While retaining the empirical observations of realism, that international relations are characterized by antagonistic interstate relations, neorealists point to the anarchic structure of the international system as the cause. They reject explanations that take account of states' domestic characteristics. States are compelled by relative gains and balance against concentration of power. Unlike realism, neo-realism seeks to be scientific and more positivist. What also distinguishes neo-realism from realism is that the former does not accept the latter's emphasis on the behavioural explanation of international relations.

Neoliberalism

Neoliberalism seeks to update liberalism by accepting the neorealist presumption that states are the key actors in international relations, but still maintains that non-state actors (NSAs) and intergovernmental organizations (IGOs) matter.

Proponents such as Joseph Nye argue that states will cooperate irrespective of relative gains, and are thus concerned with absolute gains. The growing interdependence throughout the Cold War through international institutions means that neoliberalism is also called liberal institutionalism. This also means that nations are, in essence, free to make their own choices as to how they will go about conducting policy without any international organizations blocking a nation's right to sovereignty. Neoliberalism also contains an economic theory that is based the use of open and free markets with little, if any, government intervention to prevent monopolies and other conglomerates from forming.

Post-positivist/reflectivist Theories

International Society Theory (the English School)

International society theory, also called the English School, focuses on the shared norms and values of states and how they regulate international relations. Examples of such norms include diplomacy, order, and international law. Unlike neo-realism, it is not necessarily positivist. Theorists have focused particularly on humanitarian intervention, and are subdivided between solidarists, who tend to advocate it more, and pluralists, who place greater value in order and sovereignty. Nicholas Wheeler is a prominent solidarist, while Hedley Bull is perhaps the best known pluralist.

Social Constructivism

Social Constructivism encompasses a broad range of theories that aim to address questions of ontology, such as the Structure and agency debate, as well as questions of epistemology, such as the "material/ideational" debate that concerns the relative role of material forces versus ideas. Constructivism is not a theory of IR, for example in the manner of neo-realism, but instead is a social theory.

Constructivism in IR can be divided into what Hopf (1998) calls 'conventional' and 'critical' constructivism. Common to all varieties of constructivism is an interest in the role that ideational forces play. The most famous constructivist scholar, Alexander Wendt noted in a 1992 article in International

Organization (later followed up by a book, Social Theory of International Politics (1999)), that "anarchy is what states make of it". By this he means that the anarchical structure that neo-realists claim governs state interaction is in fact a phenomenon that is socially constructed and reproduced by states. For example, if the system is dominated by states that see anarchy as a life or death situation (what Wendt terms a "Hobbesian" anarchy) then the system will be characterised by warfare. If on the other hand anarchy is seen as restricted (a "Lockean" anarchy) then a more peaceful system will exist. Anarchy in this view is constituted by state interaction, rather than accepted as a natural and immutable feature of international life as viewed by neo-realist IR scholars.

Critics, however, abound from both sides of the epistemological divide: Post-positivists say the focus on the state at the expense of ethnicity/race/class/gender makes social constructivism yet another positivist theory. The use of implicit rational choice theory by Wendt has also raised criticisms from scholars such as Steven Smith. Positivist scholars of (neo-)liberalism/realism hold that the theory forgoes too many positivist assumptions for it to be considered positivist.

Critical Theory

Critical international relations theory is the application of 'critical theory' to international relations. Proponents such as Andrew Linklater and Robert Cox focus on the need for human emancipation from States. Hence, it is "critical" of mainstream IR theories that tend to be state-centric.

MARXISM

Marxist and Neo-Marxist theories of IR reject the realist/liberal view of state conflict or cooperation; instead focusing on the economic and material aspects. It makes the assumption that the economy trumps other concerns; allowing for the elevation of class as the focus of study. Marxists view the international system as an integrated capitalist system in pursuit of capital accumulation. Thus, the period of colonialism brought in sources for raw materials and captive markets for exports, while decolonialization brought new opportunities in the form of dependence. Linked in with Marxist theories is dependency theory which argues that developed countries, in their pursuit of power, penetrate developing states through political advisors, missionaries, experts and MNCs to integrate them into the integrated capitalist system in order to appropriate natural resources and foster dependence by developing countries on developed countries.

Marxist theories receive scant attention in the United States where no significant socialist party ever existed. It is more common in parts of Europe and is one of the most important theoretic contributions of Latin American academia, for example through Liberation theology.

POSTSTRUCTURALIST THEORIES

Poststructuralist theories of IR developed in the 1980s from postmodernist studies in political science. Post-structuralism explores the deconstruction of concepts traditionally not problematic in IR, such as 'power' and 'agency' and examines how the construction of these concepts shapes international relations. The examination of 'narratives' plays an important part in poststructuralist analysis, for example feminist poststructuralist work has examined the role that 'women' play in global society and how they are constructed in war as 'innocent' and 'civilians'. Examples of post-positivist research include:

- Feminisms ("gendering" war)
- Postcolonialism (challenges the euro-centrism of IR)

CONCEPTS IN INTERNATIONAL RELATIONS

Systemic Level Concepts

International relations is often viewed in terms of levels of analysis, the systemic level concepts are those broad concepts that define and shape an international milieu, characterised by Anarchy.

Power

The concept of Power in international relations can be described as the degree of resources, capabilities, and influence in international affairs. It is often divided up into the concepts of hard power and soft power, hard power relating to the use of force, and soft power commonly covering economics, diplomacy and cultural influence.

Polarity

Polarity in International Relations refers to the arrangement of power within the international system. The concept arose from bipolarity during the Cold War, with the international system dominated by the conflict between two superpowers, and has been applied retrospectively. Consequently, the international system prior to 1945 can be described as multi-polar, with power being shared among Great powers. The collapse of the Soviet Union in 1991 has lead to what some would call unipolarity, with the United States as a sole superpower.

Several theories of international relations draw upon the idea of polarity.

The balance of power was a concept prevalent in Europe prior to the First World War, the thought being that by balancing power blocs it would create stability and prevent war. Theories of the balance of power gained prominence again during the Cold War, being a central mechanism of Kenneth Waltz's Neorealism. Here, the concepts of balancing (rising in power to counter another) and bandwagonning (siding with another) are developed.

Hegemonic stability theory also draws upon the idea of Polarity, specifically the state of unipolarity. Hegemony is the preponderance of power at one pole in the international system, and the theory argues this is stable configuration because of mutual gains by both the dominant power and others in the international system. This is contrary to many Neorealist arguments, particularly made by Kenneth Waltz, stating that the end of the Cold War and the state of unipolarity is an unstable configuration that will inevitably change.

This can be expressed in Power transition theory, which states that it is likely that a great power would challenge a hegemon after a certain period, resulting in a major war. It suggests that while hegemony can control the occurence of wars, it also results in the creation of one. It's main proponent, A.F.K. Organski, argued this based on the occurence of previous wars during British, Portugese and Dutch hegemony.

Interdependence

Many advocate that the current international system is characterised by growing interdependence; the mutual responsibility and dependency on others. Advocates of this point to growing globalisation, particularly with international economic interaction. The role of international institutions, and widespread acceptance of a number of operating principles in the international system, reinforces ideas that relations are characterised by interdependence.

Dependency

Dependency theory is a theory most commonly associated with Marxism, stating that a set of Core states exploit a set of weaker Periphery states for their prosperity. Various versions of the theory suggest that this is either an inevitability (standard dependency theory), or use the theory to highlight the necessity for change (Neo-Marxist).

Systemic Tools of International Relations

- Diplomacy is the practice of conducting negotiation between representatives of states. To an extent, all other tools of international relations can be considered the failure of diplomacy.
- Sanctions are usually a first resort after the failure of diplomacy, and are one of the main tools used to enforce treaties. They can take the form of diplomatic or economic sanctions and involve the cutting of ties and imposition of barriers to communication or trade.
- War, the use of force, is often thought of as the ultimate tool of international relations. A widely accepted definition is that given by Clausewitz, with war being "the continuation of politics by other means". There a growing study into 'new wars' involving actors other than states. The study of war in International Relations

is covered by the disciplines of 'War Studies' and 'Strategic studies'.

The mobilization of international shame can also be thought of as a tool of International Relations. This is attempting to alter states actions through 'naming and shaming' at the international level. A prominent use of this would be the UN Commission on Human Rights 1235 procedure, which publicly exposes states human rights violations.

Unit-level Concepts in International Relations

As a level of analysis the unit level is often referred to as the state level, as it locates its explanation at the level of the state, rather than the international system.

Regime Type

It is often considered that a states regime type can dictate the way that a state interacts with others in the international system.

Democratic Peace Theory is a theory that suggests that the nature of democracy means that democratic countries will not go to war with each other. The justifications for this are that democracies externalise their norms and only go to war for just causes, and that democracy encourages mutual trust and respect.

Communism justifies a world revolution, which similarly would lead to peaceful coexistence, based on a proletarian global society.

Revisionism/Status Quo

States can be classified by whether they accept the international status quo, or are revisionist, i.e. want change. Revisionist states seek to fundamentally change the rules and practices of international relations, feeling disadvantaged by the status quo. They see the international system as a largely western creation which serves to reinforce current realities. China is an example of a state that has gone from being a revisionist state to one that is satisfied with the status quo, because the status quo is now beneficial to it.

Religion

It is often considered that religion can have an effect on the way a state acts within the international system. Religion is visible as an organising principle particularly for Islamic states, whereas secularism sits at the other end of the spectrum, with the separation of state and religion being responsible for the Liberal tradition.

Individual or Sub-unit Level Concepts

The level beneath the unit (state) level can be useful both for explaining factors in International Relations that other theories fail to explain, and for moving away from a state-centric view of international relations.

- Psychological factors in International Relations - Evaluating psychological factors in international relations comes from the understanding that a state is not a 'black box' as proposed by Realism, and that there may be other influences on foreign policy decisions. Examining the role of personalities in the decision making process can have some explanatory power, as can the role of misperception between various actors. A prominent application of sub-unit level psychological factors in international relations is the concept of Groupthink, another is the propensity of policymakers to think in terms of analogies.
- Bureaucratic politics -Looks at the role of the bureaucracy in decision making, and sees decisions as a result of bureaucratic in-fighting, and as having been shaped by various constraints.
- Religious, Ethnic, and secessionist groups -Viewing these aspects of the sub-unit level has explanatory power with regards to ethnic conflicts, religious wars, and other actors do not consider themselves to fit with the defined state boundaries. This is particularly useful in the context of the pre-modern world of weak states.
- Science, Technology and Interntional Relations-How science and technology impact the global health, buisness, environment, technology, and development.

Institutions in International Relations

International institutions form a vital part of contemporary International Relations. Much interaction at the system level is governed by them, and they outlaw some traditional institutions and practices of International Relations, such as the use of war (except in self-defence).

As humanity enters the Planetary phase of civilization, some scientists and political theorists see a global hierarchy of institutions replacing the existing system of sovereign nation-states as the primary political community. They argue that nations are an imagined community that cannot resolve such modern challenges as the "Dogville" effect (strangers in a homogeneous community), the legal and political status of stateless people and refugees, and the need to address worldwide concerns like climate change and pandemics. Futurist Paul Raskin has hypothesized that a new, more legitimate form Global politics could be based on "constrained pluralism." This principle guides the formation of institutions based on three characteristics: irreducibility, where some issues must be adjudicated at the global level; subsidiarity, which limits the scope of global authority to truly global issues while smaller-scope issues are regulated at lower levels; and heterogeneity, which allows for diverse forms of local and regional institutions as long as they meet global obligations.

United Nations

The United Nations (UN) is an international organization that describes itself as a "global association of governments facilitating cooperation in international law, international security, economic development, and social equity"; It is the most prominent international institution. Many of the legal institutions follow the same organisational structure as the UN.

2

History of Political Science

While the study of politics is first found in ancient Greece and ancient India, political science is a late arrival in terms of social sciences. However, the discipline has a clear set of antecedents such as moral philosophy, political philosophy, political economy, history, and other fields concerned with normative determinations of what ought to be and with deducing the characteristics and functions of the ideal state. In each historic period and in almost every geographic area, we can find someone studying politics and increasing political understanding.

ANCIENT INDIA

In ancient India, the study of politics can be traced back to several Vedic Sanskrit texts: Rig-Veda (c. 1500-1200 BC), the Samhitas (c. 1200-900 BC), and the Brahmanas (c. 1200-900 BC). The study of politics is also found in the Buddhist Pali Canon (c. 6th century BC). Chanakya (c. 350-275 BC) was a professor of political science at Takshashila University, and later the Prime Minister of Mauryan emperor Chandragupta Maurya.

Chanakya is regarded as one of the earliest known political thinkers, economists and king-makers, and is also known as the Indian Machiavelli. He wrote the Arthashastra, which was one of the earliest treatises on political thought, economics and social order, and can be considered a precursor to Machiavelli's The Prince. It discusses monetary and fiscal policies, welfare, international relations, and war strategies in detail, among other topics on political science.

ANCIENT GREECE

The antecedents of western politics trace their roots back even earlier than Plato and Aristotle, particularly in the works of Homer, Hesiod, Thucydides, Plato, Xenophon, and Euripides. Later, Plato analyzed political systems and abstracted their analysis from more literary-and history-oriented studies and applied an approach we would understand as closer to philosophy. Similarly, Aristotle built upon Plato's analysis to include historical empirical evidence in his analysis.

ROMAN EMPIRE

During the rule of Rome, famous historians such as Polybius, Livy and Plutarch documented the rise of the Roman Republic, and the organization and histories of other nations, while statesman like Julius Caesar, Cicero and others provided us with examples of the politics of the republic and Rome's empire and wars. The study of politics during this age was oriented toward understanding history, understanding methods of governing, and describing the operation of governments.

MEDIEVAL EUROPE

With the fall of the Roman Empire, there arose a more diffuse arena for political studies. The rise of monotheism and particularly for the Western tradition, Christianity, brought to light a new space for politics and political action. During the Middle Ages, the study of politics was widespread in the churches and courts. Works such as Augustine of Hippo's The City of God synthesized current philosophies and political traditions with those of Christianity, redefining the borders between what was religious and what was political. Most of the political questions surrounding the relationship between church and state were clarified and contested in this period.

ISLAMIC WORLD

In the Middle East and later other Islamic areas, works such as the Rubaiyat of Omar Khayyam and Epic of Kings by Ferdowsi provided evidence of political analysis, while the Islamic Aristotelians such as Avicenna and later Maimonides and Averroes, continued Aristotle's tradition of analysis and empiricism, writing commentaries on Aristotle's works.

EUROPEAN RENAISSANCE

During the Italian Renaissance, Niccolò Machiavelli established the emphasis of modern political science on direct empirical observation of political institutions and actors in The Prince. Later, the expansion of the scientific paradigm during the Enlightenment further pushed the study of politics beyond normative determinations.

POLITICAL HISTORY

Political history is the narrative and analysis of political events, ideas, movements, and leaders. It is usually structured around the nation state. The first "scientific" political history was written by Leopold von Ranke in Germany in the 19th century. His methodologies profoundly affected the way historians critically examine sources; see historiography for a more complete analysis of the methodology of various approaches to history.

According to Hegel, Political History "is a concept of the state with a moral and spiritual force beyond the marerial interests of its subjects: it followed that the state was the main agent of historical change."

DIPLOMATIC HISTORY

Sometimes referred to as "Rankian History", diplomatic history focuses on politics, politicians and other high rulers and views them as being the driving force of continuity and change in history. It is the study of the conduct of international relations between states or across state boundaries.

This is the most common form of history and is often the classical and popular belief of what history should be.

Although history which might be classified as diplomatic history has been written for as long as history has been in existence -Thucydides, certainly, is among other things, highly concerned with the relations among states -the modern form of diplomatic history was codified in the 19th century by Leopold von Ranke, a German historian. Ranke wrote largely on the history of Early Modern Europe, using the diplomatic archives of the European powers (particularly the Venetians) to construct a detailed understanding of the history of Europe wie es eigentlich gewesen ("as it actually happened.") Ranke saw diplomatic history as the most important kind of history to write because of his idea of the "Primary of Foreign Affairs" (Primat der Aussenpolitik), arguing that the concerns of international relations drive the internal development of the state. Ranke's understanding of diplomatic history relied on the large number of official documents produced by modern western governments as sources.

Ranke's understanding of the dominance of foreign policy, and hence an emphasis on diplomatic history, remained the dominant paradigm in historical writing through the first half of the twentieth century. This emphasis, combined with the effects of the War Guilt Clause in the Treaty of Versailles (1919) which ended the First World War, led to a huge amount of historical writing on the subject of the origins of the war in 1914, with the involved governments printing huge, carefully edited, collections of documents and numerous historians writing multi-volume histories of the origins of the war. In general, the early works in this vein, including Fritz Fischer's controversial (at the time) 1961 thesis that German goals of "world power" were the principal cause of the war, fit fairly comfortably into Ranke's emphasis on Aussenpolitik.

In the course of the 1960s, however, some German historians (notably Hans-Ulrich Wehler and his cohort) began to rebel against this idea, instead suggesting a "Primacy of Domestic Politics" (Primat der Innenpolitik), in which the insecurities of (in this case German) domestic policy drove the creation of foreign policy. This led to a considerably body of work interpreting the domestic policies of various states and the ways this influenced their conduct of foreign policy.

At the same time, the middle of the twentieth century began to see a general de-emphasis on diplomatic history. The French Annales school had already put an emphasis on the role of geography and economics on history, and of the importance of broad, slow cycles rather than the constant apparent movement of the "history of events" of high politics. The most important work of the Annales school, Fernand Braudel's The Mediterranean and the Mediterranean World in the Age of Philip II, contains a traditional Rankean diplomatic history of Philip II's Mediterranean policy, but only as the third and shortest section of a work largely focusing on the broad cycles of history in the longue durée ("long term"). The Annales were broadly influential, leading to a turning away from diplomatic and other forms of political history towards an emphasis on broader trends of economic and environmental change. In the 1960s and 1970s, an increasing emphasis on giving a voice to the voiceless and writing the history of the underclasses, whether by using the quantitative statistical methods of social history or the more qualitative assessments of cultural history, also undermined the centrality of diplomatic history to the historical discipline.

Nevertheless, diplomatic history has always remained a historical field with a great interest to the general public, and considerable amounts of work are still done in the field, often in much the same way that Ranke pioneered in the middle years of the 19th century.

HISTORIOGRAPHY

Historiography is the study of the practice of history. This can take many forms, including the study of historical method and the historical development of history as an academic discipline. The term can also be used to refer a specific body of historical writing. For instance, "medieval historiography during the 1960s" can be taken to mean the methodological approaches and ideas about medieval history present in written history during that decade. As a meta-analysis of descriptions of the past, this third conception can relate to the first two in that the analysis usually focuses on the narratives, interpretations, worldview, use of evidence, or method of presentation of other historians.

Defining Historiography

Conal Furay and Michael J. Salevouris define "historiography" as "the study of the way history has been and is written -the history of historical writing... When you study 'historiography' you do not study the events of the past directly, but the changing interpretations of those events in the works of individual historians." (The Methods and Skills of History: A Practical Guide, 1988, p. 223.

Although questions of method have concerned historians since Thucydides, many trace the modern study of historiography to E. H. Carr's 1961 work What is History?. Carr challenged the traditional belief that the study of the methods of historical research and writing were unimportant. His work remains in print to this day, and is used in many postgraduate programs of study in the English-speaking world.

Historiography is often political in nature. For example, the Dunning school of historiography, which was sympathetic to former slave owners and leaders of the Confederacy, contended that black people, particularly former slaves, should neither be permitted to vote nor bear arms.

In the 1960s, historiography corrected the racism of the Dunning School viewpoint, and history that included the viewpoint of African Americans who had been disenfranchised by the Jim Crow political and economic system that grew up alongside the powerful Dunning School and its way of telling history from the viewpoint of former slave owners. Mid-twentieth century historians also focused on primary sources to reveal previously excluded roles of women, minorities, and labor from earlier histories of the United States.

According to these historiographers, historians in the 1930s and 1940s had a bias toward wealthy and well-connected white males. Some historians from that point onward devoted themselves to what they saw as more accurate representations of the past, casting a light on those who had been previously disregarded as non-noteworthy.

The study of historiography demands a critical approach that goes beyond the mere examination of historical fact. Historiographical studies consider the source, often by researching the author, his or her position in society, and the type of history being written at the time.

Basic Issues Studied in Historiography

Some of the common questions of historiography are:

- Who wrote the source (primary or secondary)?
- For primary sources, we look at the person in his or her society, for secondary sources, we consider the theoretical orientation of the approach for example, Marxist or Annales School, ("total history"), political history, etc.
- What is the authenticity, authority, bias/interest, and intelligibility of the source?
- What was the view of history when the source was written?
- Was history supposed to provide moral lessons?
- What or who was the intended audience?
- What sources were privileged or ignored in the narrative?
- By what method was the evidence compiled?
- In what historical context was the work of history itself written?

Issues engaged in so-called critical historiography includes topics such as:

- What constitutes an historical "event"?
- In what modes does a historian write and produce statements of "truth" and "fact"?
- How does the medium (novel, textbook, film, theatre, comic) through which historical information is conveyed influence its meaning?
- What inherent epistemological problems does archive-based history contain?
- How does the historian establish their own objectivity or come to terms with their own subjectivity?
- What is the relation of historical theory to historical practice?
- What is the "goal" of history?
- What is history?

The History of Written History

Understanding the past appears to be a universal human need and the telling of history has emerged independently in civilisations around the world. What constitutes history is a philosophical question. For the purposes of this survey it is written history recorded in a narrative format for the purpose of informing future generations about events. The earliest critical historical thought emerged in Greece, a development which would be an important influence on the writing of history elsewhere in the world.

EARLY WESTERN HISTORIOGRAPHY

Written history appeared first with the ancient Greeks, whose historians greatly contributed to the development of historical methodology. The very first historical work were The Histories composed by Herodotus of Halicarnassus (484 BC-ca.425 BC), who became later known as the 'father of history' (Cicero). Herodotus personally conducted research into the history of various Mediterranean cultures, and attempted to distinguish between more and less reliable accounts. His research confirmed for him the belief that divinity plays a crucial role in the determination of historical events. Thucydides, on the other hand, largely eliminated divine causality from his account of the war between Athens and Sparta, and the same holds true for his successors, such as Xenophon and Polybius.

Reports exist of other near-eastern histories. such as that composed by the Phoenician historian Sanchuniathon; but his very existence is considered semi-fabled and writings attributed to him are fragmentary, known only through the later historians Philo of Byblos and Eusebius, who asserted that he wrote before even the Trojan war.

Concerning the Bible, there is considerable debate about its historiographical character. To some scholars the use of a divinity to provide historical explanations contradicts the basic aim of any truly historical work, namely to provide rational explanations for events. Others argue that the Biblical search for an underlying cause of historical events is itself a characteristic of historiographical research, and point moreover to the Bible's frequent recourse to double-causation, whereby events are attributed to both human and divine causation. Controversy over this issue is complicated by the fact that the Bible is seen as an inspired text by many members of Western society today.

Writing history was popular among Christian monks in the Middle Ages. They wrote about the history of the Church and of their patrons, the dynastic history of the local rulers. History was written about states or nations during the Renaissance. The study of history changed during the Enlightenment and Romanticism. Voltaire described the history of certain ages that were important according to him, instead of describing events in a chronological order. History became an independent discipline. It was not called philosophia historiae anymore, but merely history (historiae).

Chinese Historiography

The writing of history in China began with the work of Sima Qian around 100 BC. Its scope extends as far back as the 16th century BC. Traditionalist Chinese historiography describes history in terms of dynastic cycles. In this view, each new dynasty is founded by a morally righteous founder. Over time, the dynasty becomes morally corrupt and dissolute. Eventually, the dynasty becomes so weak as to allow its replacement by a new dynasty.

Islamic Historiography

Islamic historiography began developing with the reconstruction of Muhammad's life in the centuries following his death. Due to numerous conflicting narratives regarding Muhammad and his companions from various sources, it was necessary to verify which sources were more reliable. In order to evaluate these sources, various methodologies were developed, such as the "science of biography", "science of Hadith" and "Isnad" (chain of transmission). These methodologies were later applied to other historical figures in the Islamic World. Famous Muslim historians included Urwah (d. 712), Ibn Ishaq (d. 768), Al-Waqidi (745 -822), Ibn Hisham (d. 834), Al-Tabari (838 -923), Ibn Khaldun (1332 -1406) and Ibn Hajar (1372 -1449) among others.

Ilm ar-Rijal (Arabic) is the "science of biography" especially as practiced in Islam, where it was first applied to the sira, the life of the prophet of Islam, Muhammad, and then the lives of the four Rightly Guided Caliphs who expanded Islamic dominance rapidly. Since validating the sayings of Muhammad is a major study ("Isnad"), accurate biography has always been of great interest to Muslim biographers, who accordingly became experts at sorting out facts from accusations, bias from evidence, etc., and were renowned throughout the known world for their honesty in recording history. Modern practices of scientific citation and historical method owe a great deal to the rigor of the Isnad tradition of early Muslims. The earliest surviving Islamic biography is Ibn Ishaq's Sirat Rasul Allah, written in the 8th century.

The "science of Hadith" is the process that Muslim scholars use to evaluate Hadith. The classification of Hadith into Sahih (sound), Hasan (good) and Da'if (weak) was firmly established by Ali ibn al-Madini (161 AH -234 AH). Later, al-Madini's student Muhammad al-Bukhari (810 -870) authored a collection that he believed contained only Sahih Hadith, which is now known as the Sahih Bukhari.

Modern Historiography

Modern historiography began with Ranke in the 19th century, who was very critical on the sources used in history. He was opposed to analyses and rationalizations. His adagium was writing history the way it was. He wanted eyewitness accounts and wanted an emphasis on the point of view of the eyewitness. Hegel and Marx introduced the change of society in history. Former historians had focused on cyclical events of the rise and decline of rulers and nations. A new discipline emerged in the late nineteenth century that analyzed and compared these perspectives on a larger scale and that discipline was sociology.

The French Annales School radically changed history during the 20th century. Fernand Braudel wanted history to become more scientific by demanding more mathematical evidence in history, in order to make the history discipline less subjective. Furthermore, he added a social-economic and geographic framework to answer historical questions. Other French historians, like Philippe Ariès and Michel Foucault described history of daily life topics as death and sexuality. They wanted history to be written about all topics and that all questions should be asked.

In the 1970s, some historians began to focus on case-studies. Case studies describe particular aspects of history in a thorough fashion, to describe history as it was or to measure it precisely. Several well chosen case studies can enhance or change the major picture and can bring more truth to the answers of the questions that the Annales School likes to ask. However, because case studies focus so narrowly on particular pieces of place and time, i.e., the living conditions of female agricultural workers in 15th century Sussex, their findings cannot always be applied to broader sets of data i.e., using the data from the Sussex study to postulate about conditions in Kent, or France, or in seventeenth century Sussex. Case studies are best used in addition to raw data and primary sources.

In the 1980s, American historians compared the differences and similarities between different world regions and to come to new concepts to describe them in the study of World History.

DIPLOMACY

Diplomacy is the art and practice of conducting negotiations between representatives of groups or states. It usually refers to international diplomacy, the conduct of international relations through the intercession of professional diplomats with regard to issues of peace-making, culture, economics, trade, and war. International treaties are usually negotiated by diplomats prior to endorsement by national politicians.

The word stems from the Greek word "diploma", which literally means 'folded in two'. In ancient Greece, a diploma was a certificate certifying completion of a course of study, typically folded in two. In the days of the Roman Empire, the word diploma was used to describe official travel documents, such as passports and passes for imperial roads, that were stamped on double metal plates. Later, the meaning was extended to cover other official documents such as treaties with foreign tribes. In the 1700s the French called their body of officials attached to foreign legations the corps "diplomatique". The word "diplomacy" was first introduced into the English language by Edmund Burke in 1796, based on the French word "diplomatie".

In an informal or social sense, diplomacy is the employment of tact to gain strategic advantage, one set of tools being the phrasing of statements in a non-confrontational, or polite manner.

Diplomats and Diplomatic Missions

A diplomat is someone involved in diplomacy; the collective term for a group of diplomats from a single country who are resident in another country is a diplomatic mission. Ambassador is the most senior diplomatic rank; a diplomatic mission headed by an ambassador is known as an embassy. The collective body of all diplomats of particular country is called that country's diplomatic corps.

History

The ability to practice diplomacy is one of the defining elements of a state, and diplomacy has been practiced since the first city-states were formed millennia ago. For most of human history diplomats were sent only for specific negotiations, and would return immediately after their mission concluded. Diplomats were usually relatives of the ruling family or of very high rank in order to give them legitimacy when they sought to negotiate with the other state.

One notable exception involved the relationship between the Pope and the Byzantine Emperor; papal agents, called apocrisiarii, were permanently resident in Constantinople. After the 8th century, however, conflicts between the Pope and Emperor (such as the Iconoclastic controversy) led to the breaking of close ties.

Modern diplomacy's origins are often traced to the states of Northern Italy in the early Renaissance, with the first embassies being established in the thirteenth century. Milan played a leading role, especially under Francesco Sforza who established permanent embassies to the other city states of Northern Italy. It was in Italy that many of the traditions of modern diplomacy began, such as the presentation of an ambassadors credentials to the head of state.

From Italy the practice was spread to the other European powers. Milan was the first to send a representative to the court of France in 1455. However, Milan refused to host French representatives fearing espionage and that the French representatives would intervene in its internal affairs. As foreign powers such as France and Spain became increasingly involved in Italian politics the need to accept emissaries was recognized. Soon the major European powers were exchanging representatives. Spain was the first to send a permanent representative; it appointed an ambassador to the Court of England in 1487. By the late 16th century, permanent missions became customary. The Holy Roman Emperor, however, did not regularly send permanent legates, as they could not represent the interests of all the German princes (who were in theory subordinate to the Emperor, but in practice independent).

During that period the rules of modern diplomacy were further developed. The top rank of representatives was an ambassador. At that time an ambassador was a nobleman, the rank of the noble assigned varying with the prestige of the country he was delegated to. Strict standards developed for ambassadors, requiring they have large residences, host lavish parties, and play an important role in the court life of their host nation. In Rome, the most prized posting for a Catholic ambassador, the French and Spanish representatives would have a retinue of up to a hundred. Even in smaller posts, ambassadors were very expensive. Smaller states would send and receive envoys, who were a rung below ambassador. Somewhere between the two was the position of minister plenipotentiary.

Diplomacy was a complex affair, even more so than now. The ambassadors from each state were ranked by complex levels of precedence that were much disputed. States were normally ranked by the title of the sovereign; for Catholic nations the emissary from the Vatican was paramount, then those from the kingdoms, then those from duchies and principalities. Representatives from republics were considered the lowest of the low. Determining precedence between two kingdoms depended on a number of factors that often fluctuated, leading to near constant squabbling.

Ambassadors, nobles with little foreign experience and no expectation of a career in diplomacy, needed to be supported by large embassy staff. These professionals would be sent on longer assignments and would be far more knowledgeable than the higher-ranking officials about the host country. Embassy staff would include a wide range of employees, including some dedicated to espionage. The need for skilled individuals to staff embassies was met by the graduates of universities, and this led to a great increase in the study of international law, modern languages, and history at universities throughout Europe.

At the same time, permanent foreign ministries began to be established in almost all European states to coordinate embassies and their staffs. These ministries were still far from their modern form, and many of them had extraneous internal responsibilities. Britain had two departments with frequently overlapping powers until 1782. They were also far smaller; France, which boasted the largest foreign affairs department, had only some 70 full-time employees in the 1780s.

The elements of modern diplomacy slowly spread to Eastern Europe and Russia, arriving by the early eighteenth century. The entire edifice would be greatly disrupted by the French Revolution and the subsequent years of warfare. The revolution would see commoners take over the diplomacy of the French state, and of those conquered by revolutionary armies. Ranks of precedence were abolished. Napoleon also refused to acknowledge diplomatic immunity, imprisoning several British diplomats accused of scheming against France.

After the fall of Napoleon, the Congress of Vienna of 1815 established an international system of diplomatic rank. Disputes on precedence among nations (and therefore the appropriate diplomatic ranks used) persisted for over a century until after World War II, when the rank of ambassador became the norm.

Diplomatic traditions outside of Europe were very different. A feature necessary for diplomacy is the existence of a number of states of somewhat equal power, as existed in Italy during the Renaissance, and in Europe for much of the modern period. By contrast, in Asia and the Middle East, China and the Ottoman Empire were reluctant to practice bilateral diplomacy as they viewed themselves to be unquestionably superior to all their neighbours. The Ottomans, for instance, would not send missions to other states, expecting representatives to come to Constantinople. It would not be until the nineteenth century that the Empire established permanent embassies in other capitals. As European power spread around the world in the eighteenth and nineteenth century so too did its diplomatic system.

Diplomatic Strategy

Real world diplomatic negotiations are very different from intellectual debates in a university where an issue is decided on the merit of the arguments and negotiators make a deal by splitting the difference. Though diplomatic agreements can sometimes be reached among liberal democratic nations by appealing to higher principles, most real world diplomacy is heavily influenced by raw power.

The interaction of strength and diplomacy can be illustrated by a comparison to labor negotiations. If a labor union isn't willing to strike, then the union isn't going anywhere because management has absolutely no incentive to agree to union demands. On the other hand, if management isn't willing to take a strike, then the company will be walked all over by the labor union, and management will be forced to agree to any demand the union makes. The same concept applies to diplomatic negotiations. Good diplomacy and strength go together.

Diplomatic Immunity

The sanctity of diplomats has long been observed. This sanctity has come to be known as diplomatic immunity. While there have been a number of cases where diplomats have been killed, this is normally viewed as a great breach of honour. Genghis Khan and the Mongols were well known for strongly insisting on the rights of diplomats, and they would often wreak horrific vengeance against any state that violated these rights. This was shown when, having sent an ambassador to

Persia, Genghis Khan received his ambassador's head sent by the Persians. Because of this act the Mongols invaded the whole of Persia, leading to even larger invasions by Khan in the future.

Diplomatic rights were established in the mid-seventeenth century in Europe and have spread throughout the world. These rights were formalized by the 1961 Vienna Convention on Diplomatic Relations, which protects diplomats from being persecuted or prosecuted while on a diplomatic mission. If a diplomat does commit a serious crime while in a host country s/he may be declared as persona non grata (unwanted person). Such diplomats are then often tried for the crime in their homeland.

Diplomatic communications are also viewed as sacrosanct, and diplomats have long been allowed to carry documents across borders without being searched. The mechanism for this is the so-called "diplomatic bag" (or, in some countries, the "diplomatic pouch"). In recent years, however, signals intelligence has led to this use of diplomatic bags being largely discarded.

In times of hostility, diplomats are often withdrawn for reasons of personal safety, as well as in some cases when the host country is friendly but there is a perceived threat from internal dissidents. Ambassadors and other diplomats are sometimes recalled temporarily by their home countries as a way to express displeasure with the host country. In both cases, lower-level employees still remain to actually do the business of diplomacy.

Diplomats as a Guarantee

The Middle East and other parts of the world had a very different tradition. In the Ottoman Empire, the diplomats of Persia and other states were seen as a guarantee of good behaviour. If a nation broke a treaty or if their nationals misbehaved the diplomats would be punished. Diplomats were thus used as an enforcement mechanism on treaties and international law. To ensure that punishing a diplomat mattered rulers insisted on high-ranking figures. This tradition is seen by supporters of Iran as a legal basis of the 1979 Iranian hostage crisis. In imitation of alleged previous practices supporters of the Iranian Revolution attempted to punish the United States for its alleged misdeeds by holding their diplomats hostage. Diplomats as a guarantee were also employed sometimes in pre-modern Europe and other parts of Asia.

Diplomacy and Espionage

Diplomacy is closely linked to espionage or gathering of intelligence. Embassies are bases for both diplomats and spies, and some diplomats are essentially openly-acknowledged spies. For instance, the job of military attachés includes learning as much as possible about the military of the nation to which they are assigned. They do not try to hide this role and, as such, are only invited to events allowed by their hosts, such as military parades or air shows. There are also deep-cover spies operating in many embassies. These individuals are given fake positions at the embassy, but their main task is to illegally gather intelligence, usually by coordinating spy rings of locals or other spies. For the most part, spies operating out of embassies gather little intelligence themselves and their identities tend to be known by the opposition. If discovered, these diplomats can be expelled from an embassy, but for the most part counter-intelligence agencies prefer to keep these agents in situ and under close monitoring.

The information gathered by spies plays an increasingly important role in diplomacy. Arms-control treaties would be impossible without the power of reconnaissance satellites and agents to monitor compliance. Information gleaned from espionage is useful in almost all forms of diplomacy, everything from trade agreements to border disputes.

Diplomatic Recognition

Diplomatic recognition is an important factor in determining whether a nation is an independent state. Receiving recognition is often difficult, even for countries which are fully sovereign. For many decades after becoming independent, even many of the closest allies of the Dutch Republic refused to grant it full recognition. Today there are a number of independent entities without widespread diplomatic recognition, most notably the

Republic of China, or Taiwan. Since the 1970s, most nations have stopped officially recognizing the ROC's existence on Taiwan, at the insistence of the People's Republic of China. Currently, the United States and other nations maintain informal relations through de facto embassies, with names such as the American Institute in Taiwan. Similarly, Taiwan's de facto embassies abroad are known by names such as the Taipei Economic and Cultural Representative Office. This was not always the case, with the US maintaining official diplomatic ties with Taiwan until 1979, when these relations were broken off as a condition for establishing official relations with China.

The Palestinian Authority has its own diplomatic service, however Palestinian representatives in most Western countries are not accorded diplomatic immunity, and their missions are referred to as Delegations General. Other unrecognized countries include Abkhazia, Transnistria, Somaliland, Nagorno Karabakh, and the Turkish Republic of Northern Cyprus. Nagorno Karabakh is the part of Azerbaijan Republic. Lacking the economic and political importance of Taiwan, these nations tend to be much more diplomatically isolated.

Though used as a factor in judging sovereignty, Article 3 of the Montevideo Convention states, "The political existence of the state is independent of recognition by other states."

Informal Diplomacy

Informal diplomacy (sometimes called Track II diplomacy) has been used for centuries to communicate between powers. Most diplomats work to recruit figures in other nations who might be able to give informal access to a country's leadership. In some situations, such as between the United States and the People's Republic of China a large amount of diplomacy is done through semi-formal channels using interlocutors such as academic members of thinktanks. This occurs in situations where governments wish to express intentions or to suggest methods of resolving a diplomatic situation, but do not wish to express a formal position.

Track II diplomacy is a specific kind of informal diplomacy, in which non-officials (academic scholars, retired civil and military officials, public figures, social activists) engage in dialogue, with the aim of conflict resolution, or confidence-building. Sometimes governments may fund such Track II exchanges. Sometimes the exchanges may have no connection at all with governments, or may even act in defiance of governments; such exchanges are called Track III.

POLITICAL FREEDOM

Political freedom is the right, or the capacity, of self-determination as an expression of the individual will.

Types

The concept of political freedom is closely allied with the concepts of civil liberties and human rights. Most democratic societies are characterized by various freedoms which are afforded the legal protection of the state. Some of these freedoms include (in alphabetical order):

- Freedom of assembly
- Freedom of association
- Freedom from government sanctioned discrimination
- Freedom of education
- Freedom of movement (or travel)
- Freedom of the press
- Freedom of religion (or belief)
- Freedom of speech
- Freedom of thought.

Views

Various groups along the political spectrum naturally differ on what they believe constitutes "true" political freedom. Friedrich Hayek famously noted that "liberty" and "freedom" have probably been the most abused words in recent history.

In libertarianism, freedom is defined in terms of interference with the individual pursuit of happiness either by government or other persons, where interference is defined as unreasonably preventing others from realising their will in their chosen course of action or in their use of things. Contrary to popular belief, libertarians are not pro-business. Rather, they simply oppose interference in any consenting acts between adults, including capitalist acts. Generally businesses favour regulations that protect them from competition, which requires many restrictions on consenting capitalist acts between adults. Libertarians call for freedom from coercion, governmental and civilian, in social, political, and economic matters.

On the other hand, those on the political left place more emphasis on freedom as the ability of the individual to realize one's own potential and pursuit of happiness. Freedom in this sense may include freedom from want, poverty, deprivation, or oppression.

Many anarchists with the exception of individualist anarchists, anarcho-capitalists, and particularly anarchists that don't qualify their type of anarchism see negative and positive liberty as complementary concepts of freedom. Anarchists that recognize the concepts of negative and positive liberty tend to be left-leaning anarchists such as communist anarchists.

Some treat freedom as if it were almost synonymous with democracy, while others see conflicts or even opposition between the two concepts. E.g. some argue that Iraq was free under Paul Bremer, because it was a rational, humanist, non-subjugating government, long before elections were held. While some thought that Iraq was free under Saddam because Iraq was not a colony.

Environmentalists often argue that political freedoms should include some social constraint on use of ecosystems. They maintain there is no such thing, for instance, as "freedom to pollute" or "freedom to deforest" given the downstream consequences. The popularity of SUVs, golf, and urban sprawl has been used as evidence that some ideas of freedom and ecological conservation can clash. This leads at times to serious confrontations and clashes of values reflected in advertising campaigns, e.g. that of PETA regarding fur.

There have been numerous philosophical debates over the nature of freedom, the claimed differences between various types of freedom, and the extent to which freedom is desirable. Determinists argue that all human actions are pre-determined and thus freedom is an illusion. Isaiah Berlin saw a distinction between negative liberty and positive liberty.

In jurisprudence, freedom is the right to autonomously determine one's own actions; generally it is granted in those fields in which the subject has no obligations to fulfil or laws to obey, according to the interpretation that the hypothetical natural unlimited freedom is limited by the law for some matters.

Recent Trends

In modern times the expansion of "freedom" around the world is considered by some to be synonymous with increased participation in democratic political systems.

In the 20th Century, the world observed a great reverse in terms of political situation, since the revolutionary struggles in areas of the world suddenly succeeded in establishing freedom from foreign colonialists and domination, at least in places like Africa, even though others may argue that the Cold War caused most of these new states to become puppet states for various regimes such as in Latin America, Africa, and Asia.

FREEDOM OF ASSEMBLY

Freedom of assembly is the freedom to associate with, or organize any groups, gatherings, clubs, or organizations that one wishes. It is held to be a key right in liberal democracies, whereby citizens may form or join any political party, special interest group, or union without government restrictions. In legal systems without freedom of assembly, certain political parties or groups can be banned with harsh penalties for any members. Public protests against the government are usually banned as well.

Tiered Rights

In legal or political systems where rights tend to be ranked in a hierarchy, or "tiered", such that some rights are considered more worthy of protection by the state than others, freedom of assembly is generally located on the top tier. However, the very concept of assigning relative value to rights by way of tiers tends to be controversial.

Those who consider the right of assembly to exist on the "top" tier will sometimes concede that the state may legitimately ban groups which support terrorism or violence.

This makes freedom of assembly closely linked with notions of freedom of speech. Thus, while one can be allowed to advocate the murder of the President, one is not necessarily allowed to be a member of a group that seeks to achieve this goal.

The freedom of assembly in order to protest sometimes conflicts with laws intended to protect public safety, even in democratic countries: in many cities, the police are authorized by law to disperse any crowd (including a crowd of political protesters) which threatens public safety, or which the police cannot control.

The idea is to prevent rioting. Often local law requires that a permit must be obtained in advance by protest organizers if a protest march is anticipated; the permit application can be denied. Sometimes this bureaucratic power is abused by lawmakers if the protest is not a popular one in the community or with the local government, with the permit process in some cities taking a great deal of time, organization, and even money required before a permit is issued --and then, when issued, time and location restrictions are sometimes added.

From time to time, local permit laws collide in court with the freedoms of assembly and of speech, such as in February 2003 when protests were anticipated over the exclusion of women from membership at the Augusta National Golf Club where golf's Masters Tournament is played every year.

The Richmond County, Georgia county commission implemented a new rule requiring 20 days of advance notice before a protest, and giving the county sheriff the power to approve or deny permits, and to dictate the location of demonstrations. The sheriff turned down a permit to protest in front of the golf club but approved a protest half a mile away. Two courts upheld the ordinance granting the sheriff this power.

FREEDOM OF ASSOCIATION

Freedom of association is a Constitutional (legal) concept based on the premise that it is the right of free adults to mutually choose their associates for whatever purpose they see fit. This concept has been included in several national constitutions, including the United States Constitution, the European Convention on Human Rights, and Canada's Charter of Rights.

United States

While the United States Constitution's First Amendment identifies the rights to assemble and to petition the government, the text of the First Amendment itself does not make specific mention of a right to association.

Nevertheless, the United States Supreme Court has held that the freedom of association is an essential part of the Freedom of Speech because, in many cases, people can only engage in effective speech when they join together with others. The Supreme Court has found the Constitution to protect the freedom of association in two cases:

1. *Intimate Associations:* A fundamental element of personal liberty is the right to choose to enter into and maintain certain intimate human relationships. These intimate human relationships are known as "intimate associations." The paradigmatic "intimate association" is the family.
2. *Expressive Associations:* Expressive associations are groups that engage in activities protected by the First Amendment-speech, assembly, petitioning government for a redress of grievances, and the free exercise of religion. Because the role of these relationships is central to safeguarding individual freedoms, they may receive protection from undue intrusion by the State. Thus, there is a constitutional freedom to associate as a means of preserving other individual liberties.

Limitation

However, the implicit First Amendment right of association is not a general right of association. For example, it is illegal in the United States to consider race in the making and enforcement of private contracts other than marriage or taking affirmative action. This limitation of freedom of association results from Section 1981 of Title 42 of the Civil Rights Act, as weighed against the First Amendment according to the court decision Runyon v. McCrary, 427 U.S. 160 (1976).

The holding of Runyon is that the defendant private schools were free to express and teach their views, such as white separatism, but could not discriminate on the basis of race in the provision of services to the general public. So if the plaintiff African-American children wished to attend such private schools, and were clearly qualified in all respects (but race) and were able to pay the fees, and were willing to attend despite the fact that the schools strongly disliked them, then the schools were required by Section 1981 to admit them.

The general rule to be drawn from this is that the First Amendment protects the right to express, including expression of racial discrimination, but people may not practice such ideas even within private associations.

This doctrine rests on the interpretation of a private contract as a "badge" of slavery when either party considers race in choosing the other. The phrase "badges... of slavery" is from the Circuit Court decision 109 U.S. 3 (1883) upholding the power of Congress to pass laws under the Thirteenth Amendment to the United States Constitution compensating for the legacy of slavery.

Libertarian

Freedom of association is a term popular in libertarian literature. It is used to describe the concept of absolute freedom to live in a community or be part of an organization whose values or culture are closely related to what one wants; or on a more basic level, to associate with any individual one chooses. The right-libertarian (or "free market capitalist," "minarchist") concept of freedom of association is often rebuked from a moral/ ethical context.

Under laws in such a system, businessowners could refuse custom to anyone for whatever reason. Opponents argue that such practices are regressive and would lead to greater prejudice within society. Those right-libertarians sympathetic to freedom of association, such as Richard Epstein, in a case of refusing service, a case of the freedom of contract, respond that unjustified discrimination incurs a cost and therefore a competitive disadvantage.

Workers' Freedom of Association

To most of the world, the freedom of association is a right identified under international labor standards as the right of workers' to organize and collectively bargain. The freedom of association is recognized as a fundamental human right by a number of human rights documents, including the Universal Declaration of Human Rights and International Labor Organization Convention C87 and Convention C98 --two of the eight fundamental, core international labor standards.

3

Political Philosophy

Political philosophy is the study of fundamental questions about the state, government, politics, liberty, justice, property, rights, law and the enforcement of a legal code by authority: what they are, why (or even if) they are needed, what makes a government legitimate, what rights and freedoms it should protect and why, what form it should take and why, what the law is, and what duties citizens owe to a legitimate government, if any, and when it may be legitimately overthrown-if ever. In a vernacular sense, the term "political philosophy" often refers to a general view, or specific ethic, belief or attitude, about politics that does not necessarily belong to the technical discipline of philosophy.

Three central concerns of political philosophy have been the political economy by which property rights are defined and access to capital is regulated, the demands of justice in distribution and punishment, and the rules of truth and evidence that determine judgments in the law.

HISTORY OF POLITICAL PHILOSOPHY

Ancient Period

As an academic discipline, Western political philosophy has its origins in ancient Greek society, when city-states were experimenting with various forms of political organization including monarchy, tyranny, aristocracy, oligarchy, and democracy. The first classic work of political philosophy is Plato's The Republic, which was followed by Aristotle's Politics. Roman political philosophy was influenced by the Stoics, and the Roman statesman Cicero wrote on political philosophy.

Independently, Confucius, Mencius, Mozi and the Legalist school in China, and the Laws of Manu and Chanakya and in India, all sought to find means of restoring political unity and stability; in the case of the former three through the cultivation of virtue, in the last by imposition of discipline. In India, Kautilya, in his Arthashastra, developed a viewpoint which recalls both the Legalists and Machiavelli. Ancient Chinese and Indian civilization resembled Greek in that there was a unified culture divided into rival states. In the case of China, philosophers found themselves obliged to confront social and political breakdown, and seek solutions to the crisis that confronted their entire civilization.

The early Christian philosophy of Augustine of Hippo was by and large a rewrite of Plato in a Christian context. The main change that Christian thought brought was to moderate the Stoicism and theory of justice of the Roman world, and emphasize the role of the state in applying mercy as a moral example. Augustine also preached that one was not a member of his or her city, but was a citizen of the City of God. Augustine's The City of God is an influential work of this period that refuted the thesis, after the First Sack of Rome, that the Christian view could be realized on Earth at all -a view many Christian Romans held.

Islamic Period

The rise of Islam, based on both the Qur'an and Muhammad strongly altered the power balances and perceptions of origin of power in the Mediterranean region. Early Muslim philosophy emphasized an inexorable link between science and religion, and the process of ijtihad to find truth -in effect all philosophy was "political" as it had real implications for governance. This view was challenged by the Mutazilite philosophers, who held a more Greek view and were supported by secular aristocracy who sought freedom of action independent of the mosque. By the medieval period, however, the Asharite view of Islam had in general triumphed.

Islam was widely exposed to the writings of both Plato and Aristotle, however the main political writing from the Greeks that Islam encountered was Plato's Republic. The West and

Christianity were exposed to both the Republic and Aristotle's Politics. Many credit this as to why the Middle East and the West developed differently "politically speaking".

Islamic "political philosophy", was, indeed, rooted in the very sources of Islam i.e. the Qur'an and the Sunna, the words and practices of the Prophet. However, in the Western thought, it is generally known that it was a specific area peculiar merely to the great philosophers of Islam: Kindi, Farabi, Ibni Sina, Ibn-i Bacce and Ibni Rusd. So, the political conceptions of Islam such as kudrah, sultan, ummah, cemaa -and even the "core" terms of the Qur'an, i.e. ibada, din, rab and ilah-should be taken as the very basis of an analysis. Hence, not only the ideas of the "Muslim political philosophers" but also many other "jurists" and "ulama" posed "political" ideas and even "theories." For example, the ideas of Hawarij in the very early years of Islamic history on Hilafa and Ummah, or that of Shia on the concept of Imamah deserve to be named as the proofs of "political" thought. In fact, the clashes between the Ehl-i Sunna and Shia in VII. and VIII. centuries had a genuine political character.

Muslim "political philosophy" did not ceased in the classical period. Despite the fluctuations in its original character during the medieval period, it has lasted even in the modern era. Especially with the emergence of "Islamic radicalism" as a "political" movement, political thought has revived in Muslim world. The political ideas of Abduh, Afgani, Kutub, Mawdudi, Shariati and Khomeini has caught on an ethusiasm in especially Muslim youth in 20th century.

Medieval Period

Medieval political philosophy in Europe was heavily influenced by Christian thinking. It had much in common with the Islamic thinking in that the Roman Catholics also subordinated philosophy to theology. Perhaps the most influential political philosopher of the medieval period was St. Thomas Aquinas who helped reintroduce Aristotle's works, which had been preserved in the interim only by the Muslims. Aquinas's use of them set the agenda for scholastic political philosophy, and dominated European thought for centuries.

The most influential work, however, was that which ended this period, that being Niccolò Machiavelli's The Prince, 1532. It is that work, and The Discourses, a rigorous analysis of the classical period, from which modern political philosophy is largely derived. Machiavelli was a republican, although he is falsely identified as the founder of a much harsher view of politics.

ENLIGHTENMENT PERIOD

During the Enlightenment period, new theories about what the human is and reality, along with the discovery of other societies in the Americas, and the changing needs of political societies (especially in the wake of the English Civil War, the American Revolution and the French Revolution) led to new questions and insights by such thinkers as Jean-Jacques Rousseau, Thomas Hobbes, Montesquieu and John Locke - known by most for his influential theory of the social contract.

These theorists were driven by two basic questions: by what right or need do people form "states," and what is the best form for a "state." These large questions involved a conceptual distinction between "state" and "government." Basically, "state" refers to a set of enduring institutions through which power is distributed and its use justified. "Government" refers to a specific group of people who occupy these institutions, and exercise particular policies. This conceptual distinction continues to operate in political science, although some political scientists, philosophers, historians and cultural anthropologists have argued that most political action in any given society occurs outside of its state, and that there are societies that are not organized into states which nevertheless must be considered politically.

Political and economic relations were drastically changed by these views as the guild was subordinated to free trade, and Roman Catholic dominance of theology was increasingly challenged by Protestant churches subordinate to each nation-state and which preached in the "vulgar" or native language of each region.

In the Ottoman Empire, these reforms did not take place and these views did not spread until much later. Also, there was no contact with the New World and the advanced civilizations of the Aztec, Maya, Inca, Mohican, Delaware, Huron and especially the Iroquois, who gave a great boost to Christian thought and in many cases actually inspired some of the institutions adopted in the United States: for example, Benjamin Franklin was a great admirer of some of the methods of the Iroquois Confederacy, and much of early American literature emphasized the political philosophy of the natives.

INDUSTRIALIZATION AND THE EARLY MODERN AGE

The industrial revolution produced a parallel revolution in political thought. Urbanization and capitalism greatly reshaped society. During this same period, the socialist movement began to form. In the mid-19th century, Marxism was developed, and socialism in general gained increasing popular support, mostly from the urban working class. By the late 19th century, socialism and trade unions were established members of the political landscape. In addition, the various branches of anarchism and syndicalism also gained some prominence. In the Anglo-American world, anti-imperialism and pluralism began gaining currency at the turn of the century.

World War I was a watershed event in human history. The Russian Revolution of 1917 (and similar, albeit less successful, revolutions in many other European countries) brought communism -and in particular the political theory of Leninism, but also on a smaller level Luxembourgism (gradually) -on the world stage. At the same time, social democratic parties won elections and formed governments for the first time, often as a result of the introduction of universal suffrage.

In response to the sweeping social changes that occurred in the years after the war, ultra-reactionary ideologies such as fascism began to take shape. In particular, the rise of the Nazis in Germany would later lead to the Second World War.

All political thought was deeply affected by the Great Depression, which led many theorists to reconsider the ideas they had previously held as axiomatic. In the United States, President Franklin D. Roosevelt introduced the New Deal. In Europe, both the extreme left and the extreme right gained increasing popularity.

CONTEMPORARY POLITICAL PHILOSOPHY

After World War II political philosophy moved into a temporary eclipse in the Anglo-American academic world, as analytic philosophers expressed skepticism about the possibility that normative judgments had cognitive content, and political science turned toward statistical methods and behavioralism. The 1950s saw pronouncements of the 'death' of the discipline, followed by debates about that thesis. A handful of continental European emigres to Britain and the United States-including Hannah Arendt, Karl Popper, Friedrich Hayek, Leo Strauss, Isaiah Berlin, Eric Voegelin and Judith Shklar-encouraged continued study in the field, but in the 1950s and 60s they and their students remained somewhat marginal in their disciplines.

Communism remained an important focus especially during the 1950s and 60s. Zionism, racism and colonialism were important issues that arose. In general, there was a marked trend towards a pragmatic approach to political issues, rather than a philosophical one. Much academic debate regarded one or both of two pragmatic topics: how (or whether) to apply utilitarianism to problems of political policy, or how (or whether) to apply economic models (such as rational choice theory) to political issues. The rise of feminism and the end of colonial rule and of the political exclusion of such minorities as African Americans in the developed world has led to feminist, postcolonial, and multicultural thought becoming significant.

In Anglo-American academic political philosophy the publication of John Rawls's A Theory of Justice in 1971 is considered a milestone. Rawls used a thought experiment, the original position, in which representative parties choose principles of justice for the basic structure of society from behind a veil of ignorance. Rawls also offered a criticism of utilitarian approaches to questions of political justice. Robert Nozick's book Anarchy, State, and Utopia (1974) responded to Rawls from a libertarian perspective.

Contemporary with analytic ethics-oriented work in Anglo-American thought, within Europe several new lines of philosophy directed at critique of existing societies arose between the 1950s and 1980s. Many of these took elements of Marxist economic analysis, but combined them with a more cultural or ideological emphasis. Out of the Frankfurt School, thinkers like Herbert Marcuse, Theodor W. Adorno, Max Horkheimer, and Jürgen Habermas combined Marxian and Freudian perspectives. Along somewhat different lines, a number of other continental thinkers-still largely influenced by Marxism-put new emphases on structuralism and on a "return to Hegel". Within the (post-) structuralist line (though mostly not taking that label) are thinkers such as Gilles Deleuze, Michel Foucault, Claude Lefort, and Jean Baudrillard. The Situationists were more influenced by Hegel; Guy Debord, in particular, moved a Marxist analysis of commodity fetishism to the realm of consumption, and looked at the relation between consumerism and dominant ideology formation.

Another debate developed around the (distinct) criticisms of liberal political theory made by Bernard Williams and Charles Taylor. The liberalism-communitarianism debate is often considered valuable for generating a new set of philosophical problems, rather than a profound and illuminating clash of perspectives.

Today some debates regarding punishment and law center on the question of natural law and the degree to which human constraints on action are determined by nature, as revealed by science in particular. Other debates focus on questions of cultural and gender identity as central to politics.

INFLUENTIAL POLITICAL PHILOSOPHERS

A larger list of political philosophers is intended to be closer to exhaustive. Listed below are a few of the most canonical or important thinkers, and especially philosophers whose central focus was in political philosophy and/or who are good representatives of a particular school of thought.

- *Confucius:* The first thinker to relate ethics to the political order.
- *Chanakya:* Founder of an independent political thought in India, laid down rules and guidelines for social, law and political order in society.
- *Mozi:* Eponymous founder of the Mohist school, advocated a strict utilitarianism.

- *Socrates/Plato:* Named their practice of inquiry "philosophy", and thereby stand at the head of a prominent (often called "Western") tradition of systematic intellectual analysis. Set as a partial basis to that tradition the relation between knowledge on the one hand, and a just and good society on the other. Socrates is widely considered founder of Western political philosophy, via his spoken influence on Athenian contemporaries; since Socrates never wrote anything, much of what we know about him and his teachings comes through his most famous student, Plato.
- *Aristotle:* Wrote his Politics as an extension of his Nicomachean Ethics. Notable for the theories that humans are social animals, and that the polis (Ancient Greek city state) existed to bring about the good life appropriate to such animals. His political theory is based upon an ethics of perfectionism (as is Marx's, on some readings).
- *Mencius:* One of the most important thinkers in the Confucian school, he is the first theorist to make a coherent argument for an obligation of rulers to the ruled.
- *Han Feizi:* The major figure of the Chinese Fajia (Legalist) school, advocated government that adhered to laws and a strict method of administration.
- *Niccolò Machiavelli:* First systematic analyses of: (1) how consent of a populace is negotiated between and among rulers rather than simply a naturalistic (or theological) given of the structure of society; (2) precursor to the concept of ideology in articulating the epistemological structure of commands and law.
- *Thomas Hobbes:* Generally considered to have first articulated how the concept of a social contract that justifies the actions of rulers (even where contrary to the individual desires of governed citizens), can be reconciled with a conception of sovereignty.
- *Baruch Spinoza:* Set forth the first analysis of "rational egoism" in which the rational interest of self is

conformance with pure reason. To Spinoza's thinking, in a society in which each individual is guided of reason, political authority would be superfluous.

- *John Locke:* Like Hobbes, described a social contract theory based on citizens' fundamental rights in the state of nature. He departed from Hobbes in that, based on the assumption of a society in which moral values are independent of governmental authority and widely shared, he argued for a government with power limited to the protection of personal property. His arguments may have been deeply influential to the formation of the United States Constitution.
- *Baron de Montesquieu:* Analyzed protection of liberty by a "balance of powers" in the divisions of a state.
- *David Hume:* Hume criticized the social contract theory of John Locke and others as resting on a myth of some actual agreement. Hume was a realist in recognizing the role of force to forge the existence of states and that consent of the governed was merely hypothetical.
- *Jean-Jacques Rousseau:* Analyzed the social contract as an expression of the general will, and controversially argued in favor of absolute democracy where the people at large would act as sovereign.
- *Immanuel Kant:* Argued that participation in civil society is undertaken not for self-preservation, as per Thomas Hobbes, but as a moral duty. First modern thinker who fully analyzed structure and meaning of obligation. Argued that an international organization was needed to preserve world peace.
- *Adam Smith:* Often said to have founded modern economics; explained emergence of economic benefits from the self-interested behavior ("the hidden hand") of artisans and traders. While praising its efficiency, Smith also expressed concern about the effects of industrial labor (e.g. repetitive activity) on workers. His work on moral sentiments sought to explain social bonds outside the economic sphere.

- *Edmund Burke:* Irish member of the British parliament, Burke is credited with the creation of conservative thought. Burke's Reflections on the Revolution in France is the most popular of his writings where he denounced the French revolution. Burke was one of the biggest supporters of the American Revolution.
- *John Adams:* Enlightenment writer who defended the American cause for independence. Adams was a Lockean thinker, who was appalled by the French revolution. Adams is known for his outspoken commentary in favor of the American revolution. He defended the American form of republicanism over the French liberal democracy. Adams is considered the founder of American conservative thought.
- *Thomas Paine:* Enlightenment writer who defended liberal democracy, the American Revolution, and French Revolution in Common Sense and The Rights of Man.
- *Jeremy Bentham:* The first thinker to analyze social justice in terms of maximization of aggregate individual benefits. Founded the philosophical/ethical school of thought known as utilitarianism.
- *John Stuart Mill:* A utilitarian, and the person who named the system; he goes further than Bentham by laying the foundation for liberal democratic thought in general and modern, as opposed to classical, liberalism in particular. Articulated the place of invididual liberty in an otherwise utilitarian framework.
- *Karl Marx:* In large part, added the historical dimension to an understanding of society, culture and economics. Created the concept of ideology in the sense of (true or false) beliefs that shape and control social actions. Analyzed the fundamental nature of class as a mechanism of governance and social interaction.
- *John Dewey:* Co-founder of pragmatism and analyzed the essential role of education in the maintenance of democratic government.
- *Antonio Gramsci:* Instigated the concepts hegemony and social formation. Fused the ideas of Marx, Engels,

Spinoza and others within the so-called dominant ideology thesis (the ruling ideas of society are the ideas of its rulers).

- *Herbert Marcuse:* One of the principle thinkers within the Frankfurt School, and generally important in efforts to fuse the thought of Freud and Marx. Introduced the concept of repressive desublimation, in which social control can operate not only by direct control, but also by manipulation of desire. Analyzed the role of advertising and propaganda in societal consensus.
- *Friedrich Hayek:* Advanced an analysis under which any collectivism could only be maintained by a central authority. Advocated free-market capitalism in which the sole role of the state was to maintain the rule of law.
- *Hannah Arendt:* Analyzed the roots of totalitarianism and introduced the concept of the "banality of evil" (how ordinary technocratic rationality comes to deplorable fruition). Brought distinctive elements of and revisions to the philosophy of Martin Heidegger into political thought.
- *Leo Strauss:* Strauss is known for his writings on the classical and modernity philosophers and denouncement of the modern politics.
- *John Rawls:* Revitalised the study of normative political philosophy in Anglo-American universities with his 1971 book A Theory of Justice, which uses a version of social contract theory to answer fundamental questions about justice and to criticise utilitarianism.
- *Robert Nozick:* Criticized Rawls, and argued for Libertarianism, by appeal to a hypothetical history of the state and the real history of property.

BUREAUCRATIC POLITICS

Bureaucratic politics theories or explanations of why particular public policy decisions got made the way they did stress the motivation by the relevant officials in the government bureaucracy to protect or promote their own agency's special interests (in competition with other agencies) as a major motivating factor in shaping the timing and the content of government decisions. Each bureau (or other governmental sub-division) continually strives to maximize its budget and its authorized manpower, as well as to protect or extend its operating autonomy and discretion in decision-making in the area of its assigned responsibilities. Often this can be most readily accomplished by lobbying for an expansion of the scope of the bureau's responsibilities that are prescribed by Congress or the legislature. Because bureaucratic agencies are in competition with each other for budget shares and for personnel allocations as well as for gaining responsibility for juicy new programs justifying expansion, the policies and policy recommendations generated in the executive branch of the government and passed on to both the chief executive and the legislative authorities are often better understood as the by-product of bureaucratic turf-battles and expedient compromises between bureaucratic chieftains than as the product of reasoned analysis of how most effectively and efficiently to carry out the policy commitments of the elected chief executive or to serve the public interest.

BUREAUCRACY

In ordinary usage, "bureaucracy" refers to a complex, specialized organization (especially a governmental organization) composed of non-elected, highly trained professional administrators and clerks hired on a full-time basis to perform administrative services and tasks. Bureaucratic organizations are broken up into specialized departments or ministries, to each of which is assigned responsibility for pursuing a limited number of the government's many official goals and policies - those falling within a single relatively narrow functional domain. The departments or ministries are subdivided into divisions that are each assigned even more specialized responsibilities for accomplishing various portions or aspects of the department's overall tasks, and these divisions are in turn composed of multiple agencies or bureaus with even more minutely specialized functions (and their own subdivisions). Bureaucratic organizations always rely heavily on the principle of hierarchy and rank, which requires a clear, unambiguous chain of command through which "higher" officials supervise the "lower" officials, who of course supervise their own subordinate administrators within the various subdivisions and sub-subdivisions of the organization.

Bureaucratic organizations are typically charcterized by great attention to the precise and stable delineation of authority or jurisdiction among the various subdivisions and among the officials who comprise them, which is done mainly by requiring the organization's employees to operate strictly according to fixed procedures and detailed rules designed to routinize nearly all decision-making. Some of the most important of these rules and procedures may be specified in laws or decrees enacted by the higher "political" authorities that are empowered to set the official goals and general policies for the organization, but upper-level (and even medium-level) bureaucrats typically are delegated considerable discretionary powers for elaborating their own detailed rules and procedures. Because the incentive structures of bureaucratic organizations largely involve rewarding strict adherence to formal rules and punishing unauthorized departures from standard operating procedures (rather than focussing on measureable individual contributions toward actually attaining the organization's politically assigned goals), such organizations tend to rely very heavily upon extensive written records and standardized forms, which serve primarily to document the fact that all decisions about individual "cases" were taken in accordance with approved guidelines and procedures rather than merely reflecting the personal preferences or subjective judgment of the individual bureaucrat involved.

The classic social scientific analysis of bureaucracy was that of the pioneer sociologist Max Weber in his 1922 book Economy and Society. Weber, like the good German he was, believed that a permanent, well-educated, conscientious, "non-partisan," Prussian-style bureaucracy professionally committed to implementing whatever decisions the legitimate rulers of the state might arrive at was the best organizational form yet discovered for the rational and efficient pursuit of collective social goals in a modern society with a specialized and highly complex division of labor. In his writings, Weber devoted considerable attention to showing ways in which the gradual evolution of modern bureaucratic methods and values helped to remove the formidable obstacles to economic development, social advancement and political stability that had been inherent in the much less professionalized and systematized practices of government administration in feudal Europe and most other premodern societies.

While most other social scientific students of bureaucracy have recognized the historical importance of bureaucratic organizational techniques in creating the powerful, centralized nation-states (and other very large organizations such as modern business corporations and labor unions) that predominate in the industrialized world of the 20th century, it is fair to say that they have generally been considerably less one-sidedly approving of bureaucracy than Weber was. Despite their many advantages for dealing efficiently and effectively with routine, recurring problems in a fairly stable and predictable environment, bureaucratic methods also have their dark side. Hired and promoted largely on the basis of educational credentials and seniority within the organization and protected by civil service personnel practices designed to provide a high degree of job security, bureaucratic officials tend to be very well insulated from responsibility for the external consequences of their decisions and actions as long as they stay formally within prescribed procedures.

Such sociologists as Robert K. Merton and Michel Crozier have shown that pressures on officials to conform to fixed rules and detailed procedures, when added to the narrow responsibilities of highly specialized agencies for pursuing only a select few of the many objectives that government has set, quite regularly leads bureaucrats to become defensive, rigid, and completely unresponsive to the urgent individual needs and concerns of the private citizens and outside organizations with which they come into professional contact. ("That's not my department. I cannot help you.") Because the salaries and promotion prospects of officials working in large bureaucracies seldom depend upon measurable success or efficiency by the organization in achieving its larger goals (which are often especially difficult to measure in government agencies and other non-profit oriented organizations that lack a clear "bottom line") and because any departure from established routines always requires permission from remote higher levels of the hierarchy, large bureaucratic organizations tend to be very slow and cumbersome in making important policy decisions (the "buck-passing" phenomenon) and are especially dull-witted in recognizing and responding to the consequences of major changes in economic, social and technological conditions and circumstances outside the organization itself. In other words, individual officials working under bureaucratic incentive systems frequently find it to be in their own best interests to adhere rigidly to internal rules and formalities in a ritualistic fashion, behaving as if "proper procedure" were more important than the larger goals for serving their clients or the general public that they are supposedly designed to accomplish (the "red tape" phenomenon).

INCENTIVE

Something that provides a motive for a person to choose a particular course of action. Organized cooperative activities in a social setting --such as cooperation for the purpose of economic production --depends upon each of the participants having some sort of incentive to behave in the required cooperative fashion. Different societies (and even different organizations within the same society) vary considerably in the nature of the incentive systems upon which they characteristically rely to organize their common projects. Incentives may be classified according to a number of different schemes, but one of the more useful classifications subdivides incentives into three general types: moral incentives, coercive incentives and remunerative incentives.

- A person has a moral incentive to behave in a particular way when he has been taught to believe that it is the "right" or "proper" or "admirable" thing to do. If he behaves as others expect him to, he may expect the approval or even the admiration of the other members of the collectivity and enjoy an enhanced sense of acceptance or self-esteem. If he behaves improperly, he may expect verbal expressions of condemnation, scorn, ridicule or even ostracism from the collectivity, and he may experience unpleasant feelings of guilt, shame or self-condemnation.

- A person has a coercive incentive to behave in a particular way when it has been made known to him that failure to do so will result in some form of physical aggression being directed at him by other members of the collectivity in the form of inflicting pain or physical harm on him or his loved ones, depriving him of his freedom of movement, or perhaps confiscating or destroying his treasured possessions.
- A person has a remunerative incentive to behave in a particular way if it has been made known to him that doing so will result in some form of material reward he will not otherwise receive. If he behaves as desired, he will receive some specified amount of a valuable good or service (or money with which he can purchase whatever he wishes) in exchange.

All known societies employ all three sorts of incentives to at least some degree in order to evoke from its members the necessary degree of cooperation for the society to survive and flourish. However, different societies differ radically in the relative proportions of these different kinds of incentives used within their characteristic mix of incentives. "Primitive" or "traditional" cultures such as those of hunter-gatherers tend to rely very heavily on moral incentives and make relatively little use of coercive and remunerative incentives to sustain social cooperation. More "advanced" or "modern" societies built around a much more specialized and complex division of labor tend to make much greater use of both coercive and remunerative incentives in organizing social activities, while still relying in very important ways upon moral or normative incentives. Among the more "advanced" societies, liberal societies try to rely as much as possible on remunerative and moral incentives in preference to the use of coercive incentives, while authoritarian and totalitarian societies display much less reluctance to resort to coercive incentives in securing social cooperation.

STATE

1. A specialized type of political organization characterized by a full-time, specialized, professional work force of

tax-collectors, soldiers, policemen, bureaucrats and the like that exercises supreme political authority over a defined territory with a permanent population, independent from any enduring external political control and possessing a local predominance of coercive power (always supplemented with moral and remunerative incentives as well) great enough to maintain general obedience to its laws or commands within its territorial borders. The first known states were created in ancient times in Egypt, Mesopotamia, India, China, Mexico and Peru, but it is only in relatively modern times that states have almost completely displaced alternative "stateless" forms of political organization of societies all over the planet. (Roving bands of hunter-gatherers and even fairly sizable and complex tribal societies based on herding or agriculture have existed without any full-time specialized state organization, and these "stateless" forms of political organization have in fact prevailed for all of the prehistory and much of the history of the human species.)

2. One of the component territorial political units in a larger federal state that are so called because, although they actually fall short of full independent statehood or sovereignty, they still possess a very large degree of autonomy in decision-making with respect to most of their internal affairs and are thus also legally allowed to exercise various forms of coercion over their regional populations.

Nation State

A form of state in which those who exercise power claim legitimacy for their rule partly or solely on the grounds that their power is exercised for the promotion of the distinctive interests, values and cultural heritage of a particular nation whose members ideally would constitute all, or most of, its subject population and all of whom would dwell within the borders.

Nation

A large aggregation or agglomeration of people sharing a common and distinctive racial, linguistic, historical and/or cultural heritage that has led its members to think of themselves as belonging to a valued natural community sharing a common destiny that ought to be preserved forever.

Nationalism

An ideology, or rather a whole category of similar ideologies, based on the premise that each nation (or at least the ideologist's own nation) constitutes a natural political community whose members should all live together under the authority of "their own" independent nation state. When the people of one nation live in large numbers in a multi-ethnic state or in states with government(s) dominated by political elites drawn from another nationality, nationalism often becomes an ideology justifying rebellion or secession in order to create or recreate a nation state for the heretofore subjugated nation. When substantial numbers of people seen as belonging to the nation live outside the borders of their own nation state, nationalism often becomes an ideology justifying an aggressive foreign policy striving to expand the state's borders to include them. Nationalist ideologies usually claim that their respective nation possess special national characteristics or virtues that make them morally and intellectually superior to all other nations and should qualify their nation state for a special or privileged role in the world at large.

Ideology

A comprehensive and coherent set of basic beliefs about political, economic, social and cultural affairs that is held in common by a sizable group of people within a society. Such interrelated ideas and teachings purport both to explain how political, economic, social and cultural institutions really do work and also to prescribe how such institutions ought ideally to operate. Conservative ideologies seek to demonstrate a close correspondence between "the way things are" and "the way things ought to be," thus legitimizing the existing order in the eyes of those who can be convinced to believe in the ideology. Radical and revolutionary ideologies, on the other hand, set unconventional, higher, or even utopian standards with regard to what would constitute a legitimate and supportable social-economic-political system and then demonstrate in detail that the existing order does not even come close to meeting these standards, thereby de-legitimizing the existing system and helping mobilize believers in the ideology for concerted action to reform or overthrow the existing order. (In addition to their descriptive and prescriptive functions about existing and ideal social orders, ideologies may also include more specialized doctrines regarding the most suitable political strategies and tactics to be pursued by believers in their efforts to shore up or undermine the existing order)

One useful way of categorizing ideologies from a political point of view focusses on differences in the ideologies' prescriptions for how much the government ought to be involved in directing or regulating economic, social and cultural affairs and how much individuals or voluntary organizations ought to be left alone to make their own (widely varied) decisions in these spheres of life. In this course, for example, we frequently employ a two-dimensional classification of ideologies proposed by Maddox and Lilie that is based on assessing people's preferences for government regulation versus non-regulation in:

1. Economic decisions
2. Non-economic or life-style decisions.

It should be noted that the term "ideology" often has a somewhat derogatory flavor, especially in Anglo-American societies, because it often carries the implication that "ideological" thought is unduly biased, dogmatic and distorted, an obstacle rather than an aid in perceiving how the world "really" works. ("You, sir, are an ideologue. I, on the other hand, am a pragmatic man of reason who sees things the way they really are.")

Legitimacy

The principle that indicates the acceptance of the decisions of government leaders and officials by (most of) the public on the grounds that these leaders' acquisition and exercise of power has been in accordance with the society's generally accepted procedures and political or moral values. Legitimacy may be conferred upon power holders in a variety of ways in different societies, usually involving solemn formal rituals of a religious or quasi-religious nature --royal birth and coronation in monarchies, popular election and "swearing in" in democracies and so on. "Legitimate" rulers typically require less use of physical coercion to enforce their decisions than rulers lacking in legitimacy, because most of the people are apt to feel a moral obligation to obey the former but not the latter. Consequently, people who gain or hold power by illegitimate means tend to work very hard to discover or create ways of endowing themselves with legitimacy after the fact, often by inventing a new ideology or religion and attempting to indoctrinate the people with its legitimating formulas through various forms of propaganda, thus creating moral incentives for the citizenry to obey their government.

Propaganda

Persuasive communications directed at a specific audience that are designed to influence the targeted audience's opinions, beliefs and emotions in such a way as to bring about specific, planned alterations in their behavior. The information communicated by the propagandist may be true or false, the values appealed to may be sincerely held by the propagandist or cynically manipulated, and the presentation may be either logically and dispassionately argued or rhetorically tailored to arouse the most irrational emotions and prejudices -but the message content of propaganda is always deliberately selected and slanted to lead the audience toward a predetermined mindset that benefits the cause of the propagandist.

Socialism

A class of ideologies favoring an economic system in which all or most productive resources are the property of the government, in which the production and distribution of goods and services are administered primarily by the government rather than by private enterprise, and in which any remaining private production and distribution (socialists differ on how much of this is tolerable) is heavily regulated by the government rather than by market processes. Both democratic and non-democratic socialists insist that the government they envision as running the economy must in principle be one that truly reflects the will of the masses of the population (or at least their "true" best interests), but of course they differ considerably in their ideas about what sorts of political institutions and practices are required to ensure this will be so. In practice, socialist economic principles may be combined with an extremely wide range of attitudes toward personal freedom, civil liberties, mass political participation, bureaucracy and political competition, ranging from Western European democratic socialism to the more authoritarian socialisms of many third world regimes to the totalitarian excesses of Soviet-style socialism or communism.

Communism

1. Any ideology based on the communal ownership of all property and a classless social structure, with economic production and distribution to be directed and regulated by means of an authoritative economic plan that supposedly embodies the interests of the community as a whole. Karl Marx is today the most famous early theoretician of communism, but he did not invent the term or the basic social ideals, which he mostly borrowed and adapted from the less systematic theories of earlier French utopian socialists --grafting these onto a philosophical framework Marx derived from the German philosophers Hegel and Feuerbach, while adding in a number of economic theories derived from his reinterpretation of the writings of such early political economists such as Adam Smith, Thomas Malthus, and David Ricardo. In most versions of the communist utopia, everyone would be expected to cooperate enthusiastically in the process of production, but the individual citizen's equal rights of access to consumer goods would be completely unaffected by his/her own individual contribution to production --hence Karl Marx's famous slogan "From each according to his ability; to each according to his need." The Marxian and other 19th century communist utopias also were expected to dispense with such "relics of the past" as trading, money, prices, wages, profits, interest, land-rent, calculations of profit and loss, contracts, banking, insurance, lawsuits, etc. It was expected that such a radical reordering of the economic sphere of life would also more or less

rapidly lead to the elimination of all other major social problems such as class conflict, political oppression, racial discrimination, the inequality of the sexes, religious bigotry, and cultural backwardness --as well as put an end to such more "psychological" forms of suffering as alienation, anomie, and feelings of powerlessness.

2. The specifically Marxist-Leninist variant of socialism which emphasizes that a truly communist society can be achieved only through the violent overthrow of capitalism and the establishment of a "dictatorship of the proletariat" that is to prepare the way for the future idealized society of communism under the authoritarian guidance of a hierarchical and disciplined Communist Party.
3. A world-wide revolutionary political movement inspired by the October Revolution (Red Oktober) in Russia in 1917 and advocating the establishment everywhere of political, economic, and social institutions and policies modeled on those of the Soviet Union (or, in some later versions, China or Albania) as a means for eventually attaining a communist society.

Capitalism

A form of economic order characterized by private ownership of the means of production and the freedom of private owners to use, buy and sell their property or services on the market at voluntarily agreed prices and terms, with only minimal interference with such transactions by the state or other authoritative third parties.

Market

In its original meaning, a physical coming together of a sizable number of merchants and prospective customers at a pre-arranged time and place (in medieval Europe, typically once a week on the main square of the largest village in the vicinity) for the purpose of striking deals to buy and sell a variety of goods and services. Large numbers of customers came to such organized markets because they found it convenient to be able to make many of their necessary purchases on the same day in one central location (minimizing their total travel time and other travel costs) and because the presence of many merchants offering similar wares made it much more practical to comparison shop for the best deals in terms of quality and price. Merchants were often attracted from considerable distances to participate in such markets because of the opportunity to sell so many of their wares to such large numbers of potential customers in such a short time. Modern day flea markets, farmers' markets, gun shows and crafts fairs are fairly close to the original concept.

In the language of modern industrial society, and especially in the language of professional economists, the concept of a market has been generalized and abstracted far beyond the original rather concrete and localized meaning of the term. In the more modern sense of the term, a market is the generalized name tag for the whole process that gets under way whenever a sizable number of people free to buy and/or sell a particular kind of good or service are in more or less close communication with each other (either personally and directly or else through the mediation of advertising, catalogs, news reports, postal carriers, telephone systems, computer networks, etc.) so that information about the terms of recent transactions and current offers to buy or sell is generally available to a large number of interested parties at relatively low cost--regardless of the participants' physical proximity or distance. Such technological innovations of the industrial age as ever cheaper and more rapid transportation and communications over increasing distances both have dramatically increased the size of the areas from which buyers and sellers may be brought together to do business and have greatly reduced the need for them actually to meet face-to-face in one place in order to strike a bargain. The markets for many consumers' durable goods like automobiles or TVs and major agricultural and industrial commodities like oil, natural gas, wheat, beef, steel, forest products and computer chips are now literally worldwide in extent. (Of course, for many markets there do still exist central gathering places or locations that play an especially important role in the local, national or even worldwide networks of buyers and sellers --for example, the New York Stock Exchange, the

Chicago Commodities Exchange, the seasonal women's fashions shows in Paris and Milan, regional baseball card collectors conventions and so on but in nearly all such cases, it is not really necessary for an individual buyer or seller actually to travel to the relevant marketplace in order to participate in the broader markets of which these are nowadays only a part.)

Where markets exist and are allowed to function reasonably freely, there are certain predictable consequences for the way the economy will operate. Elaboration of these consequences is the primary purpose of most of the research in the theoretical subfield of microeconomics.

MARKET ECONOMY

An economy in which scarce resources are all (or nearly all) allocated by the interplay of supply and demand in free markets, largely unhampered by government rationing, price-fixing or other coercive interference. In classifying real historical economies, the level of "marketization" is not primarily an either/or issue but rather a matter of degree. The greater the proportion of the goods and services produced in the society that are allocated by market processes (rather than by government edict or the operation of unchangeable custom), the more meaningful it is to refer to its economy as a market economy --and the more useful is the abstract economic theory of the operation of markets likely to be for understanding and even predicting economic behavior within that society.

Probably the most critical single distinction between "basically market" and "basically non-market" (socialist, feudal, hunter-gatherer, etc.) economies is whether or not the determinations of what is to be produced and of the corresponding allocation of producers' goods (land, raw materials, machinery, and other "capital," as well as the services of labor) are accomplished primarily through free markets rather than primarily through government command or unalterable custom.

The concept of a market presupposes the existence of certain sorts of property relations in the society involved. At least some goods and services must be legally or socially regarded as alienable property --that is, there must be ascertainable individuals (or group representatives) who are recognized as having not just the right to use particular scarce economic resources for their own purposes but also the discretionary authority permanently to transfer such rights of use to someone else in exchange for some mutually agreeable quid pro quo, such as money or other goods or services. Not all human societies have recognized any such rights to transfer ownership, and most historical human societies have forbidden or placed stringent limits on the transferability of at least certain kinds of recognized property rights. In many societies (including most of Europe during the Middle Ages), individual or family rights to the perpetual use of particular plots of land were well established and protected by law --but such rights only rarely could legally be sold to someone else because the land was socially regarded as fundamentally the inalienable property of either the local community as a whole or of the tribe or clan or church or perhaps of the reigning royal family. And even in the USA since 1865, while each person's ownership of his or her own body is well established, the law will still not allow you to make a binding contract to sell yourself into slavery or even to auction off your spare bodily organs for purposes of a surgical transplant.)

It is worth noting for clarity's sake that the concept of a market does not logically presuppose the existence of "private property in the means of production" in the sense that private individuals or family households are the owners of land and capital and thus the recipients of profits, interest, rent etc. One may at least theoretically conceive of an economy of market socialism, in which workers' collectives, consumers' cooperatives, village communes or even autonomous state agencies leased from the state or held actual title to land, mines, factories, machinery and so forth --so long as the socialist production organizations were free to buy and sell their output and the use of their assigned land or capital assets to each other at freely negotiated prices responsive to conditions of supply and demand (assuming, of course, they are allowed to keep effective control of the bulk of the proceeds). There are, of course, both theoretical and practical problems with market socialism, and the costs and benefits of capitalist markets cannot be uncritically attributed to such a system. The larger point is that socialist economies have historically included varying proportions of "remnant" market elements in their make-up, and the theoretical possibilities for additional "hybrid" forms are numerous.

PROPERTY RIGHTS

A property right is the exclusive authority to determine how and by whom a particular resource is used. More broadly, property rights may be seen as a bundle of separate and distinct rights over a particular good -including at least the right of personal use, the right to demand compensation as a prerequisite for its use by other people, and the right to transfer any or all of these rights to others (either permanently by sale or temporarily through some form of contractual arrangement). Property rights may be exercised by governments through their designated officials (public ownership or public property) as well as by private individuals and other sorts of non-governmental organizations (private property).

Private Property Rights

The basic rights of individuals (and organizations or associations of people functioning as a single conglomerate "legal person" such as corporations, partnerships, churches, non-profit foundations, etc.) to the peaceful possession, control and enjoyment of the things they own as well as their rights to make contracts to rent, sell or give away all or part of their various ownership rights over these possessions (or these possessions' services) to any other people willing to accept the owners' terms. The possessions over which a person has property rights may be tangible (like real estate, factory machinery, livestock, automobiles or a jack-knife) or intangible (like contractual obligations to provide goods or services at some time in the future, shares of common stock in a corporation, bonds, insurance policies, the right to broadcast over a designated radio frequency, patents, trademarks and copyrights). In highly specialized societies, property rights over particular resources may be "unbundled" and parcelled out among many individuals according to quite complex rules of division of authority over particular aspects or uses cf the resource specified in written contracts -for example, separating mineral rights from surface rights to a parcel of land, utility easements over the same land, restrictive deed covenants and so on.

Contract

A legally binding agreement between two or more competent parties fixing the precise terms and details for a voluntary exchange of goods or services over which the contracting parties possess property rights. An agreement is a legally enforceable contract if and only if:

1. The agreement must be "mutual" (all parties have the same understanding of the meaning of their agreement --there is a "meeting of the minds");
2. The agreement must be "voluntary" (none of the parties is agreeing under the influence of violent threats or fraudulent misrepresentation of the facts);
3. There must be actual "consideration" paid (that is, each party must be achieving a benefit by giving up something he controls to get something another party controls in exchange: a simple one-sided promise to give someone else a gratuitous benefit is not a contract);
4. All parties to the agreement must be "competent" (children and the severely mentally impaired or insane are assumed by the courts to be incapable of forming a coherent intent or determining their own best interests, so the courts will not enforce the agreements they make);
5. The substance of the agreement must not be "contrary to public policy" (for example, the U.S. courts will not enforce a contract that requires one or more of the parties to commit a crime, nor will they enforce a contract by which even a legally competent adult voluntarily sells himself into life-long slavery in exchange for, say, a ten million dollar payment to his children).

Factors of Production

The scarce resources that are useful not so much for direct and immediate satisfaction of human wants as for producing other goods or services. Economists often find it useful for purposes of theoretical simplification to group the millions of different sorts of factors of production into several very broad categories and then discuss them as though all the items within each category were perfectly substitutable for each other and therefore traded on a single market. The simplest such conventional categorization of the factors of production divides them into land, labor, capital, and sometimes also entrepreneurship and/or human capital.

Derived Demand

The demand for each of the factors of production is often referred to as a "derived" demand to emphasize the fact that the relationship between the factor's price and the quantity of the factor demanded by firms employing it in production is directly dependent on consumer demand for the final product(s) the factor is used to produce.

If for some reason (say, for example, a spontaneous shift in consumer tastes) the demand for men's hats increases (shifts to the right) so that more hats than before can be sold at any given price, then the "derived" demand for felt used in making hats will also increase (shift to the right) so that felt-makers will be able to sell more felt at any given price. (We would also expect the hat-makers' demand for the labor of hatters and for specialized hat-making machinery to shift to the right in a similar fashion in response to the public's greater demand for hats.)

What is the mechanism by which a shift in demand for the final product is translated into a shift in demand for the factors of production used in its manufacture? The key is the change in the price of the final product brought about by the shift in demand for it. If the demand curve for hats shifts to the right and the (upwardly sloping) supply curve remains unchanged, then the equilibrium price and quantity in the hat market will now involve both a somewhat higher price for hats and a somewhat larger quantity of hats being produced and sold to the public. (Because of the price rise, the marginal revenues earned by the manufacturers per additional hat sold will be higher, so consequently their desire to maximize profits will lead them to produce additional hats until the marginal cost for the last hat rises to equal the new higher price.) But producing more hats than before will require more of the relevant factors of production than before, which they will want to purchase from their suppliers, shifting the demand curves for each of the factors to the right. (This increase in demand for the factors in turn will tend to raise the factor prices somewhat and to increase the quantity of them sold, which then affects the factor producers' demand for their own necessary inputs and brings about further price-and-quantity adjustments throughout the economy in an ever-widening ripple effect.)

Demand

The willingness and ability of the people within a market area to purchase particular amounts of a good or service at a variety of alternative prices during a specified time period.

Other things being held constant, the lower the price of a good (or service), the greater the quantity of it that will be demanded by purchasers at any given time.

Demand Curve

A graphical representation of a demand schedule. Conventionally, the demand curve is usually drawn between axes with price plotted along the vertical axis and number of units of the good or service demanded plotted along the horizontal axis. Where the law of demand applies to the particular market under consideration, the demand curve will slope (either gently or steeply) downwards from left to right.

Demand Schedule

A table or listing showing the number of units of a single type of good (or service) that potential purchasers would offer to buy at each of a number of varying prices during some particular time period. Demand schedules may be drawn up to reflect the behavioral propensities of a single unique individual, household, or firm or, more frequently encountered in microeconomic analysis, composite demand schedules for the particular good may be derived by adding up all the demand schedules of the large number of individuals, households or firms that are active or potentially active as purchasers in the market under consideration.

Supply

The willingness and ability of potential sellers to offer various specific amounts of a good or service for sale at each of a variety of alternative prices during a particular time period.

Other things being held constant, the higher the price of a good (or service), the larger the quantity of that good (or service) that will be offered for sale in a particular time period.

Supply Curve

A graphical representation of a supply schedule. Conventionally, the supply curve is drawn between axes with price plotted along the vertical axis and number of units of the good or service supplied plotted along the horizontal axis. Where the law of supply applies to the particular market under consideration, the supply curve will slope (either gently or steeply) upwards from left to right.

Supply Schedule

A table or listing showing the exact quantities of a single type of good (or service) that potential sellers would offer to sell at each of a number of varying prices during some particular time period. Supply schedules may be drawn up to reflect the behavioral propensities of a single unique individual, household, or firm --or, more frequently encountered in microeconomic analysis, composite supply schedules for the particular good may be derived by adding up all the supply schedules of the large number of individuals, households or firms that are active or potentially active as sellers in the market under consideration.

Law of Diminishing Returns

Sometimes also referred to as the law of variable proportions, this "law" is really a generalization economists make about the nature of technology when it is possible to combine the same factors of production in a number of different proportions to make the same product. The law states:

When increasing amounts of one factor of production are employed in production along with a fixed amount of some other production factor, after some point, the resulting increases in output of product become smaller and smaller. (That is, first the marginal returns to successive small increases in the variable factor of production turn down, and then eventually the overall average returns per unit of the variable input start decreasing.) Since the law assumes that the available quantity of at least one factor of production is fixed at a given level and that technological knowledge does not change during the relevant period, the law of diminishing returns normally translates into a statement about the short-run choice of production possibilities facing a firm (since in the longer run it is virtually always possible for the firm to acquire more of the temporarily "fixed" factor --building an additional factory building, buying additional land, installing additional machines of the same kind, installing newer and more advanced machinery, and so on.)

A simple example of the workings of the law of diminishing returns comes from gardening. A particular twenty by twenty garden plot will produce a certain number of pounds of tomatoes if the gardener just puts in the recommended number of rows and plants per row, waters them appropriately and keeps the weeds pulled. If the gardener varies this approach by adding a pound of fertilizer to the topsoil, but otherwise does everything the same, he can increase the number of pounds of tomatoes the garden plot yields by quite a bit (notice the amount of land is being held fixed or constant). If he adds two pounds of fertilizer (rather than just one), probably he can get still more tomatoes per season, but the increase in tomatoes harvested by going from one pound to two pounds of fertilizer is probably smaller than the increase he gets by going from zero pounds to one (diminishing marginal returns). Applying three pounds of fertilizer may still increase the harvest, but perhaps by only a very little bit over the yields available using just two pounds. Applying four pounds of fertilizer turns out to be overdoing it --the garden yields fewer tomatoes than applying only three pounds because the plants begin to suffer damage from root-burn. And five pounds of fertilizer turns out to kill nearly all the plants before they even flower.

Another similar example of diminishing returns in an industrial setting might be a widget factory that features a certain number of square feet of work space and a certain number of machines inside it. Neither the space available nor the number of machines can be added to without a long delay for construction or installation, but it is possible to adjust the amount of labor on short notice by working more shifts and/ or taking on some extra workers per shift. Adding extra man-hours of labor will increase the number of widgets produced, but only within limits. After a certain point, such things as worker fatigue, increasing difficulties in supervising the large work force, more frequent breakdowns by over-utilized machinery, or just plain inefficiency due to overcrowding of the work space begin to take their toll. The marginal returns to each successive increment of labor input get smaller and smaller and ultimately turn negative.

The law of diminishing returns is significant because it is part of the basis for economists' expectations that a firm's short-run marginal cost curves will slope upward as the number of units of output increases. And this in turn is an important part of the basis for the law of supply's prediction that the number of units of product that a profit-maximizing firm will wish to sell increases as the price obtainable for that product increases.

Marginal Analysis

A concept employed constantly in microeconomic theory (and quite frequently in macroeconomic theory as well) is that of the marginal change in some economic variable (such as quantity of a good produced or consumed), or even the ratio of the marginal change in one variable to the marginal change in another variable. A marginal change is a proportionally very small addition or subtraction to the total quantity of some variable. Marginal analysis is the analysis of the relationships between such changes in related economic variables. Important ideas developed in such analysis include marginal cost, marginal revenue, marginal product, marginal rate of substitution, marginal propensity to save, and so on. In microeconomic theory, "marginal" concepts are employed primarily to explicate various forms of "optimizing" behavior. (Consumers are seen as striving to maximize their utility or satisfaction. Firms are seen as striving to maximize their profits.) The maximum value of such a variable is found by identifying a value of the independent variable such that either a marginal increase or a marginal decrease from that value causes the value of the dependent variable being maximized to fall. (The student of mathematics may recognize the opportunity to apply concepts from differential calculus here, with the various marginal concepts being special names given to first derivatives of particular functions.) The valuation of the benefits (utility) and the costs of any good is determined "at the margin." For the (individual or collective) decision maker pondering how many units of a good to consume or provide to the market, net total benefits (benefits minus costs) will always be maximized at that level of consumption (or provision to the market) where the marginal benefit derived from adding the last unit equals the marginal addition to total costs of producing or acquiring that last additional unit.

Optimum

The very "best" possible situation or state of affairs according to some explicit objective that provides a precise standard of evaluation. For example, if a business firm's objective is to make the biggest profits possible (as economists generally assume it is), then the firm's optimal level of output at any given level of sales prices and production costs is that at which its profits will be the highest possible. Most of economics is concerned with analyzing how individuals or groups of people or even whole societies may achieve optimal use of available resources, and it is normally assumed that the maximum satisfaction of people's individual wants or desires is the objective of the economy that provides the relevant standard of evaluation. (Social critics, moral philosophers, religious thinkers, and political power-seekers in their various ways have often disputed the validity of this individualistic standard of evaluation, of course.)

Efficiency

In an economic sense, the ratio or proportionality between the value of the human end achieved ("benefits" or "satisfactions") and the value of the scarce resources expended to achieve it (opportunity costs). When an economist calls a situation or a practice "inefficient," he is claiming that we could achieve exactly the same desired goals with the expenditure of fewer scarce resources, or, put another way, that the amount of resources being employed could potentially produce even more of the beneficial results intended than they do. Efficiency simply means making the most we can of the limited resources we have.

Notice that "efficiency" in the economist's sense is an inherently evaluative term, not a matter of mere technical or scientific measurement of objective physical quantities, as the term might be used in an engineering context (as for example, the "efficiency" of various kinds of steam engine in transforming heat energy to useful kinetic energy). "Value of" always requires some sort of answer to the question "value to whom." When we assess the efficiency of any process or social institution or practice, just whose evaluations of the means and the ends are we using? In a well-developed market economy, assessment of economic efficiency makes heavy use of the monetary values placed on the various inputs and the resulting outputs in the open marketplace. The valuations that count are thus the valuations of those who are willing and able to support their preferences by spending their money in the ways that seem to them most likely to maximize their own satisfactions or "utility" based on their own individual tastes and preferences. The evidence that any particular economic resource is being used efficiently is, in the end, the fact that no one finds it "worth his while" to bid up the price and pay more in order to divert it to some other use. The logical and philosophical elaboration of the idea that competitive market systems are highly efficient in a much broader sense even than this is the primary content of Adam Smith's classic work The Wealth of Nations (1776). Indeed the entire subdivision of today's economic science known as "welfare economics" specializes primarily in identifying and analyzing the necessary preconditions for voluntary market interactions to generate socially efficient outcomes (and in examining the possibilities for remedies by deliberate state economic policies where those necessary preconditions may not be fully met).

Cost

In the widest sense, the measure of the value of what has to be given up in order to achieve a particular objective. In everyday language, people most often use the term rather like an accountant does, as synonymous with the total money outlays actually paid out to achieve the objective, but this is not precisely what economists mean by the term. Economists are concerned with rational decision-making, and the rational decision-maker needs to estimate in advance the full range of consequences of each of the various alternative uses of his time and resources open to him, not just the portion of the costs accounted for by money outlays. For the economist, the true cost of any decision is the value of the next best outcome (of all the other possible outcomes) that is given up because of that decision. Unless otherwise specified, when economists say "cost," they mean opportunity cost --that is, the highest valued alternative that must be sacrificed to attain something or otherwise satisfy a want. For example, the opportunity cost of a spur-of-the-moment decision to go to the movies Tuesday afternoon instead of going in to work is not just the six dollars for the ticket plus the gasoline and wear and tear on the car to get there. It also includes (at least) the four hours' wages not earned, diminished prospects for being promoted at work, and possibly such additional consequences as future hostility from co-workers who had to take up the slack, unpleasant feelings of guilt or shame, and so on. In a more extreme vein, the opportunity cost of committing suicide is not simply the money outlay for the necessary equipment, but rather the value of the total range of future satisfactions one might otherwise be able to achieve.

Transaction Costs

The costs other than the money price that are incurred in trading goods or services. Before a particular mutually beneficial trade can take place, at least one party must figure out that there may be someone with which such a trade is potentially possible, search out one or more such possible trade partners, inform him/them of the opportunity, and negotiate the terms of the exchange. All of these activities involve opportunity costs in terms of time, energy and money. If the terms of the trade are to be more complicated than simple "cash on the barrelhead" (for example, if the agreement involves such complications as payment in installments, prepayment for future delivery, warranties or guarantees for quality, provision for future maintenance and service, options for additional future purchases at a guaranteed price, etc.), negotiations for such a detailed contract may itself be prolonged and very costly in terms of time, travel expenses, lawyers' fees, and so on. After a trade has been agreed upon, there may also be significant costs involved in monitoring or policing the other party to make sure he is honoring the terms of the agreement (and, if he is not, to take appropriate legal or other actions to make him do so). These are the main sorts of transaction costs, then: search and information costs, bargaining and decision costs, policing and enforcement costs.

Elementary versions of economic theorizing often make the simplifying assumption that information and other transaction costs are zero (and, indeed, in a generally law-abiding society with a stable money system, cheap transportation and cheap communications, they are often pretty negligible). But realism nevertheless demands that we keep in mind the fact that the benefits to the participants in an exchange have to be high enough to cover their transaction costs if the trade is to take place at all. Indeed, many otherwise mutually advantageous trades do not take place because of the very high transaction costs that would be involved. High transaction costs are very often at the root of the problems discussed under the heading of externalities, especially in those situations where the external costs or benefits accrue to very large numbers of third parties and therefore a contractual agreement to internalize the externality is extremely costly to negotiate.

Externality

A situation in which the private costs or benefits to the producers or purchasers of a good or service differs from the total social costs or benefits entailed in its production and consumption. An externality exists whenever one individual's actions affect the well-being of another individual --whether for the better or for the worse --in ways that need not be paid for according to the existing definition of property rights in the society. An "external diseconomy," "external cost" or "negative externality" results when part of the cost of producing a good or service is born by a firm or household other than the producer or purchaser. An "external economy," "external benefit," or "positive externality" results when part of the benefit of producing or consuming a good or service accrues to a firm or household other than that which produces or purchases it. Example: If one neighbor decides to repaint his house and spruce up his yard so he can get a better price when selling it, he also at the same time is slightly improving the market value of other houses in the neighborhood, creating a "positive externality" benefitting his neighbors. On the other hand, another neighbor who is a grade-A slob and lets the external appearance of his house run down creates a "negative externality" by depressing the attractiveness and thus the market value of the whole neighborhood.

Externalities of either the "positive" or the "negative" sort create a problem for the effective functioning of the market to maximize the total utility of the society. The "external" portions of the costs and benefits of producing a good will not be factored into its supply and demand functions because rational profit-maximizing buyers and sellers do not take into account costs and benefits they do not have to bear. Hence a portion of the costs or benefits will not be reflected in determining the market equilibrium prices and quantities of the good involved. The price of the good or service producing the externality will tend toward equality with the marginal personal cost to the producer and the marginal personal utility to the purchaser, rather than toward equality with the marginal social cost of production and the marginal social utility of consumption. Thus, normal market incentives for the buyer and seller to maximize their personal utilities will lead to the over-or under-production of the commodity in question from the point of view of society as a whole, not the socially optimal level of production. Goods involving a positive externality will be "underproduced" from the point of view of society as a whole, while goods involving a negative externality will be "overproduced" from the point of view of society as a whole. In our example above, the individual homeowner pays all the cost of sprucing up his home but realizes only part of the benefits created --so consequently each homeowner will probably not keep his house up as well as he otherwise might if his neighbors could somehow be induced or required to pay him something for their share of the benefits from his labors.

Contracts often can be worked out as a means to "internalize" potential externalities because the existence of the externality implies there is at least the potential opportunity for mutual gains if the "third party" by-standers affected can offer compensation to the buyers or sellers in exchange for adjusting production or consumption levels of the good to a more acceptableble level. For example: If each homeowner in the neighborhood will agree to be legally responsible for maintaining a high common standard of upkeep in exchange for everyone else in the neighborhood also guaranteeing to do the same, then everyone can be financially better off than they would be without the agreement which is precisely why we observe such phenomena as homeowners associations and restrictive deed covenants.

Or other homeowners in the neighborhood might even band together and agree to finance jointly the entire cost of purchasing, fixing-up, and reselling some particularly run-down homestead in the neighborhood if the expected increase in their individual property values would be greater than their share of the cost of buying out their slovenly neighbor. Unfortunately, where externalities affect very large numbers of third parties (but only to a relatively minor degree in each case), the transaction costs of negotiating such many-sided contracts among them all may often be so large as to make this contractual solution impractical.

Where the transaction costs to arrive at contractual solutions to "externality" problems are prohibitively high, complex modern societies normally provide "second best" remedies to private persons through the courts. Nearly the whole area of "tort" law (including especially law suits for "nuisance" and for "negligence") deals with externality problems in one way or another. People adversely affected by other people's activities may go to court and sue them in an effort to obtain an award of financial compensation for the damages and/or a court injunction requiring their obnoxious neighbors to change their ways in the future.

Government regulations or tax policies are often justified to the public as a means of "correcting" the outcome of the market for goods involving especially sizable externalities, especially negative externalities. The government might, for example, place a special tax or licensing fee on the production (or purchase) of a good or service believed to involve significant negative externalities, with the size of the tax or fee to be determined by some estimate of the total costs being imposed on third parties. The government charges would force the sellers (or the buyers) of the good or service to begin to start taking into account these external costs along with their own and would effectively shift the supply curve (or the demand curve) to the left, resulting in somewhat smaller quantities of the good being sold at a somewhat higher price in the new equilibrium after inauguration of the tax --and thus, somewhat fewer costs will be imposed on third parties. (But note that it is the government that gets to keep the money, not the unfortunate bystanders still suffering the damage!) In the case of a good or service involving a positive externality, government might cope in an analogous fashion by offering to pay subsidies to the producers or consumers of the good or service in question in order to encourage an appropriate expansion of production, or by using government's power to compel obedience without first negotiating mutually agreeable terms of cooperation among the affected parties, government might avoid the sizable transaction costs that would be involved in achieving a contractual solution to the problem by using its law-making or regulatory powers --for example, a city ordinance requiring all householders to keep their lawns mowed and their houses painted and forbidding them to allow trash or old automobile hulks to litter their front yards.

An important problem with the tax/subsidy approach to remedying externalities problems is, of course, that it may well be impossible or prohibitively expensive for the government to determine the size of the external costs or benefits involved and hence to determine even approximately what an appropriate tax or subsidy rate would be. More generally, there are bound to be transaction costs for all forms of government action, including regulatory or legal strategies for correcting externalities --costs of gathering information, costs of debating and making policy decisions, and costs of administration or policing once the policy has been made. It will often be the case that the costs imposed on society by government taking corrective action would be larger than the decrease in welfare to society from the externalities that the government action is supposedly designed to cure. In any given case of externality, society may well be better off by simply leaving the externality in place, unless the third-party effects of the externality are truly massive. More precisely, government policy-makers need to devote their attention to the problem of lowering total transaction costs, rather than simply focussing on "fixing" this or that externality problem regardless of costs, if their intention is to maximize social welfare.

One area in which government has a great deal of control over the size of transactions costs throughout the economy is in the design and construction of the legal system. The costs to private firms and individuals of enforcing their contracts and protecting their other property rights are largely determined by the government's arrangements for the legal system. If the legal system is costly and cumbersome and unpredictable, mutually beneficial trades may often not take place because of potentially high transactions costs involved in protecting and enforcing complex property rights and contracts once made. Moreover, negative externalities often arise because certain third party property rights have not been clearly defined or effectively enforced in some aspect of social life, and the law has mandated that social or common ownership will be imposed instead of conventional private ownership and control.

Excessive air and water pollution problems are often examples of such negative externalities from flaws in property law. For example, factory owners nearly always refrain from dumping waste products on neighboring privately-owned property for fear of the massive lawsuits they would surely lose --but they can often get by with dumping noxious waste products into "the public's air" or "the public's river" or "the public's ocean" without having to pay to secure the consent of those who later will be breathing or drinking or eating these poisons (or paying extra to remove them) precisely because the victims often have had no practical legal way of purchasing or selling a fully recognized exclusive property right in the portion of the air or rivers or the oceans (and their wildlife) on which they nevertheless depend.

Tort

Legal term. A wrongful or injurious act (other than breaking a contract) for which a civil suit may be brought in court by private persons. If the suit is successful, the court may award the victims cash compensation for damages, "punitive" damages above the actual cost of the injury in order to punish the defendent, and/or a court order banning any future repetitions of the kind of behavior giving rise to the suit. For example, a householder might sue the owners of a nearby factory for creating excessive noise or pollution that interferes unreasonably with the householder's health or the peaceful enjoyment of his property. Tort law procedures are thus one of the principal mechanisms for defining and protecting property rights short of evoking criminal law and is an important governmental mechanism for trying to overcome the problem of negative externalities.

Judicial Activism

The view that the Supreme Court justices (and even other lower-ranking judges as well) can and should creatively (re)interpret the texts of the Constitution and the laws in order to serve the judges' own considered estimates of the vital needs of contemporary society when the elected "political" branches of the Federal government and/or the various state governments seem to them to be failing to meet these needs. On such a view, judges should not hesitate to go beyond their traditional role as interpreters of the Constitution and laws given to them by others in order to assume a role as independent policy makers or independent "trustees" on behalf of society.

Judicial Restraint

The view that the Supreme Court (and other lesser courts) should not read the judges' own philosophies or policy preferences into the constitution and laws and should whenever reasonably possible construe the law so as to avoid second guessing the policy decisions made by other governmental institutions such as Congress, the President and state governments within their constitutional spheres of authority. On such a view, judges have no popular mandate to act as policy makers and should defer to the decisions of the elected "political" branches of the Federal government and of the states in matters of policy making so long as these policymakers stay within the limits of their powers as defined by the US Constitution and the constitutions of the several states.

Judicial Review

The power of the federal courts to overturn or limit the enforcement of Federal or state laws or regulations that the judges determine have violated the Federal constitution. The term also covers the power of the Federal courts to overturn or limit the enforcement of state laws or regulations that the judges determine are in direct conflict with Federal laws or regulations regarding a specific subject matter where the Federal constitution gives primary jurisdiction to the Federal government. Also the power of state courts to overturn or limit the enforcement of state laws or regulations that the judges determine have violated either the Federal constitution or the constitution of their own state.

Separation of Powers

One of the most important of the basic principles that guided the framers of the US Constitution in their design for America's future governance was the idea that the root cause and essence of tyrranical government is the concentration of control over all the powers and functions of government in the hands of the same individual or narrow political faction. The corollary the Framers drew from this was the separation of powers principle: that free popular government can best be sustained by dividing the various powers and functions of government among separate and relatively independent governmental institutions whose officials would be selected at different intervals and through different procedures by somewhat different constituencies so as to make it unlikely that the same small faction could gain control of them all at the same time. Thus, in the American federal republic the Framers designed, "the power surrendered by the people is first divided between two distinct governments [the Federal government and the governments of the several states], and then the portion allotted to each subdivided among distinct and separate departments [the executive, the legislative, and the judicial]."

The idea that concentrated political power is a mortal danger to civil liberties and popular rights remains to this day one of the most persistent and characteristic features of American ideologies and popular thinking about politics. In comparison with other advanced industrial countries, the United States possesses one of the most complex governmental structures and perhaps the most broadly diffused distribution of governmental authority among independent agencies. Not only do American governmental arrangements still allocate power to separate executive, legislative and judicial branches at both the state and federal levels, but they also feature a great variety of forms of relatively autonomous and geographically overlapping governmental bodies at the local level --including not only general purpose county and municipal governments but also a wide variety of functionally specialized mini-governments such as elected district school boards, flood control district boards, water resource planning boards, transit authority boards and the like.

Autocracy

A system of government in which supreme political power to direct all the activities of the state is concentrated in the hands of one person, whose decisions are subject to neither external legal restraints nor regularized mechanisms of popular control (except perhaps for the implicit threat of coup d'etat or mass insurrection).

Dictatorship

Government by a single person (or group) whose discretion in using the powers and resources of the state is unrestrained by any fixed legal or constitutional rules and who is (are) in no effective way held responsible to the general population or their elected representatives.

Republic

Originally, any form of government not headed by an hereditary monarch. In modern American usage, the term usually refers more specifically to a form of government (a.k.a. "representative democracy") in which ultimate political power is theoretically vested in the people but in which popular control is exercised only intermittently and indirectly through the popular election of government officials and/or delegates to a legislative assembly rather than directly through frequent mass assemblies or legislation by referendum.

Democracy

A system of government in which effective political power is vested in the people. In older usage (for example, in the writings of the classical Greek and Roman philosophers or in the Federalist Papers), the term was reserved exclusively for governmental systems in which the populace exercised this power directly through general assemblies or referenda to decide the most important questions of law or policy.

In more contemporary usage, the term has been broadened to include also what the American Founding Fathers called a republic --a governmental system in which the power of the people is normally exercised only indirectly, through freely elected representatives who are supposed to make government decisions according to the popular will, or at least according to the supposed values and interests of the population.

Oligarchy

Any system of government in which virtually all political power is held by a very small number of wealthy but otherwise unmeritorious people who shape public policy primarily to benefit themselves financially through direct subsidies to their agricultural estates or business firms, lucrative government contracts, and protectionist measures aimed at damaging their economic competitors -while displaying little or no concern for the broader interests of the rest of the citizenry. "Oligarchy" is also used as a collective term to denote all the individual members of the small corrupt ruling group in such a system. The term always has a negative or derogatory connotation in both contemporary and classical usage, in contrast to aristocracy (which sometimes has a derogatory connotation in modern usage, but never in classical).

Elite (elitist) Theory

The theoretical view held by many social scientists which holds that American politics is best understood through the generalization that nearly all political power is held by a relatively small and wealthy group of people sharing similar values and interests and mostly coming from relatively similar privileged backgrounds. Most of the top leaders in all or nearly all key sectors of society are seen as recruited from this same social group, and elite theorists emphasize the degree to which interlocking corporate and foundation directorates, old school ties and frequent social interaction tend to link together and facilitate coordination between the top leaders in business, government, civic organizations, educational and cultural establishments and the mass media. This "power elite" can effectively dictate the main goals (if not always the practical means and details) for all really important government policy making (as well as dominate the activities of the major mass media and educational/cultural organizations in society) by virtue of their control over the economic resources of the major business and financial organizations in the country. Their power is seen as based most fundamentally on their personal economic resources and especially on their positions within the top management of the big corporations, and does not really depend upon their ability to garner mass support through efforts to "represent" the interests of broader social groups. Elitist theoreticians differ somewhat among themselves on such questions as how open the power elite is to "new blood," the exact degree of agreement or disagreement that usually prevails within its ranks, and the degree of genuine concern (or lack thereof) for the broader public welfare that enters into their choices of public policy goals, but all such theorists broadly share the notion that it is these few thousand "movers and shakers" who really run the country and determine the basic directions of public policy, certainly not the manipulated and powerless masses of ordinary voters choosing among candidates at election time.

Aristocracy

A privileged social class whose members possess disproportionately large shares of a society's wealth, social prestige, educational attainment and political influence, with these advantages having been acquired principally through gift or inheritance from a long line of similarly privileged and cultivated ancestors. The term refers also to a form of government in which the state is effectively controlled by the members of such a class. The term tends to have a somewhat unsavory or derogatory connotation today in the light of democratic theories, but in classical political philosophy it meant rule by "the best people" of the society, who were expected to feel a paternalistic concern for the humbler members of the society that would keep them from ruling in a purely self-seeking fashion.

Pluralist Theory

The theoretical point of view held by many social scientists which holds that American politics is best understood through the generalization that power is relatively broadly (though unequally) distributed among many more or less organized interest groups in society that compete with one another to control public policy, with some groups tending to dominate in one or two issue areas or arenas of struggle while other groups and interests tend to dominate in other issue areas or arenas of struggle.

There tends to be little overlap between those leaders who participate most influentially in one policy area and those who are influential in other policy areas, and what linkage there is tends to come from popularly elected political officials (especially political executives and party leaders) who, by the nature of their jobs, must exercise leadership (or act as brokers) in a number of different policy areas. There is no single, unified "power elite", but rather there are many competing power elites with differing backgrounds, values and bases of support in the broader society. Government tends to be depicted as a mechanism for mediating and compromising a constantly shifting balance between group interests rather than as an active innovator or imposer of policies upon society.

Interest Group

A group of people who share common traits, attitudes, beliefs, and/or objectives who have formed a formal organization to serve specific common interests of the membership. Examples of interest groups would include such disparate organizations as the Auburn Chamber of Commerce, the Society for the Prevention of Cruelty to Animals, the elementary school P.T.A., the Teamsters Union, the Southern Baptist Convention, the American Numismatics Association, the National Association for the Advancement of Colored People, the Brangus Breeders Association, the American Civil Liberties Union, the Cosa Nostra, and the Benevolent Order of Elks. Interest groups typically have formal admission to membership, dues, elected officers, by-laws and regular meetings, and they often provide information and regular opportunities for communication through newsletters or magazines, sponsor recreational or educational activities, organize volunteer public service projects, make deals for group discounts or group insurance and so on. Larger interest group organizations may have full-time paid officers or professional staff to manage and to supplement the efforts of member-volunteers in furthering the work of the organization.

Many interest groups at least occasionally engage in some form of lobbying or other political activities with respect to issues that touch directly on the common interests that are the organization's reason for being --for example, the PTA may organize support for a bond issue election to pay for erecting a new school building. Some interest groups have political activity as their principal or only reason for being in the first place. Interest groups that exist primarily for exerting political influence as a means of affecting government policies or legislation are often referred to by the narrower term pressure groups. Since more and more activities have become politicized with the expansion of the scope of activities of the government in the 20th century, more and more interest groups find themselves drawn into politics to protect or promote the interests of their membership, and the distinction in usage between the terms interest group and pressure group has accordingly become less significant in ordinary language.

Political Party

An organized group that has as its fundamental aim the attainment of political power and public office for its designated leaders. Usually, a political party will advertise a common commitment by its leaders and its membership to a set of political, social, economic and/or cultural values (an "ideology") that distinguish it from other political parties and which supposedly provide the basis for the policies the party proposes to implement or maintain through its members who obtain public office.

A political party differs from a pressure group in that a pressure group is primarily interested in influencing whatever government officials actually happen to be in office rather than in attaining office for its own leaders, and accordingly interest groups do not normally put forward candidates for public office under their own name (although they may sometimes endorse particular candidates put forward by party organizations). In a democracy, political parties primarily function as agencies for recruiting suitable candidates to run for elective office and for organizing and conducting election campaigns. They may also become important in selecting candidates for appointive political office when winning the election has provided the party's leaders with power to appoint new officials to the cabinet and other top policy-making positions in the government bureaucracy.

Political parties may also have another function as vehicles for coordinating the day to day activities and policy decisions of their elected and appointed office-holders so as to fulfill the party's policy platform, as for example, through an organized party caucus and a full-time party leadership machinery in the parliament or other legislative assembly.

However, unless the national party organization is in a good position to reward its members for "voting the party line" after they have been elected to office or to punish them for failing to support the party platform, the party organization's preferences may often not be the most important influence on the policy decisions made by its supposed representatives. In the United States, neither the Democrat nor the Republican national convention (nor their standing national committees) have the power to deny renomination to their parties' uncooperative representatives in Congress so long as they can win renomination in local party primaries or party conventions back home in their states or districts.

The national party organizations' financial contributions to the campaign expenses of Congressional candidates (and usually those of state and local party organizations as well) tend to account for only a rather small proportion of what candidates need to be re-elected, so the party leaderships' financial leverage over their parties' office holders tends to be quite limited as well. The dominant role of "seniority" in guaranteeing individual committee assignments and personal influence in the House and the Senate, as well as the fact that the House and Senate party leaderships are elected by their own House and Senate party caucuses rather than appointed by the national party organization, considerably insulate "non-conformist" representatives from retaliation by their national party organizations.

Fascism

A class of political ideologies (and historical political regimes) that takes its name from the movement led by Benito Mussolini that took power in Italy in 1922. Mussolini's ideas and practices directly and indirectly influenced political movements in Germany (especially the Nazi Party), Spain (Franco's Falange Party), France, Argentina, and many other European and non-European countries right up to the present day.

The different "fascist" movements and regimes have varied considerably in their specific goals and practices, but they are usually said to be characterized by several common features:

1. Militant nationalism, proclaiming the racial and cultural superiority of the dominant ethnic group and asserting that group's inherent right to a special dominant position over other peoples in both the domestic and the international order
2. The adulation of a single charismatic national leader said to possess near superhuman abilities and to be the truest representation of the ideals of the national culture, whose will should therefore literally be law
3. Emphasis on the absolute necessity of complete national unity, which is said to require a very powerful and disciplined state organization (especially an extensive

secret police and censorship apparatus), unlimited by constitutional restrictions or legal requirements and under the absolute domination of the leader and his political movement or party

4. Militant anti-Communism coupled with the belief in an extreme and imminent threat to national security from powerful and determined Communist forces both inside and outside the country
5. Contempt for democratic socialism, democratic capitalism, liberalism, and all forms of individualism as weak, degenerate, divisive and ineffective ideologies leading only to mediocrity or national suicide
6. Glorification of physical strength, fanatical personal loyalty to the leader, and general combat-readiness as the ultimate personal virtues
7. A sophisticated apparatus for systematically propagandizing the population into accepting these values and ideas through skilled manipulation of the mass media, which are totally monopolized by the regime once the movement comes to power
8. A propensity toward pursuing a militaristic and aggressive foreign policy
9. Strict regulation and control of the economy by the regime through some form of corporatist economic planning in which the legal forms of private ownership of industry are nominally preserved but in which both workers and capitalists are obliged to submit their plans and objectives to the most detailed state regulation and extensive wage and price controls, which are designed to insure the priority of the political leadership's objectives over the private economic interests of the citizenry. Therefore under fascism most of the more important markets are allowed to operate only in a non-competitive, cartelized, and governmentally "rigged" fashion.

Totalitarianism

Domination by a single, like-minded governing elite of all (or virtually all) organized political, economic, social and cultural activities in a country by means of a single-party monopoly of power, police repression not only of all forms of dissent and opposition but also of all forms of independent private organizations as such, rigorous censorship of the mass media, centralized state planning and administration of the economy, and pervasive propaganda to inculcate the principles of the obligatory official ideology.

Totalitarian states differ from traditional dictatorships or despotisms primarily with respect to the broader ("total") scope of human behavior that the authorities seek to regulate in detail and with respect to their much more effective control mechanisms made possible by exploiting twentieth century breakthroughs in rapid communication and transportation, scientific psychology, pervasive mass media, surveillance technology, electronic information retrieval, and so on. The term is commonly applied both to fascist regimes and communist regimes, and occasionally by extension to other exotic cults, movements or regimes with ambitions for total control such as those led by various sorts of religious fanatics like the Rev. Jim Jones or the Ayatollah Khomeini.

Civil Rights, Civil Liberties

The rights of every citizen to freedom of thought, freedom of conscience, freedom of expression, freedom of movement, freedom to enjoy privacy and autonomy in the management of one's personal affairs, freedom of private individuals to associate voluntarily and to form organizations for pursuing common purposes, and freedom to participate politically in ways that do not infringe upon the similar rights of others.

Although the two terms overlap considerably in ordinary usage (and are often difficult to distinguish in concrete instances), the term civil liberties generally refers more specifically to the protection of the individual's rights to form and express his or her own preferences or convictions and to act freely upon them in the private sphere without undue or intrusive interference by the government, while the term civil rights emphasizes more specifically the individual's rights as a citizen to participate freely and equally in politics and public affairs in order actively to promote his/her preferred public policy alternatives through lobbying policy-makers and/or through personal participation in the electoral process.

Thus, civil liberties may be seen as the logical correlates of the goal of limited government, while civil rights are the logical correlates of the goal of popular or democratic government.

Liberalism

1. A 19th century political viewpoint or ideology associated with strong support for a broad interpretation of civil liberties for freedom of expression and religious toleration, for widespread popular participation in the political process, and for the repeal of protectionist legal restrictions inhibiting the operation of a capitalist free market economy.
2. In the 20th century US, the term has come to describe an ideology with similar views on civil liberties and personal freedom issues but now supporting a much stronger role for government in regulating and manipulating the private economy and providing public support for the economically and socially disadvantaged, though still stopping well short of full socialism.

In Europe, the term liberalism is still used more in its 19th century sense, and European liberals are rather more respectful of the values of the free market than their American namesakes, whose views sometimes more closely resemble those of Europeans styling themselves as social democrats.

Libertarianism

A contemporary 20th century political viewpoint or ideology derived largely from 19th century liberalism, holding that any legitimate government should be small and should play only the most minimal possible role in economic, social and cultural life, with social relationships to be regulated as much as possible by voluntary contracts and generally accepted custom and as little as possible by statute law. In other words, libertarians believe that the individual should be as free as is practically feasible from government restraint and regulation in both the economic and non-economic aspects of life. Thus, libertarians endorse stricter respect for private property rights, the establishment of a more laissez-faire laissez-faire capitalist economic system, rigorous separation of church and state, and greater respect for individual rights to freedom of expression and freedom of choice in personal lifestyles.

They oppose government programs for the redistribution of income, the inculcation of "politically correct" values through government schools and propaganda outlets, all forms of government-imposed censorship, the imposition of criminal penalties for the commission of "victimless crimes," and in general all forms of social, economic or cultural "engineering" by the government.

Laissez-faire

Literally, French for "Let do." The classical liberal (and modern libertarian) doctrine that the economic affairs of society are best guided by the free and autonomous decisions of individuals in the marketplace, to the near exclusion of government interference in economic matters. That is, the doctrine that government should almost always leave people alone and let them do as they please, so long as they respect the personal and property rights of others.

Welfare State

A state whose government devotes a very large proportion of its activities and expenditures to the direct provision of personal benefits to be consumed by qualifying individuals or families (as contrasted with such more traditional and less individually divisible government activities as national defense, law enforcement, controlling the money supply, economic regulation, maintaining transportation and communications nets, administering the public lands, etc.).

Welfare benefits to individuals may be in the form either of bureaucratically supplied professional services of government employees or in the form of government-issued stipends or allowances or subsidies (transfer payments) to help qualifying households pay for general subsistence or for specific categories of state-favored expenses (merit goods). Examples of such social welfare programs would include old age and disability pensions, unemployment benefits, aid to families with dependent children, income supplements for the poor, public housing and housing vouchers, health care provided in state hospitals or clinics and reimbursement for the costs of privately-provided health care, government-funded drug abuse rehabilitation programs, food stamps, public education and child care, etc.

Advocacy of extensive "welfare state" programs was at first associated mainly with socialist movements, but in most Western industrial societies today many welfare state programs are endorsed as well by non-socialist parties that nevertheless still continue to reject the socialists' traditional demands for much more extensive state ownership, state planning, and state administration of industry and commerce.

4

Essentials of Political Science

The branch of the social sciences that is primarily concerned with analyzing and explaining the functioning of political institutions (especially governmental institutions) as well as the political behavior of individuals, groups and organizations in their efforts to influence or resist the decisions and policies of government.

THE SUBJECT MATTER OF THE THEORY

Whenever a group of people collectively decide about an issue the result does not only depend on the individual group members' opinions, but also, on the decision rule used. Different decision rules can thus give different results even if the group members' opinions about the issue do not vary. One aspect of this relationship, namely the purely formal one, is quite obvious. Let us, for instance, assume that 60 % of a group's members are in favor of a certain proposal. If so, and if the group members just vote their minds, the proposal will pass if only a simple majority is required, but it will be refuted if a qualified majority of say 75 % is required. Apart from this formal aspect there is however another aspect which may be important, namely that decision rules affect more of the group members' behavior than just their voting. The rules may for instance affect the extent to which the individuals organize in various ways, their tendency to behave strategically, and so forth. The distinction made here is, by the way, the same one as made by Maurice Duverger (1964, p 224) when he discusses in particular electoral laws, namely the one between a "mechanical factor and a psychological factor". Duverger's distinction thus has a far wider application than he originally intended.

Now, a democratic constitution can be considered as a decision rule, or rather as a system of such rules, and the population of a country as a decision making group. Within such a perspective the question about the constitution's impact on the resulting decisions obviously becomes pertinent. Do different kinds of constitutions, one may ask, give significantly different results, with different welfare effects and, if so, which are the differences? Is, for example, just to mention one important question, a society's public sector more likely to expand with one type of constitution than with another one? It is this kind of questions which the theory presented here deals with. When developing that theory it will obviously be important to consider not only "mechanical factors" but to a large extent also "psychological factors" in Duverger's sense.

The questions mentioned can also be phrased in a somewhat different manner. In all societies the citizens have individual opinions about various issues and some of these issues are, in fact, decided politically. The political decisions can thus be considered as aggregations of the individual opinions, but such aggregations can be related to the pattern of individual opinions in many different ways. It is therefore natural to ask about the relation between the original set of individual opinions and the emerging final political decisions, and about the constitution's impact on this relation. Questions like this have indeed been raised now and then.

Quite some time ago William Niskanen (1971, p 27) thus wrote that "The relation between the population's demands and the collective organization's expressed demands in a particular institutional setting is one of the more important problems of political science -and one, incidentally, that is not well understood." Some ten years later Bingham Powell (1982, p 186) wrote in a similar vein that "From the point of view of democratic process, it is important that the government be doing what citizens desire and that it be responsive to their changes in preference.... The analysis and comparison of such policy responsiveness is an extremely difficult problem, worth several books in its own right." Melvin Hinich and Michael Munger (1994, p 102), somewhat later still, stress the same issue again when writing that "The fundamental challenge to the development of a scientifically valid theory of electoral competition in a democratic society is to link the perceptions and preferences of voters on political factors that they care about with the actions of candidates before, during, and after an election."

These problems, I think, are still about as unsolved as when Niskanen, Powell and Hinich & Munger expressed their concerns. The theory presented here aims at bringing them closer to a solution.

- My main concern is thus the impact of democratic constitutions of various types on the nature of the decisions taken, and on the welfare effects of those decisions. In the following I will present a number of hypotheses about these matters.
- In addition to this I am however also interested in differences in the politics, or political life, of different countries that are attributable to constitutional differences. The main reason for this interest is my contention that it is necessary, or at least highly helpful, to start by deducing differences in the political life, as an intermediary, in order to be able to deduce differences in the resulting decisions. This, however, does not preclude that the inferences about the political life may be interesting in their own right as well. Accordingly I will also present a number of hypotheses about these relationships.

Finally I should add that I will only treat constitutions that exist or have existed. Theoretically possible constitutions are not treated if they do not exist, however interesting some such constitutions may seem.

NATURE OF THE THEORY

The theory presented here, although verbal rather than formalized, aims at being a logical, deductive system. In essence this means that a number of propositions are logically derived from a limited set of basic propositions, which thus are used as axioms. Ultimately and ideally all propositions should, of course, be empirically tested. If this leads to verification that is good so far, if not that is a problem for the theory. Here, in this context, the theory should however rather be tested for logical consistency. It is of utmost importance that propositions which are presented as logical consequences of other more basic propositions really are so. To the extent that this is not case the theory, considered as theory, is a failure. If the theory does not form a logical system in the sense described it just is not a theory.

There are, I think, at least two dangerous pitfalls involved in an undertaking like this one. The first is the risk of presenting, without noticing it, circular arguments. The other is the risk of mistaking common knowledge of real matters for logical conclusions. In what follows I have, at my best, tried to be aware of these pitfalls, but I am not sure that I have succeeded in avoiding them everywhere.

At last it should be emphasized that a theory is more than an instrument for producing hypotheses. Even if it were possible, somehow, to produce hypotheses for empirical testing by other means than from a theory, the theory will still always be a necessary part of a scientific enterprise. The reason is that the logical order, and by that the predictive and explanatory power, which a theory brings to a set of empirical findings cannot be achieved in any other way. In this sense theory supports empirical results as much as empiricism supports theory. Perhaps it was something like this which the great British astronomer and physicist Arthur Stanley Eddington (1882-1944) had in mind when saying that "One should never believe any experiment until it has been confirmed by theory" (Quoted by Steven Weinberg, 1993, p 101).

LEGAL AND INFLUENTIAL POWER

In a democracy ruled by law the legally established institutions of the state, such as the legislature and the executive, have, in large and specified areas such as lawmaking, power in a very different sense than other actors in the community. That it is so is very important for a variety of reasons. In particular, in this context, it is this fact which makes possible the conception of a theory about constitutions and their effects. If legislatures and executives had not had power of a particular kind, which we may call legal power, such a theory had hardly been possible.

An important characteristic of the legal power is that it is specified by legally binding rules. If, for example, the constitution says that a majority of the legislature is entitled to institute laws of a certain kind, and a majority in fact decides to institute a law of that kind, then such a law really comes into existence. In that sense, and in this case, a majority in the legislature has all the power needed for instituting laws of the kind intended. Similarly a constitution usually stipulates the decisions or actions which can be undertaken by the executive alone, by the legislature alone, by the legislature and the executive in combination, and so on. All the power needed for these decisions is thus present in the various public institutions and the exact distribution of that power is spelled out in the constitution.

This, to be sure, does not preclude that public institutions can be influenced by other actors in the society. When for example the individual members of the legislature consider whether they, in their voting, shall favor or oppose a particular law, they are likely to take the opinions of people in their constituencies, of sponsors, of lobbying groups, and so on, into account. Of course I am not denying this. What I am saying is that if a majority of the legislature, if that is what is required by the constitution, votes in favor of a proposed law, then the proposal passes, otherwise not, independently of what lobbyists, sponsors and common voters think. Or, in other words, lobbyists, etc., cannot affect things in any other way than by influencing the relevant members of the legal public power structure. All analysis of power in a community ruled by law therefore has to start with a careful delineation of the legal power as determined by the constitution.

This principle of separating the legal power, and starting with it as a prerequisite for all other discussions about power, is at the same time so important and so overlooked, that it deserves a name of its own, for example the legalistic principle.

In order to clarify things further it is expedient to distinguish between different kinds of legal power. So far I have given examples of what might be called decision-making power. Actors who are explicitly mentioned in the decision rules enjoy that kind of power. In addition to this it is however also important to emphasize the importance of procedural power. Some actors may for example be authorized, formally, to make proposals to the decision-makers, and others may be entitled, again formally, to express their opinions about proposals. These kinds of rights related to the procedure do also constitute power, and since they are prescribed in the constitution they are examples of legal power. Some individuals have, of course, both decision-making power and procedural power.

The positions held by individuals in a legal power structure may be called legal power positions. In democracies, at the national level, there are two types of legal power positions which are particularly important, namely the positions as legislators in the legislature, and the positions in the executive. For countries which have a constitutional court, the positions as judges in those courts should be added to the legal power positions. All of these positions are associated with decision-making power. In addition, it is also common that some persons, for example heads of executives, speakers in the legislature, and chairmen of the committees in the legislature, have a considerable amount of procedural power. The constitutional rules often warrant certain competences to the incumbents of these positions.

It is important that power basically is attached to, or linked to, positions rather than to persons. Within such a structure a person thus has power only because he or she has been appointed to a certain position, and only for the period prescribed by the rules. This contrasts sharply to systems in which persons have power because they belong to a certain family, or because they have taken it, for example by violent means, and where they may keep that power for life, unless it is taken away from them by somebody else. In such systems the power is linked to a person, or a family, rather than to a position in a legal structure. This principle of linking power to positions, rather than to persons, is obviously immensely important for the functioning of democracy and for the legal security in a society.

Now, as I have already indicated, the holders of the legal power positions can, of course, be influenced, or even controlled, by outsiders such as for example unions, or big firms, or even influential individuals. Those influencing the holders of the legal power thus also have a kind of power, which we can call power of influence or influential power. Such power may be weak and partial; but it may also be complete in the sense that whenever the holder of influential power tells the holder of legal power to behave in a certain way, for example to vote in a specified manner, the holder of legal power does so. Even in this last extreme case the distinction between legal and influential power, and the existence of both, is still fundamental. This is so since the holder of influential power, according to our assumptions, can act only by influencing the holder of legal power he cannot himself do what the holder of legal power can do.

Decisive and Blocking Power

In part 2 I made a distinction between decision-making power and procedural power. Here, as a preparation for the subsequent discussion, I will continue by splitting decision-making power into the two concepts of decisive and blocking power.

For illustrating I will assume, as a very simple example, that we have a single decision making group consisting of 100 persons, and that a majority of 3/4 is required for an affirmative decision. If so, any set of 75 persons, or more, can make a proposal pass. Such a set is thus decisive, and it holds decisive power. Conversely any set of 26 persons, or more, can block the passage of a proposal -such a set is consequently blocking and it possesses blocking power. The concepts can also be described by saying that a decisive set is needed for changing the status quo, while a blocking set is enough for hindering a change of the status quo.

These concepts can, of course, also be used in more elaborated situations. Here we are for instance usually considering complexes including both an executive and a legislature, the latter possibly having two houses. In such situations it is always possible to describe exactly which composition a set must have in order to be decisive, and in order to be blocking. We just have to know the decision-rules exactly.

It is often easier to form a blocking set than a decisive one. Such, for instance, was the case in the example above, where a qualified majority was stipulated: 75 persons were required for dictating a decision whereas 26 persons were enough for blocking it. The same is true in a number of situations of interest for the discussion here. It is for instance true if there are two houses in the legislature, and a proposal, in order to pass, must be affirmed in both houses, even if only with a simple majority in each house. If so a majority in either house is enough for blocking a proposal, whereas a majority in each house is required for making it pass. Another example is a presidential system in which the affirmation of both the president and the legislature is required, even if there is only one house, and even if only a simple majority in the house is required. Obviously, in such a case, the president alone, or a majority in the legislature alone, is enough for blocking a proposal, whereas the acceptance of both the president and a majority in the legislature is needed for changing the status quo. There are, however, also situations, in which it is as difficult to form a blocking set as a decisive one. Consider for example a situation in which a simple majority in a one house legislature is enough for passing a proposal. In such a case the same kind of set, that is a simple majority, is obviously also needed for blocking the proposal.

The distinction between decisive and blocking sets is, of course, commonplace in social choice theory. Now and then it also appears in texts primarily devoted to constitutional problems. One example is Shugart & Mainwaring (1997, p 41) who call the power to change the status quo proactive power, and the power to block changes of the status quo reactive power. The concepts of positive and negative power may also be used.

The Legalistic Principle Disregarded: Examples

I wrote in part 2 that the legalistic principle is often overlooked in political science, and a few examples may therefore be in order. The principle is obviously disregarded when the power of various actors, whether they belong to the legal decision-making system or not, is treated on equal terms.

The first example of this kind of disregard is taken from V. O. Key, Jr. He writes as follows about the "American democratic order" (1964, p 6 f): "Actual authority tends to be dispersed and exercised not solely by governmental officials but also by private individuals and groups within the society.... On one matter the President's decision may govern; on another, the wishes of the heads of a half-dozen industrial corporations will prevail; on a third, organized labor or agriculture will win the day; and on still another, a congressionally negotiated compromise completely satisfactory to none of the contenders may settle the matter. Even the journalists may cast the deciding vote on some issues."

Another, very recent, example is taken from Peter Esaiasson and Sören Holmberg. In their book "Representation from above" about the Swedish democracy they devote a whole chapter to "Power in Society" (1996, chapter 9). There they discuss the power of 8 groups and institutions in exactly the same manner, and by using, for all groups, exactly the same terms. The groups or institutions are "The Cabinet", "Mass Media", "Trade Unions (LO)", "Parliament", "Civil Servants", "Employer Organisation (SAF)", "Private Business", and "The Electorate". This, again, constitutes a clear disregard of the legalistic principle.

ROLE OF POLITICAL PARTIES

When exemplifying influential power in part 2 I mentioned unions, firms, and individuals, but not political parties. The reason is that political parties, although they certainly have influential power, are very special, or even unique, organizations. Political parties play a fundamental role in the theory presented here.

What makes the political parties special and unique is that they are directly engaged in the competition for the legal power positions, and there are several expressions of this basic contention in the political science literature. Schattschneider, for instance, wrote as follows (1942, p 35): "A political party is first of all an organized attempt to get power. Power is here defined as control of the government. That is the objective of party organization. The fact that the party aims at control of the government as a whole distingusihes it from pressure groups." A few lines later (p 36) Schattschneider adds that "Since control of a government is one of the most important things imaginable, it follows that a real-party is one of the most significant organizations in society." Many years later Sartori (1976, p 63) wrote in a similar vein that "A party is any political group identified by an official label that presents at elections, and is capable of placing through elections..., candidates for public office". These conceptions of Schattschneider and Sartori correspond well to the party concept used here, and political parties are thus more directly attached to the legal power structure than any other type of organizations.

Because of this role of political parties people holding legal power positions usually belong to a party, and are thereby also controlled by that party to some extent. This control can however vary considerably from being very strong to being quite weak. This is significant since the more control a party has over its representatives in the legal decision-making bodies, the more the party as such can be considered as an actor in its own right in the political game. This also means, in other words, that strong party discipline has the important effect of reducing the number of actors in the political game considerably.

Let us consider, as a theoretical extreme, a country in which the political parties are absolutely cohesive and disciplined. In such a case the party's control of its representatives in the executive and legislature is perfect. Whenever the party wants its representatives to behave in a certain way, for example to vote in a specific manner, they will do so. Although the representatives have all the legal power they are completely in the hands of the party with its overriding influential power. In such a situation it is quite reasonable to consider the party as a unitary actor. An illustrative example; which comes close to this extreme, is given by Key (1964, p 337) when he describes the old-fashioned machine organization of political parties in US cities as follows: "The classic machine took a clearly hierarchical form, with a boss at the head of an organization of workers held together by the spoils of politics and capable of determining the party's nominations and of exerting a mighty influence in elections as well. In its most fully developed form the urban machine became the government in that many major decisions, as well as minor matters, were decided by the party functionaries who managed their puppets in public office."

The other extreme, as theoretical as the former one, is a country in which there are no political parties at all. Such a country, it should first be noted, is perfectly possible since parties, although they are defined as organizations engaged in the political competition for positions in the legal structure, are nonetheless not necessary. A situation in which individuals compete for the legal power positions by themselves, without belonging to any organization, is perfectly thinkable. In such a situation there are obviously no party actors, but rather a considerable number of individual actors.

In reality we do perhaps not find any extremes like the ones just described but there are certainly cases approaching the one extreme or the other. Thus there are countries in which the parties are very well consolidated, cohesive and disciplined. There are also countries in which the parties are very loosely organized and which thus are rather close to the second extreme. There are also countries in the middle field between the two extremes. In the following I will present hypotheses about the constitutional conditions for these different patterns.

The observation that the influential power of political parties is of a special, interesting and consequential kind is certainly not new in the political science literature. In particular it has been noted that well consolidated political parties, at least to a large extent, may cancel or nullify the intended effects of constitutional rules. In his book Political Parties Maurice Duverger (1964, p 393 ff) has, for instance, a whole section on the subject where he writes, among other things, that "The degree of separation of powers is much more dependent on the party system than on the provisions of the Constitution. Thus the single party brings in its train a very close concentration of powers, even if the Constitution officially prescribes a marked separation: the party binds very closely together the various organs of government." This, of course, is a variation of the theme that the party structure is relevant for the functioning of the legal decision-making system.

The Party in the Legislature

In spite of their importance political parties are somewhat elusive and many-faced organizations. A first point to notice is that, although political parties appear and operate in all democracies, they are usually not highlighted in the constitutional texts. They may be mentioned, and their activities may also be regulated in various ways, but that is about all. Thus, according to Sartori (1976, p 33), "(e)ven today, in most countries parties remain, juridically, private associations with no constitutional recognition. Among the few notable exceptions are the Bonn Fundamental Law and the French Constitution of 1958". Another interesting exception, though negative in a sense, is the Austrian constitution in which the parties are mentioned mainly in the stipulation that the members of the constitutional court must not be party functionaries or employees (Müller, 1994, p 24). It is also interesting to quote Schlesinger (1991, p 10 f) writing that "The United States is unique among democracies in the extent to which it has sought to regulate and define party organization. ... In countries such as Great Britain or France ... parties have been free to organize as they see fit ... ".

So, usually, the constitutions do not reveal the importance of the political parties. Still, the parties are important, and, furthermore, as will be outlined in the following, various constitutional elements play important roles in shaping the parties and the party-systems, and thereby also contribute in determining the exact roles played by the parties in the political process. Another important point is that political parties, since they work in both the legal decision-making structure and in society at large, and in a sense form links between these two worlds, have several appearances. V. O. Key has (1964, p 164), for instance, made distinctions between the party-in-the-electorate, the party-in-the-legislature, and the party-in-the-government.

- Using this terminology the kind of party I am mainly interested in here is the party-in-the-legislature. Thus, when I talk about cohesion and discipline of parties, I am primarily referring to the parties-in-the-legislature, and, in particular, I think about cohesion and discipline in voting.

The Nature of the Political Party

For the theory developed here it is enough, at least for a beginning, to state that there always are political parties in a democracy; that they are important; and that their organizational structures, and thereby their ways of acting, are significantly affected by various constitutional elements. Still it may be worthwhile, at least, to ask for the reason for the omnipresence of political parties. Why do political parties always appear?

A first comment to be made to this question is that parties may appear, or originate, in different contexts or arenas. Referring to the discussion in part 3.1 about the party-in-the-legislature and the party-in-the-electorate parties may, in fact, originate in the legislature or in the electorate. The distinction between these two kinds of origins is important and has been made, in particular, by Maurice Duverger (1964, p xxiii ff).

Having made that distinction we may however return to the question about why parties always appear, whether in the legislature or the electorate. This question has, in fact, considerable similarities with Ronald Coase's well-known question about firms. In his celebrated paper "The Nature of the Firm" he asked about the basic reasons for the existence of firms. He asked why markets, on which individuals freely operate, were not enough, and why it was advantageous also to have firms, whose inner operations are hierarchical and isolated from direct influences from the market. His answer was that the firm was advantageous since, and when, it entailed savings in transaction costs. Probably there is a similar rationale for the political party. But even so the exact and detailed answers, for parties originating in the electorate as well as for those originating in the legislature, are yet not formulated. The provision of those answers thus are important tasks still waiting for their fulfillment.

It may thus be a good idea to compare firms and parties but obviously there are not only similarities. One interesting difference has been highlighted by Harold Demsetz. According to him (1990) "a political party typically holds more stubbornly to its product mix than does a business firm". The reason is that the people active within a firm usually feel quite free to adjust the product as a means towards the end of profit maximizing. In a political party, on the contrary, the products of the party, that is its political ideas and its programme, and its candidates, are valuable in themselves for those working in the party, and therefore not likely to be basically changed in the efforts to get more votes. The products are, in Demsetz' words, laden with "amenity potential".

THE MAIN ACTOR CONCEPT

The theory presented here is strongly actor oriented. In particular the concept of main actor is important. A main actor is an actor operating in the legal system. An individual legislator may thus be a main actor, whereas a lobby group is just an actor. Things are however more complicated than this since a legislator is not necessarily a main actor, and also since a political party may be a main actor.

An individual holder of a legal power position is a main actor if he or she enjoys a significant amount of freedom in relation to his or her party. Such a person obviously has a capacity to act, in a real sense, on its own. It is for this reason, and since the person holds a legal power position, that I call such a person a main actor. Even political parties may however be main actors. If, for example, a party controls all its representatives in the legal structure, that party is a main actor (and the representatives are not main actors). The reason is that the party, in contrast to its representatives, enjoys a real freedom of its own. Obviously, however, a party need not necessarily control all its representatives, or none. Other patterns are quite conceivable. A party may, for instance, control some of its representatives, while some other ones may enjoy a considerable freedom. If so these latter representatives are main actors. As long as a party controls at least some of its representatives, to some extent, the party is however also a main actor, as the concept is used here.

- We thus have two types of main actors. An individual main actor is an individual who holds a legal power position and who, in that capacity, enjoys a substantial amount of individual freedom. A party main actor is a political party which is represented in the legal decision-making system, and which deprives at least one of its representatives there of a substantial amount of personal freedom and thus, to that extent, controls that individual.

A first obvious implication of this definition is that there is no rule saying "one main actor -one vote". A big party which controls all its representatives is for example a main actor with a lot of votes. Another implication is that the number of main actors will be big if the parties are weak and undisciplined, whereas the number will be small if the parties are cohesive and embracing in the sense of controlling all, or at least most, of their representatives. A third implication is that the voting result is known when the positions of all main actors on a particular issue, together with the decision rule, is known. Finally it should perhaps be said that a particular main actor may regularly happen to be a member of defeated minorities. A main actor is therefore not necessarily a powerful actor in this sense.

MAIN TYPES OF CONSTITUTIONS

In the preceding parts I have argued that a legal decision-making system's way of functioning to a large extent depends on its constellation of main actors, which in turn depends on the properties of the political parties. In the following I will furthermore show that some constitutional traits are important determinants of these properties. Thus we will see that it matters how the executive is appointed, and how the legislators are appointed.

There are two main methods for appointing the executive, the one used in parliamentary systems, the other one in presidential systems. According to the parliamentary method the people first elects the legislature, which, in turn, appoints the executive. In a pure parliamentary system the executive, furthermore, can remain in office only as long as it enjoys the support, or confidence, of a majority in the legislature. This requirement is often referred to as the parliamentary principle. According to the presidential method separate popular elections are held for appointing a president and, thereby, the rest of the executive. In a presidential country, there are thus two main types of popular elections, those for electing the executive and those for electing the legislature. As for methods for appointing the members of the legislature there are, again, essentially two types of methods. First there are the majoritarian methods using single-member constituencies and giving, in each constituency, the mandate to the candidate who, according to some set of rules, gets most votes. Second there are the proportional methods which use multi-member constituencies and distributes the mandates to the parties in proportion to their votes.

Now, by combining the methods for appointing the executive, and the legislators, we get the following four types of constitutions.

- Parliamentary constitutions with proportional elections.
- Parliamentary constitutions with majoritarian elections.
- Presidential constitutions with proportional elections.
- Presidential constitutions with majoritarian elections.

This fourfold classification includes the main types of democratic constitutions dealt with in the theory presented here. The classification is thus of fundamental importance, and a few comments on it are in order.

First, the actual distribution of the different types of constitutions exhibits a discernible pattern. The main examples of parliamentary constitutions with proportionalism are found in Western Europe; parliamentarism combined with majoritarianism is characteristic for the United Kingdom and some other countries in the Commonwealth; presidentialism combined with proportionalism is mainly met with in Latin America; and finally, the main example of presidentialism combined with majoritarianism is the US.

Second, the classification is not completely exhaustive. In particular constitutions which simultaneously have elements of presidentialism and parliamentarism, as for example the French constitution, are not represented -although they are gaining popularity. I do however hope, and believe, that the classification is fruitful in spite of this deficiency. The reason is my contention that it is expedient to analyze the simple and clear-cut cases before turning to the more complex, mixed forms. Third, the fourfold classification of constitutions presented here is not totally absent in the political science literature. It is thus clearly indicated in for example Powell (1982) and Sartori (1994), and it is explicitly emphasized in Lijphart (1991). None of these authors do, however, stress the importance of the classification for the shaping of parties and party systems.

Majoritarian Elections

The plurality method, also called the first-past-the-post method, is used when the problem is to elect one member from each constituency, and it is the simplest method serving that purpose. The candidate which gets most votes, that is a plurality, wins. If for example candidate A gets 20 000 votes, candidate B 15 000 votes, candidate C 15 000 votes and candidate D 25 000 votes, then candidate D wins.

The method has been criticized on the ground that a candidate who in reality enjoys only quite a weak support may be elected. Suppose, for instance, that all people who support A, or B, or C in the example above prefer anyone of these candidates to D. If so A, or B, or C would get 50 000 votes if put alone in a contest against D, who still would get just 25 0000 votes. D:s winning in the original example is thus, in a sense, due to the opposition's division.

Several methods have been designed in order to mitigate this problem and the double ballot method is one of them. As the name indicates the method stipulates the use of two ballots separated by some time, for example a week. If some candidate gets an absolute majority in the first ballot, then that candidate is elected. Otherwise there will be a second ballot, and in that second ballot plurality is enough for winning.

Illustrating with the same example as above, and assuming that the figures represent the result of the first ballot, we see that none of the four candidates A, B, C and D has an absolute majority. Therefore there will be a second ballot. What happens there is, however, impossible to predict without further assumptions. We may for example assume that the candidates B and C are politically rather close to each other, that both are somewhat distant from A, and that both are very hostile towards D. If so B and C may make the agreement that C shall withdraw from the second ballot and urge its supporters in the first ballot to vote for B in the second ballot. If they succeed with that A will get 20 000 votes in the second ballot, B 30 000 votes and D 25 000 votes. B thus gets a plurality and wins. There is a variant of the method, it should be mentioned, in which the second ballot is restricted to the two candidates with the highest number of votes in the first ballot, and thus it is ensured that the final winner gets an absolute majority of the votes.

It is important to note that neither the plurality method, nor the double ballot method, presupposes any political parties. The candidates may be supported by, or even appointed by, parties, but they may, also, be free, independent individuals who, on their own, decide to compete. The methods work perfectly well in both cases.

Proportional Elections

Proportional methods are used when several representatives from each constituency are to be elected. They are motivated by a quest for proportional representation of existing political opinions, or fair representation as some would say. If, for example, there are 70 % socialists among the constituency's voters, and 30 % liberals, then the ambition is to elect representatives in the same proportions. Exact proportionality is not always possible but the larger the number of representatives from the constituency is, the easier it is, of course, to come close to that goal. From this point of view large, and consequently few, constituencies, is desirable. In the extreme the whole country may form one single constituency.

In principle the proportional methods are quite simple. Let us start by considering a method according to which the political parties, in each constituency, present lists with their candidates in sequence. Thus, on each party's list, there is a first candidate, a second candidate, and so on. The voters cast their votes on the parties, each voter voting for his or her favored party. The election result is thus, primarily, a distribution of votes on parties. Representatives are then, according to this method, taken from the parties' lists, in proportion to the number of votes they have got, starting, for each party, with its first candidate, and so on. Elections of this kind are usually called list elections. This general method may be varied, or complemented, in various of ways. In countries where the ideal is a very exact proportionalism it may thus be considered important to "correct", nation-wide, the perhaps somewhat erratic combined result of all the individual constituencies. Such a correction can be achieved by distributing a number of additional mandates in a proper way. In other countries it may, on the contrary, be considered desirable to make big parties' shares of the representatives somewhat bigger than their shares of the votes. This purpose may be achieved by using an appropriate formula, designed for the purpose, for the distribution of the mandates. In some countries it may also be considered expedient to discourage very small parties, which can be done by means of a threshold-rule of some kind.

Furthermore, it is sometimes considered desirable to give the voters a chance to express their feelings about particular candidates, for example by adding, or by erasing, names on the list of the party they are voting for. A candidate added, or erased, by a sufficient number of voters, may thus win, or lose, a place in the legislature in spite of the original list. Electoral systems like this may in fact be made completely independent of ordered lists of candidates. In Finland, for instance, the parties just nominate their candidates, without ordering them, and the voter then writes the name of one single candidate on his or her voting paper, which is blank from the beginning. Each vote thus becomes a vote both for a party and for a candidate. Within each party the candidates are then ordered according to the number of votes they have got, and each party becomes represented, from the top of the list determined by the voters and downwards, according to the number of votes it has got. This system thus gives the voters a very substantial influence over the composition, in terms of individuals, of the legislature.

But even if the proportional methods, as we have seen, can be varied in many ways, they all have one very important property in common, namely that they presuppose political parties. First the parties are needed for making the lists of candidates, or at least for nominating candidates. Second, and more basic, the very idea of proportionalism presupposes that there is something in the electorate, which can be proportionally represented in the legislature. It is the political parties which constitute that something. Proportional methods are therefore unthinkable without political parties.

Having said that it should however also be noted that there are electoral methods, which may be used in multi-member constituencies, and which do not presuppose parties. The single transferable vote method is an example. Certainly such methods are sometimes called proportional but, since there is nothing that is represented proportionally, that terminology is hardly appropriate.

Parliamentarism

The parliamentary principle, requiring that the executive enjoys a continous confidence from the legislature, may take slightly different forms. First there is a distinction between positive and negative parliamentarism, the former meaning that the executive must be actively supported by a majority of the legislature, the latter that it is enough for the executive not to be actively opposed by a majority of legislators. It may also be stipulated that the incumbent executive cannot be dismissed without the simultaneous appointment of a new one. This is usually referred to as a constructive vote of no confidence. The parliamentary principle can thus be varied within certain limits. For all of these varieties it is, however, for their proper functioning, of crucial importance that the political partygroups in the legislature are stable, centralised and cohesive.

This condition is, as far as I know, universally acknowledged. Some authors express it quite distinctly and I am not aware of anyone who objects. Sartori says (1994, p 94, his italics), for example, that "... parliamentary democracy cannot perform - in any of its varieties -unless it is served by parliamentary fit parties, that is to say, parties that have been socialized (by failure, duration, and appropriate incentives) into being relatively cohesive and/or disciplined bodies.... indeed, disciplined parties are a necessary condition for the 'working' of parliamentary systems."

But even if this is so it is hardly obvious why. The basic reason for the necessity of stable, disciplined, parties, is, I think, that the parliamentary confidence, in order to be reliable and lasting, cannot be anonymous. The confidence has to be expressed by a few stable and identifiable actors, which, in effect, means political parties. In such a case there are also substantial organisational links between the part of the legislature supporting the executive and the executive itself, which, of course, facilitates, the confidence problem. The relevant part of the legislature may even to some extent control the executive, should the need appear. All of this is, in fact, implicit in the concept fusion of power, which was introduced by Walter Bagehot (1826-77).

If, on the other hand, no political parties are present things become quite different. If, under such conditions, an executive gets a declaration of confidence from a majority of the assembly, that majority will necessarily be an ad hoc-majority which may perish at any moment, and because of any kind of dissatisfaction with the executive. This, in fact, means that the country really does not have an executive at all. Rather, the executive's functions are, in a sense, performed by ad hoc-majorities in the assembly, which is hardly in accordance with the ideas of parliamentarism.

In a parliamentary democracy it is thus important that political parties exist, and that they are stable, cohesive and disciplined enough, since otherwise a stable executive cannot be formed, and the system will not function as intended. This, by itself, does however not imply that such parties are likely to exist. There is no guarantee that a system, such as a parliamentarian one, automatically will function as intended. A system may obviously fail to work. What seems to be required therefore is that the properties which the parties acquire, when their functionaries and other supporters try to fulfil their ambitions, coincide with the properties required for the system's functioning. This may or may not be the case. I will return to this important topic in the following.

Here I will just finish by saying that the distinction between what parliamentarism requires for its functioning, and what in fact it brings about, is often disregarded. Peter Esaiasson, for instance, says (2000, p 51) that legislators in a parliamentary system may be looked upon "as more or less anonymous members of a cohesive party collective, and thus best analyzed as a group", and that the "main argument" for this position "of course, is that parliamentary systems require cohesive parties in order to function." Here, what is, and what is needed, is obvioulsy treated as one and the same thing. But there are also authors who honor the distinction. Michael Laver and Kenneth Shepsle thus write (1996, p 29 f, my italics) that "The effective operation of parliamentary democracy, in short, both depends upon and encourages disciplined behavior by political parties in the government formation process."

Presidentialism

Presidents can be appointed in popular elections in different ways. In essence, however, the whole country may, in a presidential election, be considered as one single-member constituency. The methods used are therefore usually variants of the plurality method or the double ballot method. When those methods are used there is, as we saw in part 5.1, and just considering the character of the method, no need for political parties at all, but still parties usually do play important roles.

In part 5.3 we saw that parliamentary systems depend, for their proper functioning, on cohesive and disciplined parties. With presidential systems it is the other way round. There stable, cohesive parties, rather, are a problem since they may impede or block the proper decision-making. Such mechanisms will be further discussed when we come to the presidential systems in the following. The mechanisms, it should be noted, are observed by some political scientists. Sartori, for instance, remarks (1994, p 94, my italics) that in a presidential system "under conditions of divided government stalemate is avoided precisely by party indiscipline".

SIX HYPOTHESES ABOUT THE SHAPING OF PARTIES

In the preceding parts I have said that the constellation of main actors is dependent on the number of political parties, and their discipline and cohesion, in particular as manifested by the voting patterns in the legislature. Accordingly it is important to consider mechanisms which shape parties and party systems in these respects. In particular mechanisms with a constitutional basis, if there are any, are relevant in this context. Here, I shall present six hypotheses about such mechanisms -the first five are related to the constitutional traits identified. Then, I will discuss the hypotheses in more detail. This discussion will however be confined to the hypotheses' logical foundations, and their places in the logical structure, or theory, developed here. The issue about the hypotheses' empirical truth will, on the whole, not be dealt with.

- The first hypothesis says that majoritarian elections tend to reduce the number of parties. Or, in other words, a democracy with majoritarian elections should, under otherwise equivalent conditions, have fewer parties than one with proportional elections.

This hypothesis is often referred to as Duverger's law. The French political scientist Maurice Duverger was certainly not the first one to entertain the idea, but he was the first to give it a sharp formulation and, simultaneously, to maintain its status as a scientifically valid generalisation, and he also collected and systematically arranged a lot of empirical information in order to prove its truth (Riker, 1986, p 26). The hypothesis has been, and continues to be, extensively and explicitly discussed in political science, and it remains controversial.

- The second hypothesis (part 6.2) says that parliamentarism, in particular in combination with proportional elections, gives the political parties strong incentives for discipline and cohesion. In a presidential system there is no corresponding incentive-creating mchanism.
- The third hypothesis (part 6.3) says that proportional elections put strong means of discipline in the hands of the leaderships of political parties. Under otherwise equivalent conditions these means are thus more efficient than those in a system with majoritarian elections.
- The fourth hypothesis (part 6.4) says that parliamentarism, in contrast to presidentialism, also gives some means of discipline to the leaderships of the political parties.

These three last hypotheses, as we see, deal with the discipline of political parties -and, again, it is in particular the discipline in legislative voting which is at issue. These hypotheses are not at all discussed in the same systematic way as Duverger's law. Rather, there are just occasional references, in passing as it were, to the hypotheses or similar ideas. Furthermore the distinction made here between means and incentives is never, to my knowledge, done explicitly. Sometimes the distinction is not even made implicitly and the idea expressed is rather that parliamentarism leads to discipline, or something like that. A few examples may illustrate this.

Lipset, for instance, quoting a paper of his own from 1976, talks about "the tight national party discipline imposed by a parliamentary as compared with a presidential system" (1990, p 199). Some authors also hold that the cohesion of the parties in a parliamentary system is, indeed, so strong that the parties can be treated as individual, or unitary, actors. In a discussion mainly devoted to other matters Hinich & Munger (1994, p 134) thus suddenly claim that "The same model holds for parliamentary systems, where parties, rather than individual candidates, are the main actors in elections." Similarly Laver & Shepsle (1994), although they admit (p 309) that they "have not gone into the mechanisms of party discipline" emphasize (p 301) "the role of the parliamentary-party machine in enforcing party discipline, and hence in enhancing the party to function as a single monolithic actor."

But even if most of the authors, who talk about the matter at all, thus seem to agree that parliamentarism enhances party discipline, there are also exceptions. Sartori, for instance, bluntly states (1994, p 95, his italics) that "... party solidification and discipline (in parliamentary voting) has never been a feedback of parliamentary government. If a system is assembly-based, atomized, unruly, magmatic, on its own intertia it will remain as it is. I cannot think of any party system that has evolved into a veritable 'system' made of strong, organization-based mass parties on the basis of internal parliamentary learning."

I do take side with those who claim that parliamentarism encourages discipline. In order to get deeper into the relevant mechanisms I have however found it productive to make a distinction between the incentives for discipline, and the means for enforcing it. Within this perspective discipline does not come about unless both incentives are present, and means available. The incentives are the subject matter of the second hypothesis, and the means are dealt with in the third and fourth hypotheses.

The two last hypotheses, number five and six, deal, without making the distinction between incentives and means, with mechanisms impeding party discipline.

- The fifth hypothesis (part 6.5) says that presidentialism is likely to impede party discipline somewhat.
- The sixth hypothesis (part 6.6) says that some popular democratic techniques are likely to impede party discipline.

The Number of Parties

When stating his law Duverger wrote (1964, p 217, his italics) that "Only individual investigation of the circumstances in each country can determine the real origins of the two-party system. The influence of such national factors is certainly very considerable; but we must not in their favour underestimate the importance of one general factor of a technical kind, the electoral system. Its effect can be expressed in the following formula: the simple-majority single-ballot system favours the two-party system. Of all the hypotheses that have been defined in this book, this approaches the most nearly perhaps to a true sociological law."

Part of the controversies about Duverger's law are, I think, a consequence of his formulation that majoritarianism "favours" a two-party system. Since a law should be law this has been interpreted as a claim that majoritarianism leads to a two-party system. After that, since it is easy to find exceptions such as India and Canada, it is also easy to conclude that Duverger is just wrong. But that is hardly sensible. What can be claimed is that majoritarianism, in contrast to proportionalism, involves strong forces tending to reduce the number of political parties. From this, by thinking in terms of equilibrium processes and taking countervailing forces into account, it is perfectly reasonable to conclude that, on the whole, we should expect fewer parties in countries with majoritarian elections than in those with proportional elections. This is a strong and important statement, which is perfectly compatible with Duverger's text, and it is this statement which I here call Duverger's law.

Our main interest here concerns the mechanisms behind Duverger's law. Why, other things being equal, should we expect fewer parties in a majoritarian system than in a proportional one? Duverger himself answered this question by referring (p 224) to "a mechanical factor and a psychological factor". The first one consists in the pure mathematical effects of the application of the electoral rule -essentially the suppression of all parties but the biggest in each constituency. The second factor consists in the parties' and voters' reactions, and adaptations, to this suppression.

Duverger's idea about a mechanical and a psychological factor is of course perfectly reasonable even if the mechanisms behind the law can be described in a more detailed manner. In particular it is important to distinguish between the constituency level, where the important mechanisms work, and the national level where the result we are interested in is manifested. Duverger himself was well aware of this and wrote (1964, p 223) that "the true effect of the simple-majority system is limited to local bipartism."

Starting at the constituency level we can assume, as an example, that we have a constituency with five candidates representing the parties P1-P5. Let us furthermore assume that these parties, in an imagined first election, get 30, 25, 20, 15, and 10 % of the votes respectively. We shall also assume that these votes reflect the real preferences of the voters, and that these preferences remain constant over time.

P1	P2	P3	P4	P5
30 %	25 %	20 %	15 %	10 %

In the first election P1 thus gets a plurality and its candidate will consequently represent the constituency in the legislature. That result may make P1 and its voters happy, but the other parties, and their voters, are hardly likely to repeat their behavior exactly in the ensuing elections. Various adaptations are likely to take place. Thus at least some of the voters, who are not satisfied by merely expressing their opinion, but really want to affect things, may change their votes from the most preferred party to their second or even third preference, if that party is considered better than the incumbent P1 and is also judged to stand a better chance than their first preference to beat P1. As the years pass, and the number of effectuated elections increases, this means that some parties, perhaps the initially smallest ones, will become still smaller, while a few, perhaps just two, main combatants will increase their vote support. In the long run the voters themselves, by departing from their initial first preferences, are thus likely to concentrate their votes on a few main combatants having real chances to win.

As for the parties and their candidates, assuming that they really want to take part in decision-making and thus are not content with just manifesting their existence, a corresponding behavior is likely. The parties, which remain small, and perhaps even decrease, as the years pass, are thus likely to withdraw from the competition altogether.

The combined behavior of the voters, and the parties, is thus likely to bring about a long term equilibrium with just a few parties, say two or three. If, at some time, there are considerably more parties than that, some of them are consequently likely to be eliminated in the long run.

After this the consequences at the national level may be considered. Let us assume that we have a country in which, initially, there are 10 parties. We shall also assume that all constituencies in important respects have the same properties. They thus have the same size, and the same patterns of political opinions. Initially all ten parties are thus represented in each constituency. After this we should thus expect, over the years and in each constituency, an equilibrium process of the kind. Since the constituencies have the same properties the process will be the same everywhere. Therefore, if it ends with for instance two parties in one constituency, it will end with the same two parties in each constituency, and thus also nationwide. In this case therefore, and due to the assumptions made, what happens in one constituency happens in the same way in the other ones, and consequently nationwide as well. Everywhere there is a reduction from 10 to two parties.

Things may however be different. Let us change the assumption that the constituencies have similar properties into its opposite, namely that all constituencies, due to important regional differences, are very different from each other. Let us also specify that there are five constituencies altogether. As for the rest everything is as before. From the beginning there are thus ten parties, which we may call p1-p10, all of which are represented in each constituency. Now, as in example above, and as the years pass, the number of parties will be reduced in each constituency. Since the constituencies are different in this example the reduction will however affect different parties in the different constituencies. We may for instance assume that, in the end, there will only be two parties in each constituency, and that these remaining parties are p1 and p2 in the first constituency, p3 and p4 in the second, p5 and p6 in the third, p7 and p8 in the fourth, and p9 and p10 in the final and fifth constituency. In this example therefore, and although the number of parties in each constituency has again been reduced from 10 to two, there is no reduction at all on the national level.

These two examples are, of course, extremes. What they have in common is that the number reducing process in the individual constituencies is the same in both cases, and the same as in the description of the mechanisms at the constituency level above. The difference is that in the first example, where all constituencies have the same properties, the national number of parties is reduced as much as the number in each constituency, whereas in the other example, where the constituencies are utterly dissimilar, the national number of parties is not reduced at all. In real situations, where there are some differences between different constituencies, but also a lot of similarities, the result is likely to be something in between. When the mechanisms operating in the constituencies reduce the number of parties there, the national number of parties is also likely to be reduced, but not as much as in the individual constituencies.

The discussion about the effects on the national level has, so far, only considered the logical effects of similarities, or differences, between constituencies. No further mechanisms other than the ones operating at the constituency level have been introduced. Mechanisms operating at the national level are, however, also imaginable. Economies of scale may for instance be important. The formation of parties, and of party opinions and positions, are thus likely to be demanding tasks requiring considerable basic investments which are independent of the number of constituencies involved. Therefore, and in order to make these investments pay off, a certain minimum number of constituencies may be required. If so, we have a mechanism which is likely to reduce the number of parties nationally as well. This mechanism, however, is as relevant for proportional as for majoritarian elections, and therefore we need not consider it further here.

Summing up we may say that the numbers of parties is likely to be smaller in a majoritarian system than in a proportional one, other things being equal. The basic mechanisms leading to this result operate at the constituency level. The result will however, even if attenuated, remain at the national level, provided that differences between the constituencies are not too many and too great.

A Corollary

Presidents, as we saw in part 5.4, are usually appointed by some kind of majoritarian method. In presidential elections there are therefore forces operating which tend to reduce the number of parties. Now, since the same political parties usually appear in presidential elections and in elections for the legislature, the forces affecting the parties in presidential elections are likely to be relevant for the elections to the legislature as well. Presidentialism will thus have some tendency to reduce the number of parties generally.

Incentives for Party Discipline

The second hypothesis, that parliamentarism gives political parties strong incentives for cohesion and discipline, has not, to my knowledge been systematically discussed anywhere. I will therefore start from scratch with the logical foundations of the hypothesis as I see them.

Using the concepts of decisive and blocking sets it seems natural that legislators in general are trying to form, or become members of, decisive sets in favor of their own ideas or positions. If they do not succeed with that they will at least try to bring about sets which are able to block proposals they are against.

Now, it is an important property of a parliamentary system that most decisive constellations necessarily consist of the executive, or at least has the executive as a constituent part. It is thus not possible that the executive is excluded from most decision-making constellations since that would be tantamount to regular no-confidence votes, and thus against the parliamentarian principle. The legislators thus have incentives to make the system work, and therefore, since stable, cohesive and disciplined parties according to part 5.3 is a prerequisite for that, to form such parties.

The incentives may however be stronger in a proportional parliamentary system than in a majoritarian one, in particular if the majoritarian system (because of the operation of Duverger's law) comes close to being a two party-system. This is so because the majority, in a two party situation and for statistical reasons, often is considerably bigger than the minority. The majority which supports the executive therefore can afford some defectors and still deliver the necessary confidence. In proportional systems, on the contrary, where coalition executives are the rule the executive's marginals are usually much narrower and discipline therefore more important. (The nature of these reasons, both the statistical mechanisms in the majoritarian case, and the mechanisms behind the narrow margins in the proportional case, will be treated in more detail later on.)

Anyway, the existence of incentives among the legislators is not enough for cohesive and disciplined parties to appear. Without some further mechanism, such as reasonably effective means for enforcing discipline at the party leaderships' disposal, the parties are likely to remain rather loose and unconsolidated organizations. This is so since the parties, in spite of being parties, are likely to harbor, within themselves, considerable differences of opinions, which it is difficult to erase. The establishment of common clear-cut party positions is likely to require some kind of organizational power.

Means of Discipline Related to Proportionalism

There is, to my knowledge, no systematic discussion about the third hypothesis that proportionalism gives strong means of discipline to the party leaderships. Rather there are just occasional assertions of the hypothesis, or similar ideas. Duverger (1964, p 183), for instance, writes that "proportional representation with fixed lists and the ranking of candidates in strict order naturally makes parliamentary representatives dependent on the leaders within the party who prepare the lists and determine the order of the names." Similarly Matthew Shugart and John Carey (1992, s 173) write about "mechanisms, such as a closed party list, by which party leaders exert discipline over their rank and file." But even if the references to the hypothesis are scattered and few, they all seem to go in the same direction. I have not come across any denials of the hypothesis, and it is thus, as it seems, uncontroversial.

Still, the mechanisms behind the hypothesis can hardly be as simple as indicated in the quotations above, namely that those deciding about the lists easily can eliminate obstinate candidates. This argument applies equally well to the majoritarian case, since also there those responsible for the nominations obviously can exclude those who do not follow the group. We have to look for more fundamental mechanisms.

The main point seems to be that the incentives for campaigning are very different in the two types of systems. In a majoritarian system the efforts of the local party organization in the constituency, as well as the efforts, and the personality, of the individual candidate, are of great importance for the result. The campaigning efforts of a candidate in a single-member constituency will to a very large extent favor the candidate himself. If the candidate campaigns successfully the voters will vote for just him. Therefore, to a considerable extent, a legislator in a majoritarian context is the architect of his or her own fortune.

When considering the corresponding mechanisms in proportinal systems I will start with list systems. In such a system an imagined campaigning candidate in a constituency -which always is a multimember one -does not work for himself but rather, and necessarily, produces a collective good. The obvious reason is that the voters cannot reward an appreciated campaigner individually -they have to vote for his party rather than for the candidate himself. Things being like that it is interesting to ask more exactly about the nature of the collective good produced by the imagined local candidate.

At first it may then be stated that he works for his party rather than for himself. Furthermore, and to the extent that his constituency party organization is not a meaningful unit for the voters, he will be working for the national party rather than for the constituency organization. For that kind of work he is, however, because of his local, low level, position, probably most unfit. The amount of the collective good produced by his campaigning will therefore be quite small, and it will also be diffusely spread out, to a considerable extent beyond the borders of his own constituency. Thus, from the imagined candidate's own point of view, his efforts will in all likelihood seem wasted. The conclusion is that the imagined candidate will remain imagined. There will not be much local campaigning at all. This, incidentally, is exactly what the theory of collective action (Mancur Olson, 1965) tells us: the incentives for producing collective goods are notoriously weak.

At the summits of the parties in a proportional list system things are however different. For the party leaderships residing there campaigning may very well be profitable. Their campaigning is at first relatively effective since they are in the proper positions for that kind of work. Furthermore, on the whole, they will reap the fruits of their own efforts. True, it may be argued that a party's candidates in all constituencies benefit from what the leadership is doing, but even so the leadership itself also benefits more the more candidates it really gets into the legislature. It is usually better to belong to the leadership of a big party than to that of a small one.

It is this necessary dominance of the party leaderships in campaigning in proportional list systems, I would argue, which also supplies the leaderships with power over their legislators. If the leadership of a party wants control a certain legislator or candidate, by sticks or by carrots, the latter usually has no personal resources of his own, such as for instance popularity among voters, to mobilize for resistance.

This argument applies however, as I have said, primarily to pure list elections. In other kinds of proportional systems, in which the candidates' individual campaigns matter to some extent, for instance because the voters can add or erase names on the lists, or because (as in the Finish case as described in part 5.2) there are no lists at all, the effects described are more or less attenuated. Or, in other words, the means of discipline become weaker and more similar to those in majoritarian systems.

Means of Discipline Related to Parliamentarism

According to the fourth hypothesis there is also another mechanism of discipline, which is related to parliamentarism rather than to proportionalism. This mechanism has been discussed now and then since long.

Gary Cox (1987, p 80 ff) thus gives an account of an interesting discussion in which Walter Bagehot (1826-77) notices and explains the discipline of the British parties. According to Bagehot the legislators were afraid of voting against the executive, since thereby, through the dissolution of the Parliament, they might lose their places there. This explanation was however refuted in the discussion on the ground that it did not explain the cohesion of the opposition party. Duverger gives a slightly different version of the same argument when he asserts (1964, p 404) that the British government often uses the vote of confidence, and thereby the threat of dissolution, and a new election, as a disciplinary weapon within its own party. Later still Shugart & Carey write (1992, p 173) that "Where parliamentary systems have become fully developed, the existence of the institution of the vote of no-confidence has mandated an imposition of discipline. This party discipline in an archetypal parliamentary system (such as the United Kingdom, New Zealand, or Norway, for example) is sure to be far stronger than in a typical presidential system's assembly... ".

Obviously there may be a mechanism like this, even if it also seems correct that it does not explain the discipline of opposition parties. But perhaps the discipline of the opposition, in parliamentarian and majoritarian systems, really is lower than that of the party, or parties, in power.

Anyway, there is an interesting and important difference between the means of discipline discussed here and those related to proportionalism treated in part 6.3. The difference is that the latter are discriminating in the sense that they could be used against a single legislator or candidate, whereas those discussed here are non-discriminating and usable only against the governing party's parliamentary group as a whole.

A Mechanism Impeding Party Discipline Related to Presidentialism

Presidential elections may affect the inner structures of the parties. Since presidential candidates usually have to win a majority of the votes in order to be elected they may, one could suspect, modify or attenuate their parties' programs considerably in order to get more votes. This may lead to tensions within the parties, and to a degradation of the party programs.

Mechanisms Impeding Party Discipline Related to Primaries, Referendums and Initiatives

Some democratic techniques or institutions, such as primaries, referendums and initiatives, give additional power to the ordinary voter. For this reason these institutions also may impede party discipline.

Popular primary elections, by which candidates for political posts are nominated, obviously deprive party leaderships of important power and thereby impede party cohesion and discipline.

The relation between referendums and party cohesion is a somewhat more complicated issue since referendums sometimes can be used in the service of party cohesion. Imagine for example that in a parliamentary country, in which party cohesion is essential, an important issue which divides the parties appears. If, in such a case, the referendum institute is used for the decision making, rather than the regular machinery, a potential threat to party cohesion is bypassed, which serves the system's functioning.

Referendums may however also be used frequently and regularly with the main purpose of reaching decisions, without any regards for party cohesion. If so the popular initiative is also an interesting institute, which may be made available for the citizens. Now, if referendums and initiatives are used without any regard for the parties, it is still interesting to ask whether, in fact, they are likely-to affect the parties in any substantial way. I think they are, and the hypotheses is that the parties' consolidation and cohesion is likey to be undermined. The reason is that the parties, in order to be consolidated and cohesive also must have some importance, which means that they must be allowed to handle as many issues as possible. If a lot of issues are taken away from the parties' dominating influence, and are given away to people's direct initiatives and decisions, the parties will, I think, disintegrate.

FOUR MAIN ACTOR CONSTELLATIONS

Using the hypotheses about party-shaping mechanisms it is now possible to derive conclusions, also hypothetical, about the constellations of main actors in the four constitutional systems.

The upper, left part of the figure illustrates the main actor constellation in parliamentary systems with proportional elections. Here, there is no strong constitutional mechanism reducing the number of parties, and hence we are likely to find considerably more than two parties, perhaps five to ten. Furthermore the incentives for upholding party discipline are strong, since the system is parliamentarian, and effective means towards that end are also available, due to the proportional elections. The parties are thus likely to be disciplined and cohesive. Looked at from outside they may be considered as unitary actors. This is the reason why the party-actors are indicated by solid circles in the figure.

In the upper, right part of the figure we have parliamentary systems with majoritarian elections. The number of parties shall, on the average, and because of the number-reducing tendency of the majoritarian elections, be smaller than in the former group of constitutions. The figure shows a case for which the reduction has been very effective, and where, as a result, there are only two parties. Obviously, and even with the number-reducing mechanism operating, there may however be more than two parties. Anyway, the parties are likely to be less disciplined than in the former case. One reason is that the incentives given by parliamentarism, according to the hypothesis in the preceding part, are weaker than in case of proportionalism. Another reason is that the means for enforcing discipline are weaker than in a proportional system. Since the discipline is less than perfect the party actors are indicated by broken circles in the figure.

Turning then to the lower parts of the figure, which show presidential systems, it may at first be noted that the actors are placed in two levels rather than one. The presidential executive is placed at an upper level, whereas the actors in the legislature are indicated at a lower level. The basic reason for placing the president at a separate level is that the rules regulating his or her actions usually differ in important respects from the rules for the legislative actors -particularly by giving the president much more power. Furthermore, as will be developed in the following, the president's general incentives may differ considerably from those of the legislative actors. The president may, for instance, sometimes be endowed with incentives for favoring the common good rather than partisan interests. Now, the lower, left part of the figure, shows the constellation of actors in presidential systems with proportionalism. Here, in the elections for the legislature, there are no strong constitutional forces reducing the number of parties, and consequently we may expect quite a lot of them, as indicated. As for incentives for discipline, there are obviously no ones of the same nature as those in a parliamentary system, but perhaps there are other ones. Anyway, the means for discipline are there, since we are dealing with a proportional system. The parties may thus be disciplined and cohesive, but it may also be the other way round. In order to settle this issue additional assumptions about the incentives for discipline are required. So far, I have however not introduced any such assumptions, and the resulting ambivalence is illustrated in the figure by some broken, and some solid, circles.

THE MAIN ACTORS' INTERACTIONS

Having put the main actors on the stage it is now time to consider their actions, and the results of those actions. In this part, and the next two ones, I will introduce three topics related to these actions. These topics will then be treated in detail in the discussions about each one of the four main types of constitutions.

- The topic introduced in this part concerns the main actors' interactions. How do the main actors relate to each other? What kinds of decision-making patterns will they form? And by which mechanisms or processes? And why? These are typical questions related to this topic. The answers to the questions, as we will see in the following, will to a large extent depend on the type of constitution considered.

In part 2.1 the concepts of decisive and blocking sets were introduced. Those concepts may, of course, be used for main actors as conceived here. Doing so it is now possible to state that a very important aspect of the political competition in a democratic society consists in the main actors' efforts, by positioning and bargaining and so forth, to form and enter, depending on the circumstances, decisive or blocking sets, and thereby further their ambitions.

The possibilities to act like this vary however considerably from case to case, depending among other things on the constitutional setting. For the discussion of these matters, which largely are of a behavioral nature, it may be useful to consider the degree of coordination among the main actors. Imagine, as an extreme example, a decision-making assembly which has so many main actors, and takes new decisions so often, that it is virtually impossible for the actors communicate with each other about what is going on. When a proposal is presented for such an assembly each actor thus have to vote for or against the proposal without any prior discussions with its fellow-actors. This voting behavior is thus completely uncoordinated. In the opposite extreme the number of main actors is so small, and other factors enhancing cooperation so favorable, that it easy for the actors to communicate extensively, and negotiate, about all proposals, and about the votes for the proposals. In such a case we should thus expect a very coordinated main actor behavior. When the conditions for coordination are favorable the coordination, it may be noted, is not necessarily limited to a single decision, or a few related decisions. If the interests of the actors concerned so dictate, the coordination may very well be extended over a considerable time period such as, for instance, a complete election period. The topic of coordination will be further discussed "Two kinds of compromises".

Two Kinds of Compromises

In previous part I said that the actors' behavior was uncoordinated when they just voted their minds, whereas coordination involved discussion and negotiations between the actors. When coordinating, the actors are thus likely to adjust their positions and behavior in various ways in order to achieve benefits, for instance by forming and entering favorable decisive constellations, or at least blocking ones. That of course requires compromises, but political compromises may be of different kinds and the differences are of considerable interest. Here I will describe two kinds of compromises.

Imagine two actors, A and B, which respectively have the opinions, or take the positions, a1-am and b1-bn. Now, for any pair of positions with one position from each actor, it is interesting to ask whether the positions are compatible or not. Each cell in the figure below represents one such comparison, and a few answers are also inserted as illustrations. Thus the positions a2 and bn, and a3 and b2, are compatible, whereas the positions a1 and b1, and am and b2, are not compatible.

Now, in politics, both compatibility and non-compatibility are common. In principle the issue of compatibility has to be judged in each individual case, but two general rules, with possible exceptions, may however be hypothesized.

- Different ideological positions are likely to be in conflict with each other, and thus not compatible. A society can, for instance, not be built in accordance with both socialistic and capitalistic principles. It has to be the one way or the other. Socialism and capitalism are not compatible. Or, to take another example, a position on a spatial left-right scale is not compatible with another position on the same scale. Thus, an actor cannot adopt several positions on such a scale, it has to be just one.
- Positions about interests may, on the contrary, very well be compatible. The position that a certain group in

society, say small farmers, should be supported is thus perfectly compatible with the position that another group, say widows with small means, should also be supported. There is no problem in adopting the two positions simultaneously.

Now compromises between political actors about political positions may be of two types.

- The first type of compromise consists in agreeing about a common program involving compatible positions from the actors concerned. Using the example in the figure the actors A and B may for example compromise about a program involving A's positions a2 and a3 and B's positions b2 and bn. The common policy or program thus is a2 + a3 + b2 + bn +.... Such a compromise is likely to be quite easy to reach, since no adjustments of original positions are needed. It is only required that all actors feel that a fair amount of their original positions are included in the final common policy.
- The second type of compromise, which in the general case should be much more difficult to reach, requires adjustments of positions which originally are incompatible. An example would be a compromise between A and B in the figure about the positions a1 and b1. If both actors adjust their positions they may finally become compatible, or perhaps even identical, and thus represent a possible compromise. a1 and b1 may for instance be two different positions on a spatial left-right scale, and the actors may agree to settle for a specific position between a1 and b1. This is however likely to be difficult since it requires that both actors change their original positions in favor of a new one.

A conclusion to be drawn from the reasoning here thus is that political compromises about interests are likely to be easier than compromises about ideological matters.

THE MAIN ACTORS AND THE VOTERS

In the preceding part I said that the main actor interaction constituted an important aspect of the political competition in democratic societies.

- Another equally important aspect of this competition is the fight for votes.

The voters obviously are of crucial importance for the main actors. A main actor without electoral support is unthinkable. Each main actor is supported by voters, and without that support the main actor would not be a main actor. For this reason electoral support can never be substituted completely by, or traded for, other goods appreciated by the main actor such as, for instance, beneficial relations with lobbyists or extensive and favorable publicity in media. Such goods are subordinated to votes, even if they may be used in the hunt for votes. Ultimately, and in the final count, a main actor depends on its electoral support.

- The topic introduced in this part concerns the relationships between the main actors and the voters. What will individuals and parties aspiring to get into the legal decision-making system, and thus to become main actors, do in order to get the necessary votes? What will the incumbent main actors do in order to keep their electoral support, and thereby their positions? How will the voters react to messages from campaigning individuals or parties, and choose between them? These are typical questions within this topic, and again we will see that the answers to a considerable extent will vary with the constitutional type considered.

Trying to attract voters a campaigning actor may use various ideological arguments, support various interests, or, if we are dealing with an individual actor, emphasize its own personal qualities. Furthermore, the actor may address the electorate at large, or, perhaps, particular target groups within the electorate. In these activities, however, the actor obviously also runs the risk of repelling voters, and it is therefore important to keep the net result positive. A good strategy attracts more voters than it repels.

As for the voter, the decision about which actor to vote for may be quite complex. The voter may consider the actors' positions on various ideological or interest-related issues, or the actors' personalities when the actors are individuals. The voter may also entertain ideas about the relative importance of these different aspects, and so forth. By weighing all this together the voter reaches a decision about how to vote. We may call this kind of voting compound voting. The contrast is voting on a single issue, for example in a referendum. In such a case the voting is straightforward rather than compound. The citizen just votes its position on the issue to be decided, and that is all. Voting, which aims at appointing main actors, is however usually compound.

In order to bring the analysis further ahead it is necessary to be more detailed about the relations between voters and politicians. In politics, and political analysis, it is common to talk about mandates from voters to politicians. Using another, and perhaps more modern terminology, it may also be said that the relationship between voters and politicians is a principal-agent relation, the voters being the principals and the politicians the agents (for an introduction to this terminology see, for instance, Milgrom & Roberts). The relation can take different forms. It is convenient to distinguish between two main types of such forms, namely delegation and instruction.

Delegation is, in a way, the simpler of the two relationships and many people have experience of it from everyday life. When people in typical voluntary associations like the local sports club or charity association elect presidents, cashiers, secretaries, and so on, they usually do not require more than having confidence in the persons elected. They just want to be able to rely on them to act in a way that is in accordance with common sense and the purposes of the club. Feeling such confidence they delegate the decision-making to the people elected. This rather simple kind of relationship is present not only in clubs and the like, but to a considerable extent also in politics.

Instruction, on the other hand, prevails when the voters do not limit themselves to a simple confidence in the ones elected but rather require that they shall execute a certain program, which may be worked out in a rather detailed way. Therefore, at the same time as people are elected, a program, or an instruction, which the ones elected shall realize, is adopted. It should be noted that the program may very well be, and often is, formulated by the people who wants to get elected. Different candidates for political positions thus offer voters to carry through different programs if elected. Even so, however, and as soon as a candidate is elected, the program can, from a formal point of view, be considered an instruction from the voters to the elected.

Here delegation and instruction have been presented as two rather pure, or archetypal, relationships. In reality, however, it is easy to see that mixtures of the two types often appear. Sometimes the element of delegation may dominate, sometimes the element of instruction, and it is interesting to ask about the reasons why. Before taking up that issue it should however be noted that instructions may be of different kinds. They may be specific or general. This distinction is closely is related to the one between generality and particularity made by Buchanan (1993).

General instructions may be based on ideological ideas about the ideal character or construction of society, or they may be derived from ideas about the common, or public, or general, interest. Often general instructions are about new rules or laws, and those supporting such new laws tend to emphasize the incentives created by the laws. The likely ambition is to create incentives which enhance the societal development, and people's general welfare, in the long run.

Specific instructions, on the other hand, are independent of notions about ideal societies, or about the common good. If general instructions often deal explicitly with rules and incentives, specific instructions are, rather, interventionistic. Their implementation usually means that some people, on purpose, satisfy their special interests at the expense of others. In these cases, therefore, the incentives created are not a main concern of those favoring the interests, and there is usually not much talk about incentives. But obviously some incentives will be affected, or created, as unintended side-effects of the instructions, and those incentives are worth investigating. They may very well be destructive.

Now, in their campaigning, the political actors may try to establish relationships of delegation, or instruction, or some mixture of the two. When considering what they are likely to do it is important to realize that the possibilities to effectuate instructions, that is to deliver, to a large extent depend on the constitutional setting. These matters will be dealt with in detail in the following parts, but generally speaking it may be said the possibilities to deliver are, on the whole, greater when the conditions for coordination are good than when they are not. Furthermore, if the possibilities to deliver are slim, it is likely to be more prudent for the actor to strive for a relationship of delegation rather than instruction. From this point of view we should therefore expect delegation, at least to a large extent, to be associated with individual main actors and instruction with party main actors.

In addition to this there is another argument which points in the same direction. The argument is that a consolidated party, with a recognizable identity over a considerable time span, has great, and perhaps even crucial, advantages in relation to individuals for developing and "marketing" instructions, and in particular such a bundle of instructions which constitute a political program.

- We should thus, on the whole, expect party main actors to rely on instructions, and individual main actors to strive for delegation.

THE MAIN ACTORS AND THE LOBBYISTS

It is commonplace in politics that various actors which do not belong to the legal decision-making system, and which in that sense are external, try to enhance their goals by influencing the main actors. Such actors are called lobbyists, and their activity is known as lobbying.

- The topic introduced in this part concerns the activities of the lobbyists, and the relationships between them and the main actors. Who are the lobbyists? How do they work in order to become effective and influential? Why do the main actors yield to their demands when they do so? These are typical questions within this topic, and the answers depend on the constitutional setting.

The actors engaged in lobbying may be of many different kinds. They may be single individuals, business firms, unions, interest groups or many other kinds of organizations (other than, by definition, political parties). The targets of lobbying are actors which have a potential for influencing the outputs of the legal decision-making system. This means, as I have already taken for granted in a few formulations above,-that the lobbyist are likely to approach the main actors, which may be individuals or parties.

Furthermore the lobbyists may either try to influence incumbents, or to affect the appointment of new main actors. Both activities are important and common. In the latter case the lobbyists may for example, because of sympathy with their policies, add to their campaign efforts. There are also mixtures between these two activities. A lobbyist may thus, while supporting an actor's campaign, at the same time try influence the actor's future behavior.

The lobbyists, since they are not political parties, are likely to pursue interests rather ideologies or other general issues. Furthermore, within this general kind of ambition, the lobbyists are likely to limit their efforts to what can reasonably be achieved. If, for instance, it seems possible to influence decisive constellations of main actors, or to stimulate the creation of such constellations, and thus to change the status quo, the lobbyists are likely to do so. But if that is not within reach the lobbyists may confine themselves to stimulating the creation of blocking constellations, and thus to impede changes of the status quo.

It is interesting to note that, in constitutional settings where lobbyists are unlikely to be able to bring about changes of the status quo, and thus are restricted to blocking strategies, laws favoring various interests are likely to stimulate the creation of, and thus to precede, organizations defending them. In a setting where the lobbyists realistically may hope to change the status quo organizations are, on the contrary, likely to be created in order to bring such changes about, and thus to precede the changes.

It may also be noted that lobbying organizations sometimes may find it advantageous to form close relations, even in an organizational sense, with main actors. An obvious prerequisite for this is that we are dealing with party main actors rather than individual main actors, but this is not enough. It is also required, at least for organizational ties to develop, that the political parties themselves have enough of organizational structure, or, in other words, that they are cohesive and consolidated enough. It is difficult to imagine a close relationship between a well organized interest group and a party which is just a very loose conglomerate.

Sometimes lobbying organizations are called "pressure groups". This, I think, is a highly misleading term. It gives the impression that the organization uses some kind of almost physical force for driving the resisting main actor backwards, which is, I submit, a completely wrong idea about the nature of the relationship between the two parties. The lobbyists just do not have any power like that. When a main actor yields to a lobbyist's demand it does so rather because it finds its own interests enhanced thereby -if it were not for that it would not yield at all. We thus have to think about the two parties as reaching a mutually beneficial agreement. The understanding of lobbying is tantamount to knowledge about the relation between the two parties, which has to be analyzed in as detailed a way as is done, for instance, with sellers and buyers on a market in economic theory. Each party gives something away, gets something else in return, and comes out in a better state.

The benefits of the lobbyist always consist in favorable public decisions. The costs, on the contrary, may be of different kinds. One type of costs occur if the lobbyist, which in this case may be an organization, exercises its influence over its members to vote for the lobbied main actor. If so the costs do not only consist in the efforts made to get the members to change their votes, but also, for the members themselves, in the benefits foregone by not voting in the way they had originally intended to do. Another type of costs occur if the lobbyist provides money in cash in order to support the lobbied actor's election campaign. That, of course, is also a way of furnishing votes, albeit an indirect one. The lobbyist thus can fulfil his part of a bargain either by exercising influence over voters, or by supplying money, and it is, of course, of great interest to find out when and why the one or the other possibility is used. Finally it should be said that the lobbyist obviously also may supply money, or other valuables, for the lobbied actor's private use. Such manners, however, are obviously corrupt.

Within the perspective applied here the widely spread idea, which is given support by the term pressure group, that an organization is necessarily more effective the bigger, and the better organized, it is, seems dubious. Big and well administered organizations could quite conceivably lack influence, for example if the political counterpart does not see any benefits, such as votes, to result from yielding. On the other hand even a very weak organization may get influence simply by informing legislators about its position, and thereby about ways to get votes. In fact, it seems quite possible for groups of citizens, for example marginal voters, to be influential without being organised at all, and one might therefore even speak about implicit organizations or lobbyists. So far I have just taken for granted that both political parties, and interest organizations, usually exist in a democratic system. Still it is important to ask why this is so. Which is the division of labor between political parties and interest organizations?

The Division of Labor Between Political Parties and Lobbying Organizations

Why, one may ask, are both lobbying organizations and political parties always present in a democratic political system? Why is it not enough with the organizations working close to the legal structure, that is the political parties? Why are there, in addition to that, interest groups? Which functions do the latter have which cannot, at least not conveniently, be fulfilled by the parties? Which is the division of labor between them? The answers to these questions are, again, dependent on the constitutional setting and therefore not fit for a detailed treatment in this chapter. Two general points may, however, be made.

First, while political parties usually have at least some ideological inclination, although it may be weak, lobbying organizations focus strongly on interests. This point is emphasized by the fact that the majority rule, which is important in all democracies, makes it possible to further special interests of various kinds. In a context dominated by the unanimity rule interests would, on the contrary, usually be defeated, and there would thus not be any room for lobbying organizations.

Second, while political parties come and go from incumbency to opposition, lobbying organizations, by being free from the parties, can always direct their demands towards the incumbents.

PARLIAMENTARY CONSTITUTIONS WITH PROPORTIONAL ELECTIONS

In this constitutional setting the main actors are, as we have seen, likely to be cohesive and disciplined political parties. Some of these actors or parties are furthermore likely to form an executive, and they are also likely, to rely to a considerable extent on instructions, and bundles of instructions or programs, in their efforts to get votes.

Now, when discussing the formation of an executive it is essential that the number of main actors, although they are few, most likely are more than two. Each party therefore knows that in all likelihood it will have to make deals with other parties. Thus, the main actors must adopt strategies which are instrumental in bringing them into coalitions, and in affecting the policies of those coalitions. What kind of strategies are these? What kind of matters are the parties to a coalition likely to agree about? In part 9 we concluded tentatively that the parties to a large extent will rely on instructions in their electoral strategies. This topic will finally be discussed in part 12, but assuming so far that the tentative conclusion is correct, the coalition agreements are likely to be about instructions as well. But what kind of instructions?

A first point is that specific instructions, rather than general, are likely to be particularly important in these agreements. There are two reasons for this contention.

The first one is that it is easier for political parties to make deals about specific instructions than about general ones. If, for instance, one party is committed to a particular specific instruction, and another party to another one, they can easily agree about supporting each other -if you support my instruction, I support yours. General instructions, on the contrary, are often in conflict with each other and, if so, not easily reconciled. This first reason is thus related to the compatibility of various political positions as such.

The second reason, on the other hand, has to do with the acceptability for those concerned of a reconciliation. This problem, as it happens, is the subject matter of a theorem saying that a coalition executive cannot have a purely ideological foundation (Moberg, 2000). Following the terminology used here it may also be said that a reconciliation of two general instructions, even if such a reconciliation, in spite of the technical difficulties, is reached, is not likely to be accepted by the parties concerned

But even if compromises based only on general instructions from the different parties are unlikely, there may be deals in which a general instruction of one party is knit together with a specific instruction of another party. They may agree that the first party supports the second party's specific instruction, if the second party supports, or perhaps just tolerates, the first party's general instruction. This, however, requires that the general instruction involved is not too offensive but rather attenuated or pragmatic enough. It may also be argued that general instructions, which give a prominent and far-reaching role to the state, are more easily reconciled with specific instructions than those giving a limited role to the state. The reason is that specific instructions often are natural parts of state interventionism. From these general arguments we can now infer the following hypotheses about the parties' programs:

- Specific instructions are likely to be frequent in all parties' programs.
- All parties do not necessarily have general instructions in their programs, and when such instructions appear they are likely to be pragmatic or attenuated.

We also get these hypotheses about the executive coalitions likely to emerge, and about their governmental programs:

- A governmental program containing only specific instructions is perfectly possible.
- A small party may be committed to some general instructions, but it is not likely to get them included in a governing coalition's program.
- If a governmental program contains general instructions, and in that sense has an ideological inclination, those

instructions are likely to have come directly from a big, dominating party's program. Either that party has been able to form an executive of its own, or it is the main participant in an executive involving one or a few small extra coalition members. In this latter case there may be a deal saying that the dominating party will support some specific instructions of the smaller parties, if they support, or tolerate, the dominating party's general instructions

- Parties with articulated (in contrast to pragmatic or attenuated) and conflicting general instructions on their programs are not likely to be able to make deals about specific instructions with each other. The freedom of such parties is thus somewhat restricted.

- A party not having any general instruction in its program is completely free in choosing its partners, irrespective of their general instructions. Such a party is often able to play a pivotal role in coalition building processes. It can, for example, credibly threaten to leave, and thereby destroy, a coalition to which it presently belongs in order to join another one. Such threats can be used for enforcing concessions from the other members of the first coalition, or from the members of the second potential coalition, and thus for giving favors to the supporters of the party itself. For operating in that way a party need not be very big -in fact a moderate size may by an advantage since the party, thereby, fits into more places and thus gets more opportunities to have its specific instructions implemented.

- A party with strongly held, articulated and controversial general instructions in its program, for example a party with an extreme ideological inclination, may affront most other parties. If so the party may be excluded from all possible coalitions, and thus from all influence.

The purpose of the negotiating parties is, as I have mentioned above, to form a durable executive. This means that, in this constitutional setting, the main actor interaction, and thereby also the real decision making, to a large extent occurs in the government formation process. After that the executive will just go on presenting its agreed upon program, bit by bit, for the legislature. The real decision making is thus a batch process rather than a continuous process. The interval between the batches may be as long as the whole election period. This obviously also means that the majorities are fairly constant over the same long time periods. There is no constant recomposition of decisive majorities.

Matters may, however, turn out somewhat differently if a minority executive, rather than a majority executive, is formed. Even such an executive depends, for its existence, on the support of a majority, but that majority, by definition, will contain parties which do not belong to the executive proper, and therefore the membership of that majority may shift to some extent, for example from decision to decision in the legislature, or from time to time. This means that the decision-making will become somewhat more of a continuous process, and also that the composition of the majorities may change to some extent.

Another conclusion is that a big party may dominate the politics of its country for a long period even if it suffers occasional electoral recessions and, indeed, even if it never has a majority of its own. The party can stay in the executive all the time just by making deals about some specific instructions favored by one or two small parties, and then govern together with them. Most likely such a party continuously appoints the prime minister and the heads of a number of key ministries. This possibility for ideological influence may, in fact, be an important driving force for big parties to suppress internal divisions, or to live with them in one way or another, in order to remain big. If so we should expect to find an important ideological component in the programs of big parties like that.

We may also conclude that an organized opposition, in the form of for instance a shadow cabinet, is unlikely. The reason is that a new governing coalition, since the parties can combine in many ways, not necessarily consists exclusively of the former outsiders. Rather, some former outsiders may join some former incumbents in a new executive. In order not to jeopardize any such possibilities the present outsiders are therefore not likely to form an organized group and thereby link their destinies. For a party aiming to develop and keep a pivotal position this consideration is particularly important. Finally it may be concluded that the executive coalitions formed are likely to be minimal winning in William Riker's sense (Riker, 1962). The reason is the important roles played by interests and specific instructions in the coalition agreements. Thus, and in other words, the executive coalitions are likely to exploit their outside minorities.

Some Conditions for the System's Proper Functioning

A parliamentary system depends, for its proper functioning on cohesive, disciplined political parties. Therefore some constitutional elements or constructions, which from a logical point may seem possible are, nevertheless, destructive in real politics.

First, it is important that the proportional technique used for appointing the legislators is of a pure list character, or at least rather close to that. A system without any lists at all - such as the Finish system is hardly useful in a purely parliamentary setting. The reason, of course, is that it may be difficult for the party leaderships to maintain party discipline within such a system..

Second, it is important that the popular techniques of primaries, referendums and initiatives are not frequently used. The reason is that these techniques, as explained in part 6.6, are detrimental to party discipline. Still, and in some particular and rare cases, referendums may be used for upholding party discipline, as is also mentioned in part 6.6.

The Impossibility of a Coalition with a Purely Ideological Foundation

In previous part I said that a coalition executive cannot have a purely ideological foundation. This, in fact, is a theorem which says that it is impossible to account for the formation of the executive only in terms of a simple a left-right scale, or, in somewhat more technical terms, that it is impossible to account for the formation of the executive within the framework of the spatial model, at least in its one-dimensional version.

In the figure below we see a situation which can be used for proving the theorem. The figure represents a legislature with six political parties, P1-P6, each one with a certain position on the left-right scale and with a certain number of representatives in the assembly with altogether 300 members. Now, we may at first assume that there is no executive at all. If so the decisions taken by the legislature will be determined by the median voter theorem. This means that the decisions will become m, which is the ideological position of the party P3 and also the median position.

For proving the theorem we may compare this situation with one in which there is an executive. Clearly, if the executive is to make any difference at all, and thus to be of any interest for its members, its policy must diverge somewhat from m. We may for example think about an executive which has the policy indicated by l, and thus a leftist inclination, and which is supported by the majority composed of P2 and P3.

Now, it is easy to see that l is worse than m for P3. P3 is therefore in fact disfavored by belonging to the executive. Therefore, contrary to our assumption, P3 will not be member of the executive or support it. Our assumption that P3 belongs to the executive, since it is advantageous to do so, thus leads to a contradiction. This kind of argument is usually called a reductio ad absurdum. If it is possible to show that an assumption leads to a contradiction, then it is also fair to conclude that the assumption is unreasonable or absurd.

So far I have only dealt with the particular example in the particular figure above. Obviously we have to ask if other examples, with other possible party constellations in the legislature, also lead to contradictions for the same reasons. The answer is in the affirmative since the examples, however they are varied, will always have two crucial properties. First, the executive's policy must always diverge from m since otherwise the executive would not matter at all and, consequently, it would not be important to be a member of it. Second, since the constellation supporting the executive has to be a majority, it necessarily includes the median member of the assembly. (This, of course, presupposes that the coalition supporting the executive is connected, but departing from this assumption does hardly add anything of interest.) Thus, contrary to our assumptions, the executive will always include at least one party member for whom the membership is a unfavorable. We are thus entitled to draw the general conclusion that it is impossible to account for the formation of the executive within the framework of a simple, one-dimensional ideological model.

As a contrast, it is easy to account for a coalition executive in terms of interests. Thus, the parties belonging to an executive can, for instance, agree to tax those outside the coalition and share the spoils between themselves.

Let us consider the following scenario. A party A tries, in an election campaign, to attract a particular group of voters by offering them some advantages at the expense of other voters. This offer, or proposal, which we can call P, is thus a specific instruction. Then some members of the target group, who appreciate the proposal, vote for A, which thereby becomes somewhat bigger than it otherwise would be. After the election A will be considered a possible executive member and, in the negotiations preceding the formation of the executive, A promises to support important points in the other prospective member parties' programs in return for their support of P. The parties reach an agreement along these lines and form an executive. P thus becomes part of the executive's program and will, accordingly, become implemented. Is this kind of scenario, we may ask, likely, or even typical, of a parliamentary democracy with proportionalism? My answer is in the affirmative.

A first prerequisite for this answer is that the parties are able to deliver in the way described, and this condition, as we have seen, is fulfilled. This, however, does not settle the issue. It is obviously not sufficient for the parties to be able to act in the way described -they must also find it expedient to do so, it must pay in terms of votes. More exactly, the behavior must be expected to result in a net gain in votes -the number of voters attracted from other parties must be greater than the number of voters repelled.

In principle this is quite possible. The negative effects may for example be spread out so thinly, and over so many people, that those hit hardly notice. With some shrewd maneuvering it may even be possible to allocate the negative effects mainly on voters who would not have voted for the party anyway. This is so since the campaigning politicians, in a setting in which specific interests are important, are likely to be able to recognize "their own people" to a considerable extent. In a presidential setting with plurality, on the contrary, and as I will later argue, such a behavior is hardly imaginable. There, as we will see, it is imperative for all campaigners not to hurt anybody.

In addition to these problems about the management of the negative effects it is, however, also necessary to consider the reactions of those favored by the proposal. Are they really likely to feel attracted and thus to change their minds in favor of the proposing party? Some may perhaps do so immediately, but there may also be those in the target group who, although favored by the particular proposal, generally dislike the system of politically distributed goods and clientelism, and therefore want to change the system rather than to use it.

Such a voter, according to the terminology used here, favors some general instruction rather than the specific instruction at issue. But perhaps there is no party committed to the general instruction which the voter endorses, or if there is such a party its chances of becoming big enough for getting the instruction into a governmental program may be slim. Such dilemmas are, in fact, as we saw in part 11, quite likely. Our voter may thus find it best to play safe and vote for the party offering the favors. Voting for the second best may, after all, seem more prudent since it may give a payoff even if the favored party, after the election, still is quite small.

- The conclusion thus is that electoral strategies including specific instructions about favors to particular target groups may be quite profitable in the parliamentary, proportional setting.

From a methodological point of view it is, I think, important to note that I have not assumed any kind of rational ignorance among the voters in order to reach this conclusion. Rational ignorance, we remember, is the kind of ignorance that ordinary citizens have about public matters, since it does not pay to keep informed. The likelihood that a particular citizen voter will become pivotal in a general election is infinitesimal, and therefore the efforts needed for finding out about the campaigners programs are not worthwhile. The idea put forward here, that small target groups of voters may be favored at the expense of others, may thus be supported by the assumption that these others are rationally ignorant, and that, in fact, is often done. That assumption is however not necessary. The redistribution can, in fact, as I have shown, be explained as a consequence of perfectly enlightened and rational voter behavior within the institutional structures present. Such an explanation tells as much more about the situation than one relying on rational ignorance, and is therefore much more interesting. It is therefore, I would say, a good research strategy to avoid assumptions about rational ignorance as long as possible. In addition to this I would like to argue that ignorance, in the situation described, with several parties and a lot of interests involved, is more limited than usually assumed. People, in particular since they are not only voters but often also rent-seekers, are likely to know quite a lot about the favors offered by the political system. Another interesting point is that relations between voters and campaigners in the particular setting discussed here have important similarities with a market type contract relation.

Having said this it is however also important to emphasize, since we are dealing with compound voting, that other approaches to the voters than the one illustrated are by no means excluded. The campaigning parties may, for instance, try to attract ideologically committed voters with various ideological arguments, they may support various general instructions, or they may just refer to their achievements in the past hoping to get the voters confidence. But even if various strategies thus may be useful, they can usually not be used without due regards. A party may for example be hurt if its various messages and promises do not form a reasonably coherent totality. If, for instance, some promise given to a group of marginal voters is to strikingly at odds with the party's ideology, some voters belonging to the party's core may leave the party. This importance of coherence has been emphasized by, among others, Downs (1957, pp 109 ff).

The Quasi Contractual Relations between Parties and Voters

In the constitutional setting discussed here, the parties have a considerable capacity for delivering. It may also be said that they have a considerable capacity for credible commitment towards the voters, and from there it is not long to think about tacit deals, or quasi contracts, between the parties and their voters in various target groups.

In a real deal, or a contract, as we know, each of the parties undertakes to do something in return for the undertakings of the other parties. Here we may think of a contract like this: The party says that it will give favors to the members of the target group in return for their votes, and the members of the target group say that they will vote for the party in return for the favors. Obviously there is no contract like this, but there is something that may be considered as an approximation, and it is interesting to see how this approximation differs from the imagined real contract.

In the imagined real contract situation the party would not go ahead fulfilling its promises without making sure that the voters had fulfilled theirs. In the political situation there is obviously no such possibility -voting is anonymous and the party has no way of controlling the voters. A main rationale for anonymity, in fact, is to prevent parties and voters from bargaining. Joseph Schlesinger, for instance, writes (1991, p 146) that "... benefit seekers need some mechanisms to assert their claims.... One of the principal arguments for the secret ballot is that it makes it difficult for benefit seekers to prove their support and be paid for their vote". But even if anonymity certainly makes real contracts impossible it cannot prevent quasi contracts universally.

In such a quasi contract situation the party, in its own interest, is likely to go ahead in good faith once it has made its commitment. It will try to get into the executive, and it will try to get the promise incorporated in the executive's program. Or, in short, it will behave as in a real contract situation and thereby, for future needs, enhance its own credibility.

The voters, in contrast to the party, have not even made a public commitment, but just listened to the party. Still, even they, to the extent they are attracted by the offer, are likely to behave as in a real contract situation, and thus vote for the party. True, a voter might speculate that she will get the favor anyway, and therefore use her vote for some other purpose. But that means taking a risk and if the voter really wants to add the party in its efforts to fulfil its part of the deal, the best the voter can do is to vote for the party and thereby contribute to its chances of becoming a member of the executive, and to get the proposal included in the governmental program.

Obviously there is no real contract in the situation described. There is no formal agreement, no control, and no enforcement. Still the parts are likely to behave as if they were parts to a real contract, and it is therefore quite reasonable to talk about a quasi contract between the party and the attracted voters in the target group. The factor which mainly accounts for the possibility of such a quasi contract is the party's capacity for delivering, or for credible commitment. That capacity is linked to the particular constitutional setting dealt with here.

According to the discussion the main actors are the likely targets for lobbying. In this constitutional setting, it is thus the political parties, which essentially means the party leaderships at the summits of the party hierarchies, which will be approached by the lobbyists. Since these targets are few and powerful the lobbying will become a very concentrated, and possibly closed, activity. Furthermore, and since this constitutional setting to such a large extent is tuned towards interest politics, it should be a very fertile ground for lobbying activities. The lobbying is thus also likely to very effective.

- Our first conclusion thus is that the lobbying activities are likely to be concentrated, possibly closed, and very effective.

I argued that the lobbyists are likely to demand what they can reasonably get. Here, since that is possible, the lobbyists are likely to ask for changes of status quo -they will not be confined to merely blocking.

- From this -and following the argument in part 10 -it may be concluded that the interest organizations are likely to be long lasting and formed before the laws, which support their interests, are created.

One interesting possibility is that trade unions, which are formed for negotiating with their counterparts about wages and other conditions of labor, are likely to become important lobbyists as well. Since the unions are likely to be able to influence the voting behavior of their members to some extent, they may even, by playing a mediating role, enforce the contract character of the relation between parties and voters.

> Another conclusion, which follows form the fact that the prerequisites for organizational ties between parties and organizations as stated in part 10 are fulfilled, is that such ties are quite possible -and perhaps even likely.

This conclusion, it should be noted, is further supported by the fact that politics in the constitutional setting at issue here is likely to be strongly interest oriented. Thus not only the organizational prerequisites for alliances between parties and interest organizations are present, but also strong positive incentives for that kind of collaboration.

Parliamentary Constitutions with Proportional Elections: In this constitutional setting we are likely to get several political parties since the elections for the legislature are proportional. Furthermore it is important for the parties to get into the executive, since in a parliamentarian system most decisive constellations include the executive. Since there are numerous parties the executive is likely to be a coalition.

A party aspiring for a place in a coalition executive is greatly helped by being cohesive and disciplined, and therefore the parties will be so, if effective means for discipline are available. In a proportional system that is the case, and thus the parties are likely to become cohesive and disciplined. The main actors will consequently be party main actors.

As for their policies the basic important fact is that the parties are capable of delivering, or, in other words, have a capacity for credible commitment towards the voters. In their relations to the voters they are therefore likely to strive for instruction rather than delegation. Furthermore, and since it is much easier to agree about specific instructions than about general ones when forming a coalition executive, specific instructions are likely to be particularly important components of policies. Politics will to a large extent be interest politics. Since lobbyists are expected to approach the main actors they will, in this constitutional setting, turn to the leaderships of the cohesive political parties.

The lobbying activities will thus be very concentrated, and to some extent perhaps also closed or secret. Since politics to such a large extent is tuned towards interests, lobbying is also likely to be quite effective. The interest organizations, which may have organizational ties with the parties, are likely to get interests satisfied in exchange for votes from their members.

This, so far, is a short summary of some earlier main points. In addition to this a few further conclusions may be added. I will start from the contention that the main actors, in this constitutional setting, are political parties, and that politics therefore, on the whole, is party politics. It may also be said that we are dealing with a partyocracy.

- Now, since the parties are just parties, this means that there is no democratically appointed main actor with a responsibility for the common good. All actors represent primarily, and basically, their own interests.
- Another related conclusion is that all proposals for decisions are made by those directly interested in them. The making of proposals, and of decisions, are in a sense inseparable aspects of one and the same process. Almost everything is done when the executive is formed, and by the parties taking part in that process.

The fact that the main actors are parties, does not, of course, mean that individuals are unimportant. The parties do obviously consist of individual human beings and this fact should certainly, and in accordance with methodological individualism, be recognized. The individuals do however almost exclusively play their roles within, or on behalf of, the parties. Thus, and when it comes to dealings with actors outside the party, for example with other parties, or with the electorate in campaigns, or with lobbyists, it is usually the individuals belonging to the party leaderships which acts on behalf of their parties. Party positions on political issues are of course also determined by the individuals who belong to the party, usually with more influence the higher up in the party hierarchy they are:

An important conclusion of this, since the individuals essentially play their roles within, or on behalf of, the parties, is that political careers, in this type of system, always are party careers.

Since the parties are likely to be well developed organizations, and to have an easily recognized identity over time, they will be able to develop successively, and to harbor, more and more elaborated, and more and more comprehensive, party programs.

- Furthermore, since the programs are likely to favour the interests of particular groups of voters, long-lasting, mutually supportive relations between parties and voters tend to develop. The party leaderships will thus to a large extent be able to recognise their own people in the electorate.

I have already said several times that politics in this constitutional setting tends to be focused on special interests.

- Another formulation of this conclusion, which alludes to the well known Gresham's law in economics ("cheap money drives out good"), is that specific instructions drive out general ones.

This does not mean that general instructions are altogether eradicated -we have for example seen that general instructions in a big party's program may prevail. Specific instructions are, however, much less threatened, and even encouraged by the system. Most parties, as it seems, will have to deal extensively with specific instructions in order to survive. Specific instructions are thus, in a sense, forced upon politics. This may also impede the voters from favouring ideological positions, and reduce them to interest seekers. All of this, it may be noted, is to a large extent in agreement with Buchanan's contention (1993) that "Political players who might seek to further some conception of an all-encompassing general, or public, interest cannot survive". Buchanan is however discussing democratic constitutions in general, whereas the focus here is on parliamentary constitutions with proportional elections.

- One implication of this focussing on special interests is that the turnout in elections is likely to be high. Since people are stimulated to pursue their own private or personal interests by political means, the turnout is likely to be greater than in other types of democratic systems.

Another implication is that the system is likely to exhibit the kind of properties which are usually associated with the so called "tragedy of the commons". There, we remember, the single farmer, since he is unable to affect the general handling of the common pasture, will have to put his cow on the pasture as quickly as possible if it shall get any grass at all. Consequently, and since all farmers are driven to behave in the same way, the pasture will be destroyed. In the political system discussed here the incentives of politicians and voters will bring them to treat common societal resources in a similar destructive way.

PARLIAMENTARY CONSTITUTIONS WITH MAJORITARIAN ELECTIONS

As I mentioned in previous part, there may also be more than two parties. Here, in this part, and in the following parts, I will however concentrate on the two-party case. The reason is that this case has important unique properties, since there will not be any coalition building. If, on the contrary, there are more than two parties we are likely to get coalition politics, and the analysis, although different in some respects, will also have important similarities with the analysis of proportional, parliamentary systems.

The most important fact in the two-party case is that there is normally no interaction at all between the main actors. The biggest party, that is the party which won the last general election, is likely have a safe majority of its own. That party will thus form the executive single-handedly. There will not be any need for the party to cooperate with the other party. The governing party will act alone. In this respect the system differs starkly from the three other main types of constitutional systems we are considering here.

There may, however, be exceptions to this general rule. Thus, if the biggest party's majority is narrow, relatively strong and independent, individual legislators of the governing party may be able to challenge the party leadership. Such legislators may for example force the party leadership to change some proposal in some way, or to deliver some other kind of favor, for example for the legislators' local constituencies. In these situations individual main actors thus become important, and the governing party main actor will have to deal with them. This, of course, is tantamount to main actor interaction.

Here, after having said what tnere is to say about main actor interaction in a narrow sense, I could end this part. It does, however, seem fitting to add a few consequences of the general rule of no main actor interaction at all, since they constitute contrasts to the preceding proportional variety of parliamentarism. Here are two consequences of that kind.

- First, the governmental process may be more continuous, and less of a batch process, than in the proportional variety of parliamentarism. The reason is that the proposals, which are presented for the legislature, are prepared by the governing party alone. The governmental program may therefore develop gradually during the electoral period.
- Second, in this system, there is always a clear-cut opposition. The party which does not govern is the opposition. There is no ambiguity in that sense, and there is nothing to be lost, such as valuable pivotal positions, by organizing the opposition. The establishment of a shadow cabinet should therefore cause no surprise.

The Cube Rule

In a majoritarian system the party getting most votes usually becomes over-represented in the legislature to a very considerable extent, and the party getting least votes is usually, and consequently, largely under-represented. The so called cube rule is the result of efforts to find a simple relationship, in a majoritarian system, between the quantities involved here. Originally it was formulated in 1909 by J. P. Smith in a report to the British Royal Commission on electoral systems. Let us assume that there are two parties which get V1 and V2 votes in an election, counted nationwide, and after that, using the plurality method, get M1 and M2 mandates respectively in the legislature. Then, according to the cube rule, (M1/M2) = (V1/V2)3. This rule has given a fairly good picture of the development in England during certain periods.

Some Conditions for the System's Proper Functioning

We saw that a parliamentary system, for its proper functioning, depends on disciplined and cohesive parties. This requirement is however probably more important in a proportional system than in a majoritarian one. The reason is that the dominating party in a two-party system usually represents a considerably greater majority in the legislature than a governing coalition in a multiparty-system. The somewhat lesser discipline which is likely in a majoritarian system may therefore be compensated for the smaller number of parties.

It therefore seems reasonable to assume that both proportional and majoritarian electoral systems can sustain a parliamentary regime, but the requirement is that the electoral system is of an appropriate variety. We saw that a proportional system, when that is used, basically has to be of the list kind. Here, a similar condition is that the majoritarian method used probably has to be of the first-past-the-post type, whereas the double ballot method probably is unsuitable. The reason is that this latter method is likely to give a considerable number of parties with rather low discipline. The number of parties is thus likely to be greater than if the first-past-the-post method is used, and their discipline is likely to be considerably less than in the case of proportional list elections. A parliamentary system using the double-ballot method is thus likely to fail.

Furthermore, and for the same reasons as in the proportional, parliamentary setting, the popular techniques of primaries, referendums and initiatives are alien to the system and thus not likely to be used. Indeed, even the possibility of using referendums occasionally for saving the parties from dealing with potentially splitting issues, which was real in the proportional context. The reason is that, in this majoritarian context, it is important for the parties, in order to demonstrate a capacity for governing, to have a complete governmental program.

THE POSSIBILITY OF PURELY IDEOLOGICAL SINGLE PARTY EXECUTIVES

As we saw it is impossible to account for the appearance of a coalition executive within the framework of an one-dimensional spatial model. If there are just two parties in the legislature, as we are now assuming (or if one party has a majority of its own), the executive may very well have an ideological foundation. Consider, for example, the situation. There P2 can easily, by itself, form an executive, and that executive is obviously able to pursue a policy equivalent to P2's position on the ideological scale. In a parliamentary-majoritarian context with two main parties it is thus perfectly possible to account for the executive formation in purely ideological terms.

Here, as always when we are talking about general elections in democracies, we have to do with compound voting. The parties may thus mix various specific or general instructions in their programs, and they may try to obtain some elements of delegation in the relations to the voters, and each individual voter will have to react to all this in his or her personal way. So far everything is the same as in the parliamentary, proportional. Since we are dealing with parliamentary systems, with fairly cohesive and disciplined parties, it also seems reasonable to conclude that the parties, as in the proportional setting, have a clear capacity for credible commitment towards the voters in general, or towards particular segments of the electorate. A main problem, however, concerns the extent to which they are likely to make use of this latter capacity, the one related to specified target groups.

In the parliamentary, proportional setting, the voters, we remember, could be deterred from voting for general instructions, for example ideological ones, since such votes were easily wasted. In many situations the voters would rather settle for the second best and vote for some specific instruction. Here, these mechanisms are clearly different. Since we are dealing with one-party executives rather than coalition executives, the winning party will have no difficulty in implementing its general instructions, and therefore a voter, who likes a party's general principles, is not deterred from voting for it. The conclusion drawn in the previous chapter, that specific instructions tend to drive out general instructions, is thus not valid here. General instructions will obviously have a place in the election campaigns.

After that conclusion it is tempting to continue by asking whether, in fact, general instructions even tend to drive out specific instructions. I believe that there will be, at least, some such tendency. The reason is that the two parties in this setting, since either of them is going to form the executive single-handedly, must show some fitness for being able to govern, for statesmanship, or, in other words, for caring about general things, in order to get votes. The voters know that they are voting, directly, for a government. In the proportional setting that is not so. There the formation of the executive is, exclusively, a matter for the parties. The voters are devoid of means of influence in that respect, and to a large extent restricted to expressing their interests. Thus, in this situation, where the voters are, in fact, voting for a government, they are likely to be interested in, and to respond to, ideological signals from the campaigning parties.

Ideology may thus be important and politics may therefore be quite well represented by models such as the one in the figure in part 15.3. The implication is that politics is mainly about ideological matters, and that the ideologies represented by the two parties are fairly close to each other, and also close to the median position on a single scale, which may be a left-right scale. The ideologies are thus not extreme. This kind of politics could be called median voter ideological politics.

This leads to some important conclusions. A first one is that phrases such as "the winner takes all", or "majoritarian politics", which are sometimes used for describing the parliamentarian, majoritarian setting, are wrong, at least to the extent that we are dealing with median voter ideological politics. Rather, and since all voters in a sense contribute to determining the median position, it may be appropriate to talk about ideological consensus. Another conclusion is that we should not necessarily expect very narrow, or minimal, majorities in the legislature. Broad majorities, if they occur, should not be a surprise.

For countries characterized by median voter ideological politics we may, furthermore, conclude that a regular change of the governing party is likely to occur. The reason is that the parties take positions close to the median position and there will always, ex ante, be a considerable uncertainty about the electoral payoff of the positioning. In addition to that the mechanisms illustrated by the cube rule will usually make sure that small differences in electoral payoff are transformed into big differences in the legislature. The possibilities for a big party to dominate a country's politics for long periods, as in the parliamentary, proportional case, are consequently slim.

So far I have only talked about the parties' efforts to win elections but it is, since we are dealing with single member constituencies, and as I have already mentioned several times, also necessary to consider the individual candidates' efforts. These candidates, to the extent that they engage in campaigns of their own, will, as it seems, have to rely on emphasizing their own personalities in various ways. Consequently we shall expect, in this system, beside instructions, a certain amount of delegation as well.

Parliamentary Constitutions with Majoritarian Elections

Since we are dealing with a parliamentary system lobbying will, on the whole, occur at the summits of the party hierarchies. It is however likely to be less influential than in the parliamentary-proportional case, because interests plays a less important role in the politics of this system. In particular, since the governing party is likely to change, and since the programs of both parties are likely to be close to the median, and thus quite similar, fusions of interest organizations and parties are not likely to occur.

In this constitutional setting we are likely to get fewer parties than in the parliamentary, proportional setting. In the extreme case we will get just two dominating parties and that is the case I am dealing with here.

Since we are dealing with a parliamentary system it is important for the parties to be cohesive and disciplined. The requirements in this respect are, however, less far-reaching than in the parliamentary, proportional setting, since the bigger party usually, is considerably bigger than the smaller party in the legislature. Therefore it should not be a problem that the means of discipline are somewhat weaker than in the proportional case.

Furthermore, and since there are just two parties, the one or the other will single-handedly form the executive and we will thus not get any coalition politics. This is likely to be quite consequential since it opens the door for ideological politics concerned with general instructions rather than interest politics concerned with specific instructions. We are likely to get median voter ideological politics.

The fact that the parties try to occupy positions close to the median voter's position, in combination with the tendency for the bigger party to become grossly over-represented in the legislature, is also likely to lead to frequent changes of power. The mechanisms in the parliamentary, proportional setting which allow a party to dominate its country's politics over extended periods are not operating here.

Since there are just two parties, the one forming the executive and the other the opposition, we are also likely to get a shadow cabinet. This, again, is in contrast to the situation in the parliamentary, proportional context, where some parties' wish to obtain pivotal positions was likely to prevent the emergence of a shadow cabinet.

Here, as in the proportional context, the lobbying organizations are likely to approach the party leadership's with their demands. Since the politics is less likely to be tuned towards interests, the politicians in the parties are, however, likely to be less inclined to listen to the lobbyists and make deals with them.

PRESIDENTIAL CONSTITUTIONS WITH PROPORTIONAL ELECTIONS

Here, as in the other systems we are studying, the main actors will try to further their ambitions by forming, or by just supporting, various decisive or blocking sets. In the presidential systems -this one as well as the majoritarian variety -the president has a particularly important role in these interactions. This is due to the following three aspects of the presidential power.

1. The inclusion of the president is often required for making a set decisive. Sometimes that requirement is dropped, but if so the requirements for a decisive set composed only of legislators is usually sharper. Some kind of qualified majority of legislators may for example be required.
2. The president is usually equipped with special, legal procedural power for making proposals.
3. The president may command resources of various kinds which may be used for giving favors, or compensations, to legislators in order to make them support a presidential proposal.

In the presidential, proportional system discussed here there may, as I have already mentioned, be some party main actors. Even so, however, there will also in all likelihood be quite a number individual main actors. The total number of main actors will therefore be rather great, and the conditions for coordination are consequently not the best. The main actor interaction is therefore likely to be characterized by a lot of uncoordinated behavior. Furthermore, and from the legislators' point of view, coordination, to the extent that it is possible at all, will be considerably easier when it aims at creating blocking sets rather than decisive sets. In particular this is so if there are two houses in the legislature. Now, taking all of this, into account, the following hypothetical conclusions can be drawn about the main actor interaction in proportional, presidential systems:

- The reactions to the proposals presented, whether they come from the president or the legislature, will to a large extent be uncoordinated. This means that the voting pattern, at least to a considerable extent, will vary from decision to decision. It also means that occasional majorities which are considerable larger than minimal winning should cause no surprise. It furthermore means that the political process will be continuous, rather than of the batch type. It also means that an organized opposition is unlikely.

  Proposals for new legislation require, in order to pass, the creation of decisive sets, and they will therefore, in fact, often come from the president. This is a consequence of the aspects 1 and 2 above. The president has an advantage in creating decisive sets.

But even if it is difficult for the legislators to initiate new legislation, they may be successful in the much easier task of creating blocking sets. This is particularly so in this proportional setting, where some party groups in the legislature may be quite consolidated. The purpose may be to bring about some wanted changes in the proposal blocked. The purpose may however also be obstructive -the proposal may be blocked even by legislators symphatizing with the proposal. If so the idea of the blocking legislators may be to blackmail the president -to force him to give favors to themselves, or to their constituencies, in exchange for an end to the blocking. What makes this kind of blackmail possible, and attractive, is, of course, the fact indicated in point 3 above that the president controls resources of various kinds. Thus, and since the legislature does not dispose of any resources of the kind mentioned, we will never see any blackmailing in the opposite direction -the president will not try to blackmail the legislature.

Some Conditions for the System's Proper Functioning

For the other three main types of constitutional systems treated in this theory it seems possible to consider some kind of functioning as the proper functioning, and therefore also to talk about the conditions for this proper functioning. In this case it is, however, not so clearly like that. I am rather inclined to say that this constitutional system, inherently, is inept and unlikely to function properly. The reason is that presidentialism, which requires party indiscipline is combined with proportional elections, which, at least if we are considering list elections, provide means for enforcing party discipline. Blocking and obstruction are thus likely to be frequent.

Pure list elections thus seem to be incompatible with the systems proper functioning, but perhaps it may work in combination with other kinds of proportional systems, which give the voters influence on the fate of individual candidates.

The Finnish system is an example. The use of primaries may also, take power away from the party leaderships, and thus enhance the functioning of the system. Frequent use of initiatives and referendums may also have similar effects.

The upshot of all this is that presidential systems with proportional elections contain a kind of tension, or balance on a very thin edge. As we saw that proportional elections require that political parties of some kind exist. Still, and according to the argument just presented, the constitutional system treated here requires, for its proper functioning, that the parties are not too homogenous, or too disciplined, or, in other words, that they are not too much of parties.

Presidential Constitutions with Proportional Elections: When discussing the relation between the main actors and the voters in this case it is, at first, necessary to distinguish between the presidential elections and the elections for the legislature.

The position for which presidential candidates are striving is, of course, even if the candidates belong to political parties, an individual main actor position. According to the final conclusion we should therefore expect the presidential candidates to strive for a relation of delegation, rather than instruction, with the voters. In their campaigns they will therefore concentrate on their own personalities and personal qualities rather on detailed political programs. Furthermore, since a candidate in order to win has to win a majority of the votes, or, depending on the circumstances and the exact rules, at least almost a majority, he or she has to treat all members of the electorate as potential supporters. The campaign messages are thus not likely to offend any voters, for instance by attacking their interests.

The nature of the election campaigns for the legislature will depend on whether we are dealing with pure list elections or not. In the case of list elections, the party leaderships are likely to do a main part of the campaign work. Furthermore, the campaigning will mainly be about instructions or political programs. These conclusions are valid, I think, independently of the extent to which the party leaderships choose to discipline their "troops" in the legislature. Thus, if we have pure list elections, the party leaderships will dominate the campaigns, and the message will be about instructions and programs, even if, after that, the party leaderships give the individual legislators a considerable amount of freedom in their activities in the legislature.

If, however, we are not dealing with pure list elections, but with some other proportional method which makes it possible for the voter to choose, to some extent, among individual candidates, things become different. If so we will also see some individual campaigning and consequently, also, more of delegation and less of instruction.

Taking everything into account we are thus likely to see, side by side, very different kinds of campaigning in this constitutional setting, in particular if pure list elections are used for legislature. If so the presidential campaigns will emphasize delegation and personal qualities, whereas the campaigns for the legislature will emphasize instruction and party programs.

PRESIDENTIAL CONSTITUTIONS WITH PROPORTIONAL ELECTIONS

In this constitutional setting, as well as in the other ones, the lobbyists are likely to approach the main actors. Furthermore, the purposes of the lobbyists may either be to get new legislation into being, or to prevent the removal of existing legislation.

In the former case, since the problem is to bring about a decisive constellation, the lobbyist may find it best to approach the president. In the latter case, which is easier since the creation of a blocking constellation is enough, the lobbyist may however also find it worthwhile to approach party main actors in the legislature. Lobbyists approaching individual main actors in the legislature is, however, likely to be an infrequent phenomenon. At least this is so if there are any suitable party main actors in the legislature.

Since the lobbyists thus may either try to initiate new legislation, or to prevent the removal existing legislation, we may, se both lobbying organizations, which are formed in order to bring changes about, and thus prior to any such changes, and organizations which are formed after some beneficial legislation, in order to prevent its removal.

Finally, and since some of the parties may be well consolidated, organizational ties between such parties and lobbying organizations should not be excluded.

The main characteristic of this constitutional system is that its two main components -that is the president or the presidency on one side, and the legislature on the other -are likely to be ill-matched.

The politics of the legislature is likely to be party politics to a large extent. This means that party main actors are likely to play dominant roles. It also means that all legislators, in all likelihood, are people making party careers.

Candidates aspiring for the presidency do not, however, necessarily have to belong to a political party. Their careers are not necessarily party careers. Still, of course, an elected president does have a personal mandate of some kind of his or her own.

The important main implication of this incongruous pattern is that clashes between the president and the legislature are likely and, in particular, that main actors in the legislature may try to blackmail the president.

In this system all main actors are likely to be individuals -we are not likely to find any party main actors. Therefore, although there are some similarities with the presidential, proportional system, there are also some differences.

The president's role is important for the same reasons as in the presidential, proportional setting, but it is considerably more difficult for the main actors in the legislature to co-ordinate their behavior. The reason, of course, is that individual main actors dominate in this system.

This means that the first two conclusions for presidential, proportional systems, as presented in part 19, will be the same here. Thus:

- The reactions to the proposals presented, whether they come from the president or the legislature, will to a large extent be uncoordinated. This means that the voting pattern, at least to a considerable extent, will vary from decision to decision. It also means that occasional majorities which are considerable larger than minimal winning should cause no surprise. It furthermore means that the political process will be continuous, rather than of the batch type. It also means that an organized opposition is unlikely.

- Proposals for new legislation require, in order to pass, the creation of decisive sets, and they will therefore, in fact, often come from the president. The president has an advantage in creating decisive sets.

The main difference concerns the third conclusion in part 19. Here -in contrast to the situation there -organized blocking, fund thus obstruction, will be less frequent.

Some Conditions for the System's Proper Functioning

Since the main actors in the legislature are likely to be individual main actors the threats to the system's functioning, in the form of clashes between the legislature and the president, that is blocking and obstructive behavior in the legislature, are much smaller here than in the presidential, proportional setting.

Still some such threats may exist. If so, the likely reason is that the legislators for some reason are dependent on political parties, and that the party leaderships somehow manage to discipline their troops. A corrective may be the introduction of primaries, and perhaps also of referendums and initiatives.

Imagine a person running for the presidency, or for a seat in the legislature. In both cases everybody knows that the person, after the election, and however great the electoral success, will not, without anything further, be in a position to implement his or her delivered campaign proposals, since she also has to deal with the heterogeneous legislature. Exactly for that reason it would not be particularly clever, and perhaps even somewhat ridiculous, to let detailed proposals dominate the campaign. It seems more expedient for the candidate to emphasize his or her own personal very general political inclinations, and personal qualities, thereby indicating a capacity for prudent action in various future situations which, at the moment of the election, are impossible to foresee. The candidate's capacity for credible commitment towards the voters is very limited indeed. The relation between voters and politicians will thus be more of delegation than of instruction.

Furthermore, in this system, with no clear opposition, and without elaborated party programs, it is difficult, or impossible, for the politicians to distinguish between their own voters and the other ones. All citizens are potential supporters and it is therefore important to avoid repelling any voters. All policies which are distinctly harmful for specific groups of voters must be avoided. For this reason a politician may be ill advised to propose the canceling of favors which already happen to exist.

In contrast to the situation in parliamentary systems there is a very large number of targets for lobbying in this setting. The president is obviously a main target. There may also be key persons in the legislature with a lot of procedural power, for example chairmen of committees, which are likely to be approached. In addition to this all individual members of the legislature are also interesting targets. The lobbying activities are thus likely to be spread out, rather than concentrated, and therefore they are also likely to be very costly, or inefficient. If a lobbying organization, for instance, strives for getting a decisive constellation behind a proposal it favors, it will have to approach a great number of different individuals, one by one, rather than one or a few consolidated parties as in a parliamentary system.

This, in turn, may mean that it is considerably easier to lobby for blocking, than to lobby for changes of the status quo. The reason is not only that the constellations needed for blocking usually are smaller than the ones needed for a positive decision. In addition, as we saw in the preceding section, the politicians must be careful not to offend any voters. That should make it wise to abstain from supporting a proposal which a lobbyist wants to see defeated. Lobbying for change of status quo may preferably be directed towards the president.

Since the parties, considered as organizations, are too loose to be able to be parts in joint organizations, the lobbyists are likely to be free in relation to them. In contrast to the case in the parliamentary, proportional setting we will thus not see any fusions between political parties and interest organizations. There is also, a possibility that lobbyists form after reforms are implemented, rather than the other way round.

In this system political parties are significantly less important than in the other three system types. Political parties are not even necessary for the system's functioning since all elections, the presidential ones as well as those for the legislature, are majoritarian. Even so, parties may appear. The system's functioning is however not hampered, and it may indeed be improved, if the parties activities are constrained by for instance primaries.

An important consequence of this restricted role for political parties is that political careers do not have to be party careers, and that individual main actors are more important than in any other constitutional setting.

It may, in fact, be argued that this constitutional type, more than any other type, resembles an ordinary association, say a sports club or a charity association. In such an association, as we know, there are usually no parties. The main decision-makers, or decisions-making bodies, of such an association may be a president, a board, and a general congress. These entities, and their workings, may correspond quite closely to the president with his executive, and the legislature, in this constitutional setting.

5

Politics

Politics is the process by which groups make decisions. Although the term is generally applied to behavior within governments, politics is observed in all human (and many non-human) group interactions, including corporate, academic, and religious institutions. In general, politics can be considered the art of navigating through tensions among multiple "I"s and the "we" to achieve collectively desired ends.

The study of politics originated in Greek political philosophy. For the Greek philosophers, politics was the means by which philosophy came into practicality. Political philosophy concerned the life of man in the polis (Greek roughly meaning "city").

Today, Political Philosophy is the study of what politics is and what the best regime is. Political science (also political studies) is the study of political behavior and examines the acquisition and application of power. Government may refer to the study of particular political regimes and practices, though "government" is sometimes used as a synonym for political science. In practice, political philosophy, politics as a social science and/or practical concerns may be integrated in various kinds of political studies.

A NATURAL STATE

There are many debates as to who was the first person to study politics, many credit Socrates with the first study of politics, while others credit Aristotle. One of the first works concerning politics was Plato's. In Plato's concept, the polis was the way in which man became virtuous. His student and successor Aristotle went on to right the Politics (book) Politics, where he asserts that the city is, by nature, and that man is, by nature, a political animal. Though he does not define it in this manner, Aristotle's assertions point to the natural state of man as being in the city. Only through the city can man become totally self sufficient and thus truly human. These two positions held supreme until the dawn of Modernity (a reaction to the Classical and Scholastic view of philosophy). Machiavelli was among the first political philosophers of Modernity. His most famous work was the Prince (book) Princewhere he discusses the nature of principalities. The idea of "ends justify the means" came from this book, along with the idea of harsh politics. Many people misunderstand Machiavelli's most well known work, believing him to be a fan of strong princes with absolute control. In fact, Machiavelli was a well known republican (one who believes in republican government) and praises it in his Discourses on Livy (book) Discourses on Livy. Modernity thinkers (Enlightenment thinkers), believed that man by nature was not born into a polis, separating from the classical view of Plato and Aristotle. The idea of politics changed from what can the state do for you to what can you do for the state. It became man's job to perfect nature. In 1651, Thomas Hobbes published his most famous work, Leviathan, in which he proposed a model of early human development to justify the creation of a government.

Hobbes described an ideal state of nature wherein every person had equal right to every resource in nature and was free to use any means to acquire those resources. He claimed that such an arrangement created a "war of all against all" (bellum omnium contra omnes). Further, he noted that men would enter into a social contract and would give up absolute rights in exchange for certain protections. Hobbes' During the latter half of the 1600's and into the 1700's an Englishman named John Locke wrote his first and second Treatises on Government (book) first and second Treatises on Government. In the first, Locke argues against the idea of divine right monarchy. He goes to great lengths to prove that no man is by nature placed over another man. In the second treatise (much more well known), Locke asserts that the state of nature consists of every man being equal to every other and all of nature was in common for every one else.

Unlike Hobbes, this state of nature did not mean a state of war. Locke believed that man by nature possesses reason (which he calls the Law of Nature) and only when he separates from that reason does he enter a state of war. Man leaves the state of nature, according to Locke, because in nature there are no general laws, no common judge, and no one to enforce the laws. By the end of the 1700's the Enlightenment was ending and on the cusp of Post-Modernity sat Jean-Jacque Rousseau. Rousseau asserted that man by nature was utterly free to do what he wished, and is not a social animal. When man leaves the state of nature and enters civil society he becomes sort of a slave to the state.

While each era of political thought changed the state of nature, man must leave nature and enter into societies. Politics then is the study of how humans interact with each other and cooperate to become self sufficient.

DEFINITIONS

- Power Max Weber defined power as the ability to impose one's will upon another, while Hannah Arendt states that "political power corresponds to the human ability not just to act but to act in concert."
- Authority is the ability to enforce laws, to exact obedience, to command, to determine, or to judge.
- A government is the body that has the authority to make and enforce rules or laws.
- Legitimacy is an attribute of government gained through the acquisition and application of power in accordance with recognized or accepted standards or principles.
- Sovereignty is the ability of a government to exert control over its territory free from outside influence.

CLASSIFICATION OF POLITICAL IDEOLOGIES

PRAGMATIC VIEW OF POWER

Samuel Gompers' maxim, often paraphrased as,"Reward your friends and punish your enemies," hints at two of the five types of power recognized by social psychologists: incentive power (the power to reward) and coercive power (the power to punish). Arguably the other three grow out of these two.

Legitimate power, the power of the policeman or the referee, is the power given to an individual by a recognized authority to enforce standards of behavior. Legitimate power is similar to coercive power in that unacceptable behavior is punished by fine or penalty.

Referent power is bestowed upon individuals by virtue of accomplishment or attitude. Fulfillment of the desire to feel similar to a celebrity or a hero is the reward for obedience.

Expert power springs from education or experience. Following the lead of an experienced coach is often rewarded with success. Expert power is conditional to the circumstances. A brain surgeon is no help when your pipes are leaking.

GOVERNMENT

A government is a body that has the authority to make and the power to enforce laws within a civil, corporate, religious, academic, or other organization or group. In its broadest sense, "to govern" means to administer or supervise, whether over a state, a set group of people, or a collection of assets.

The word government is ultimately derived from the Greek kybernan, which means "to steer" or "to control".

Typically, "the government" refers to the executive function of the state. In many countries (particularly those having parliamentary systems), the government refers to the executive branch of government or a specifically named executive, such as the Blair government (compare to the administration as in the Bush administration in U.S. usage). In countries using the Westminster system, the party in government will also usually control the legislature.

FORMS OF GOVERNMENT

Governments are often classified according to the number of people who hold political power.

- In Autocracies one individual holds all the power. This category includes absolute monarchies as well as dictatorships with an all-powerful president or other central figure.

- In Oligarchies political power is held by a small group of individuals who share interests. For example a plutocracy is composed of the wealthiest members of society.
- Democracies are governments where the people as a whole hold political power. It may be exercised by them (direct democracy), or through representatives chosen by them (representative democracy).

The lines between some of the above forms of government can sometimes be ambiguous. For example, during the 19th century, most self-proclaimed "democracies" restricted voting rights to a minority of the population (e.g. property-owning males). This could qualify them as oligarchies rather than democracies. On the other hand, the voting minority was often quite large (20-30% of the population) and its members did not form the compact group with common interests that is the hallmark of most oligarchies. Thus, this form of government occupied a space between democracy and oligarchy as they are understood today.

Ideas about the Origin of Government

There are a wide range of theories about the reasons for establishing governments. The four major ones are briefly described below. Note that they do not always fully oppose each other -it is possible for a person to subscribe to a combination of ideas from two or more of these theories.

Force Theory

Many political philosophies that are opposed to the existence of a government (such as Anarchism, Nihilism, and to a lesser extent Marxism), as well as others, emphasize the historical roots of governments -the fact that governments, along with private property, originated from the authority of warlords and petty despots who took, by force, certain patches of land as their own (and began exercising authority over the people living on that land). Thus, it is argued that governments exist to enforce the will of the strong and oppress the weak, maintaining and protecting the privilege of a ruling class. It states that the government emerged when all the people of an area were brought under the authority of one person or group!

Order and Tradition

The various forms of conservatism, by contrast, generally see the government as a positive force that brings order out of chaos, establishes laws to end the "war of all against all", encourages moral virtue while punishing vice, and respects tradition. Sometimes, in this view, the government is seen as something ordained by a higher power, as in the divine right of kings, which human beings have a duty to obey.

Natural Rights

Natural rights are the basis for the theory of government shared by most branches of liberalism (including libertarianism). In this view, human beings are born with certain natural rights, and governments are established strictly for the purpose of protecting those rights. What the natural rights actually are is a matter of dispute among liberals; indeed, each branch of liberalism has its own set of rights that it considers to be natural, and these rights are sometimes mutually exclusive with the rights supported by other liberals. As a result, there is some debate between natural rights theorists, ranging from modern writers such as Tibor Machan to Enlightenment thinkers such as Locke, Kant, or Jefferson.

Social Contract

One of the most influential theories of government in the past two hundred years has been the social contract, on which modern democracy and most forms of socialism are founded. The social contract theory holds that governments are created by the people in order to provide for collective needs (such as safety from crime, poverty, illiteracy) that cannot be properly satisfied using purely individual means. Governments thus exist for the purpose of serving the needs and wishes of the people, and their relationship with the people is clearly stipulated in a "social contract" (a constitution and a set of laws) which both the government and the people must abide by. If a majority is unhappy, it may change the social contract.

If a minority is unhappy, it may persuade the majority to change the contract, or it may opt out of it by emigration or secession. This theory is based on the idea that all men live in a state of nature which is not ideal to perfect harmony. It is also an agreement among the members of an organized society or between the governed and the government defining and limiting the rights and duties of each. Thomas Hobbes, John Locke, Jean-Jacques Rousseau are three of the most famous philosophers of contractarianism. Today, natural rights are the basis for many issues involving the constitution and ones right to privacy under the government.

Governmental Operations

Governments concern themselves with regulating and administering many areas of human activity, such as trade, education, or medicine. Governments also employ different methods to maintain the established order, such as secrecy, censorship, police and military forces (particularly under despotism, see also police state), making agreements with other states, and maintaining support within the state. Typical methods of maintaining support and legitimacy include providing the infrastructure for administration, justice, transport, communication, social welfare, etc.; claiming support from deities; providing benefits to elites; providing shops for important posts within the state; limiting the power of the state through laws and constitutions; and appealing to nationalism. Different political ideologies hold different ideas on what the government should or should not do. The modern standard unit of territory is a country. In addition to the meaning used above, the word state can refer either to a government or to its territory. Within a territory, subnational entities may have local governments which do not have the full power of a national government (for example, they will generally lack the authority to declare war or carry out diplomacy).

Size of Government

The scale to which government should exist and operate in the world is a matter of debate. Government spending in developed countries varies considerably but generally makes up between about 30% and 70% of their GDP. One major exception is the United States, where central government spending takes up less than 20% of GDP.

World Government

Some speculate that technological changes such as the Internet and the global English language would bring a World Government into existence. Some consider some governments such as the European Commission as trends towards such a system; however, others do not see this as possible.

CONSTITUTION

A constitution is a system, often codified as a written document, that establishes the rules and principles whereby an organization or political entity is governed. In the case of countries, this term refers specifically to a national constitution defining the fundamental political principles, and establishing the power and duties, of each government. Most national constitutions also guarantee certain rights to the people. Historically, before the evolution of modern-style, codified national constitutions, the term constitution could be applied to any important law that governed the functioning of a government. Constitutions are found in many organizations. They are found extensively in government, at supranational (e.g. United Nations Charter), national (e.g. Constitution of Japan), and sub-national or provincial (e.g. Constitution of Maryland) levels. They are found in many political groups, such as political parties and pressure groups, including trade unions (labour unions). There are many non-political groups and entities that may have constitutions of a sort such as companies and voluntary organisations.

Etymology

The term constitution comes from Latin, referring to issuing any important law, usually by the Roman emperor. Later, the term was widely used in canon law to indicate certain relevant decisions, mainly from the pope.

General Features

Generally, all constitutions confer specific powers to an organization on the condition that it abides by this constitution or charter limitation. The Latin term ultra vires describes activities that fall outside an organisation's or legislative body's legal or constitutional authority.

For example, a students' union may be prohibited as an organization from engaging in activities not concerning students; if the union becomes involved in non-student activities these activities are considered ultra vires of the union's charter. An example from the constitutional law of nation-states would be a provincial government in a federal state trying to legislate in an area exclusively enumerated to the federal government in the constitution.

For example, in the United States, any attempt by a state legislature to ratify a treaty with a foreign nation would be considered ultra vires of Congress' constitutional authority, being contrary to the constitution. In both cases, "ultra vires" gives a legal justification for the forced cessation of such action, which would be enforced by the judiciary in government.

Governmental Constitutions

Most commonly, the term constitution refers to a set of rules and principles that define the nature and extent of government. Most constitutions seek to regulate the relationship between institutions of the state, in a basic sense the relationship between the executive, legislature and the judiciary, but also the relationship of institutions within those branches.

For example, executive branches can be divided into a head of government, government departments/ministries, executive agencies and a civil service/bureaucracy. Most constitutions also attempt to define the relationship between individuals and the state, and to establish the broad rights of individual citizens. It is thus the most basic law of a territory from which all the other laws and rules are hierarchically derived; in some territories it is in fact called "Basic Law".

KEY FEATURES

The following are features of democratic constitutions which have been identified by political scientists to exist, in one form or another, in virtually all national constitutions.

Codification

A fundamental classification is codification or lack of codification. A codified constitution is one that is contained in a single document, which is the single source of constitutional law in a state. The classic example of this is the Constitution of the United States. An uncodified constitution is one that is not contained in a single document, consisting of several different sources, which may be written or unwritten. The Constitution of Australia is an example of a constitution in which constitutional law mainly derives from a single written document, but other written documents are also considered part of the constitution. The Constitution of the United Kingdom is an example of an uncodified constitution which consists of both written and unwritten sources and has no single written fundamental document.

The term written constitution is used to describe a constitution that is entirely written, which by definition includes every codified constitution. However, some constitutions are entirely written but, strictly speaking, not entirely codified. For example, in the Constitution of Australia, most of its fundamental political principles and regulations concerning the relationship between branches of government, and concerning the government and the individual are codified in a single document, the Constitution of the Commonwealth of Australia. However, the presence of statutes with constitutional significance, namely the Statute of Westminster, as adopted by the Commonwealth in the Statute of Westminster Adoption Act 1942, and the Australia Act 1986 means that Australia's constitution is not contained in a single constitutional document. The Constitution of Canada, which evolved from the British North America Acts until severed from nominal British control by the Canada Act 1982 (analogous to the Australia Act 1986), is a similar example.

The term written constitution is often used interchangeably with codified constitution, and similarly unwritten constitution is used interchangeably with uncodified constitution. As shown above, this usage with respect to written and codified constitutions can be inaccurate. Strictly speaking, unwritten constitution is never an accurate synonym for uncodified constitution, because all modern democratic constitutions consist of some written sources, even if they have no different technical status than ordinary statutes. Another term used is formal (written) constitution, for example in the following context: "The United Kingdom has no formal constitution". This usage is correct, but it should be construed to mean that the United Kingdom does not have a written constitution, not that the UK has no constitution of any kind, which would not be correct.

Codified Constitution

Most states in the world have a codified constitution. Only three nations, Israel, New Zealand and the United Kingdom, have uncodified constitutions as of October 2006. Codified constitutions -unlike uncodified constitutions, which are the product of an "evolution" of laws and conventions over centuries -are usually the product of dramatic political change, such as a revolution. For example, the US constitution was written and subsequently ratified less than 25 years after the American Revolution. The process by which a country adopts a constitution is closely tied to the historical and political context driving this fundamental change. This becomes evident when one compares the elaborate convention method adopted in the United States with the MacArthur inspired post war constitution foisted on Japan. Arguably the legitimacy (and often the longevity) of codified constitutions are tied to the process by which they are initially adopted.

The most obvious advantage of a codified constitution is the coherent and easily understood body of rules. A codified constitution at the least is simple to read, being a single document. Although (entrenched) codified constitutions are relatively rigid, codified constitutions still yield a potentially wide range of interpretations by constitutional courts.

States that have codified constitutions normally give them supremacy over ordinary statute law. That is, if there is a conflict between a legal statute and the codified constitution, all or part of the statute can be declared ultra vires by a court and struck down as unconstitutional. Second, an extraordinary procedure is required for constitutional amendments that may involve obtaining ? majorities in the national legislature, the consent of regional legislatures, a referendum process or some other procedure that makes obtaining a constitutional amendment more difficult than passing a simple law.

Uncodified Constitution

By contrast, in the Westminster tradition which originated in England, uncodified constitutions include written sources: e.g. constitutional statutes enacted by the Parliament (House of Commons Disqualification Act 1975, Northern Ireland Act 1998, Scotland Act 1998, Government of Wales Act 1998, European Communities Act 1972 and Human Rights Act 1998); and also unwritten sources: constitutional conventions, observation of precedents, royal prerogatives, custom and tradition, such as always holding the General Election on Thursdays; together these constitute the British constitutional law. In the days of the British Empire, the Judicial Committee of the Privy Council acted as the constitutional court for many of the British colonies such as Canada and Australia which had federal constitutions.

In states using uncodified constitutions, the difference between constitutional law and statutory law (i.e. law applying to any area of governance) in legal terms is nil. Both can be altered or repealed by a simple majority in Parliament. In practice, democratic governments do not use this opportunity to abolish all civil rights, which in theory they could do, but the distinction between regular and constitutional law is still somewhat arbitrary, usually depending on the traditional devotion of popular opinion to historical principles embodied in important past legislation. For example, several Acts of Parliament such as the Bill of Rights, Human Rights Act and, prior to the creation of Parliament, Magna Carta are regarded as granting fundamental rights and principles which are treated as almost constitutional.

Entrenchment

The presence or lack of entrenchment is a fundamental feature of constitutions. Entrenchment refers to whether the constitution is legally protected from modification without a procedure of constitutional amendment. Entrenchment is an inherent feature in most written constitutions. The US constitution is an example of an entrenched constitution, and the UK constitution is an example of a constitution that is not entrenched.

The procedure for modifying a constitution is often called amending. Amending an entrenched constitution requires more than the approval of the national legislature, it requires wider acceptance. Sometimes, the reason for this is that the constitution is considered supreme law, such as according to the supremacy clause in the US constitution. Regardless of whether a constitution has this technical status, all states with an entrenched constitution recognise the difference between constitutional law and ordinary statutory law. Procedures for ratification of constitutional amendments vary between states. In a federal system of government, the approval of a majority of state/provincial legislatures may be required. Alternatively, a national referendum may be required in some states, such as in Australia.

In constitutions that are not entrenched, no special procedure is required for modification. In the small number of countries with un-entrenched constitutions, the lack of entrenchment is because the constitution is not recognised with any higher legal status than ordinary statutes. In the UK, for example, passing laws which modify sources of the constitution, whether they are written or unwritten, are passed on a simple majority in Parliament. The concept of "amendment" does not apply, as the constitution can be altered as easily in terms of procedure as any national law.

Distribution of Sovereignty

Constitutions also establish where sovereignty is located in the state. There are three basic types of distribution of sovereignty: federal, unitary and confederal. A federal system of government will inevitably have a constitution that recognizes the division of sovereignty between the centre and peripheral/provincial regions of the state. The Canadian Constitution is an example of this, dividing power between the federal government and the provinces. A unitary constitution recognises that sovereignty resides only in the centre of the state. In the

UK, the constitutional doctrine of Parliamentary sovereignty dictates than sovereignty is ultimately contained at the centre. Confederal constitutions are rare, and there is often dispute to whether so-called "confederal" states are actually federal. In a confederacy, sovereignty is located in peripheral regions/ provinces and only limited power is granted to the centre. A historical example of a confederal constitution is the Swiss Federal Constitution.

Separation of Powers

Constitutions vary extensively as to the degree of separation of powers, usually meaning the constitutional separation of the executive, legislative and judicial branches of government. The United States constitution has a full separation of powers, with each branch having particular enumerated powers. For instance, Congress, the US legislature, has the power of impeachment, which cannot be exercised by another branch.

Lines of Accountability

Lines of accountability are a common feature in all democratic constitutions. In presidential systems of government, such as the United States, and semi-presidential systems, such as France, department secretaries/ministers are accountable to the president, who has patronage powers to appoint and dismiss ministers. The president is accountable to the people in an election. In parliamentary systems, such as the United Kingdom and Australia, ministers are accountable to Parliament, but it is the prime minister whc appoints and dismisses them (in Westminster systems this power derives from the monarch, a component of Parliament). There is the concept of a vote of no confidence in many countries with parliamentary systems, which means that if a majority of the legislature vote for a no confidence motion, then the government must resign, and a new one will be formed, or parliament will be dissolved and a general election called.

Facade Constitutions

Italian political theorist Giovanni Sartori noted the existence of national constitutions which are a façade for authoritarian sources of power. While such documents may express respect for human rights or establish an independent judiciary, they may be ignored when the government feels threatened or entirely dishonoured in practice. An extreme example was the Constitution of the Soviet Union that on paper supported freedom of assembly or freedom of speech; however, citizens who acted accordingly were summarily imprisoned. The example demonstrates that the protections and benefits of a constitution are provided less through its written terms, but more through deference by government and society to its principles.

Constitutional Courts

The constitution is often protected by a certain legal body in each country with various names, such as supreme, constitutional or high court. This court judges the compatibility of legislation with the provisions and principles of the constitution, which is termed "constitutionality". Especially important is the court's responsibility to protect constitutionally established rights and freedoms. In constitutions without the concept of supreme law, such as the United Kingdom constitution, the concept of "constitutionality" has little meaning, and constitutional courts do not exist.

A "constitutional violation" is an action or legislative act that is judged by a constitutional court to be contrary to the constitution, that is, "unconstitutional". An example of constitutional violation by the executive could be a politician who abuses the powers of his constitutionally-established office. An example of constitutional violation by the legislature is an attempt to pass a law that would contradict the constitution, without first going through the proper constitutional amendment process.

A constitutional court is normally the court of last resort, the highest judicial body in the government. The process of judicial review is then integrated into the system of courts of appeal. This is the case, for example, with the Supreme Court of the United States. Cases must normally be heard in lower courts before being brought before the Supreme Court, except cases for which the Supreme Court has original jurisdiction. Some other countries dedicate a special court solely to the protection of the constitution, as with the German Constitutional Court.

Most constitutional courts are powerful instruments of judicial review, with the power to declare laws "unconstitutional", that is, incompatible with the constitution. The effect of this ruling varies between governments, but it is common for the courts' action to rule a law unenforceable, as is the case in the United States. However, many courts have the problem of relying on the legislative and executive branches' cooperation to properly enforce their decisions.

For example, in the United States, the Supreme Court's ruling overturning the "separate but equal" doctrine in the 1950s depended on individual states cooperation to enforce. Some failed to do so, prompting the federal government to intervene. Other countries, such as France, have a Constitutional Council of France which may only judge the constitutionality of laws before the ratification process.

Some countries, mainly those with uncodified constitutions, have no such courts at all -for example, as the United Kingdom traditionally functions under the principle of parliamentary sovereignty: the legislature has the power to enact any law it wishes.

However, through its membership in the European Union, the UK is now subject to the jurisdiction of European Community law and the European Court of Justice; similarly, by acceding to the Council of Europe's European Convention on Human Rights, it is subject to the European Court of Human Rights. In effect, these bodies are constitutional courts that can invalidate or interpret UK legislation, first established as a principle by the Factortame case.

History and Development

Excavations in modern-day Iraq by Ernest de Sarzec in 1877 found evidence of the earliest known code of justice, issued by the Sumerian king Urukagina of Lagash ca. 2300 BC. Perhaps the earliest prototype for a law of government, this document itself has not yet been discovered; however it is known that it allowed some rights to his citizens.

For example, it is known that it relieved tax for widows and orphans, and protected the poor from the usury of the rich.

After that, many governments ruled by special codes of written laws. The oldest such document still known to exist seems to be that of Ur-Nammu of Ur (ca. 2050 BC). Some of the more well known among these include the code of Hammurabi of Babylonia, the Hittite code, the Assyrian code, Mosaic law, and likewise the commandments of Cyrus the Great of Persia.

In 621 BC, a scribe named Draco wrote the laws of the city-state of Athens; and being quite cruel, this code prescribed the death penalty for any offense. In 594 BC, Solon, the ruler of Athens, created the new Solonian Constitution. It eased the burden of the workers, however it made the ruling class to be determined by wealth, rather than by birth. Cleisthenes again reformed the Athenian constitution and set it on a democratic footing in 508 BC.

Aristotle (c. 350 BC) was one of the first in recorded history to make a formal distinction between law and constitutional law, establishing ideas of constitution and constitutionalism, and attempting to classify different forms of constitutional government. The most basic definition he used to describe a constitution in general terms was "the arrangement of the offices in a state".

In his works Constitution of Athens, Politics, and Nicomachean Ethics he explored different forms of constitutions. He classified both what he regarded as good and bad constitutions, and came to the conclusion that the best constitution was a mixed system, including monarchic, aristocratic, and democratic elements. He also distinguished between citizens, who had the exclusive opportunity to participate in the state, and non-citizens and slaves who did not. The Romans first codified their constitution in 449 BC as the Twelve Tables. They operated under a series of laws that were added from time to time, but Roman law was never reorganised into a single code until the Codex Theodosianus (AD 438); later, in the Eastern Empire the Codex Justinianus (534) was highly influential throughout Europe. This was followed in the east by the Ecloga of Leo III the Isaurian (740) and the Basilica of Basil I (878).

Many of the Germanic peoples that filled the power vacuum left by the Western Roman Empire in the Early Middle Ages codified their laws. One of the first of these Germanic law codes to be written was the Visigothic Code of Euric (471).

This was followed by the Lex Burgundionum, applying separate codes for Germans and for Romans; the Pactus Alamannorum; and the Salic Law of the Franks, all written soon after 500. In 506, the Breviarum or "Lex Romana" of Alaric II, king of the Visigoths, adopted and consolidated the Codex Theodosianus together with assorted earlier Roman laws. Systems that appeared somewhat later include the Edictum Rothari of the Lombards (643), the Lex Visigothorum (654), the Lex Alamannorum (730) and the Lex Frisionum (c. 785).

Japan's Seventeen-article constitution written in 604, reportedly by Prince Shotoku, is an early example of a constitution in Asian political history. Influenced by Buddhist teachings, the document focuses more on social morality than institutions of government per se and remains a notable early attempt at a government constitution. Another is the Constitution of Medina, drafted by the prophet of Islam, Muhammad, in 622.

The Gayanashagowa, or 'oral' constitution of the Iroquois nation, has been estimated to date from between 1090 and 1150, and is also thought by some to have provided a partial inspiration for the US Constitution.

In England, King Henry I's proclamation of the Charter of Liberties in 1100 bound the king for the first time in his treatment of the clergy and the nobility. This idea was extended and refined by the English barony when they forced John to sign the Magna Carta in 1215. The most important single article of the Magna Carta, related to "habeas corpus", provided that the king was not permitted to imprison, outlaw, exile or kill anyone at a whim --there must be due process of law first. This article, Article 39, of the Magna Carta read:

No free man shall be arrested, or imprisoned, or deprived of his property, or outlawed, or exiled, or in any way destroyed, nor shall we go against him or send against him, unless by legal judgement of his peers, or by the law of the land.

This provision became the cornerstone of English liberty after that point. The social contract in the original case was between the king and the nobility, but was gradually extended to all of the people. It led to the system of Constitutional Monarchy, with further reforms shifting the balance of power from the monarchy and nobility to the House of Commons.

Between 1220 and 1230, a Saxon administrator, Eike von Repgow, composed the Sachsenspiegel, which became the supreme law used in parts of Germany as late as 1900.

In 1236, Sundiata Keita presented an oral constitution federating the Mali Empire, called the Kouroukan Fouga.

Meanwhile, around 1240, the Coptic Egyptian Christian writer, 'Abul Fada'il Ibn al-'Assal, wrote the Fetha Negest in Arabic. 'Ibn al-Assal took his laws partly from apostolic writings and Mosaic law, and partly from the former Byzantine codes. There are a few historical records claiming that this law code was translated into Ge'ez and entered Ethiopia around 1450 in the reign of Zara Yaqob.

Even so, its first recorded use in the function of a constitution (supreme law of the land) is with Sarsa Dengel beginning in 1563. The Fetha Negest remained the supreme law in Ethiopia until 1931, when a modern-style Constitution was first granted by Emperor Haile Selassie I.

The earliest written constitution still governing a sovereign nation today may be that of San Marino. The Leges Statutae Republicae Sancti Marini was written in Latin and consists of six books. The first book, with 62 articles, establishes councils, courts, various executive officers and the powers assigned to them. The remaining books cover criminal and civil law, judicial procedures and remedies. Written in 1600, the document was based upon the Statuti Comunali (Town Statute) of 1300, itself influenced by the Codex Justinianus, and it remains in force today.

In 1639, the Colony of Connecticut adopted the Fundamental Orders, which is considered the first North American constitution, and is the basis for every new Connecticut constitution since, and is also the reason for Connecticut's nickname, the Constitution State.

The Commonwealth of Massachusetts adopted its constitution in 1780, before the ratification of the Articles of Confederation and the United States Constitution. It is probably the oldest still-functioning nominal constitution, that is, where the document specifically declares itself to be a constitution. The United States Constitution, ratified 1789, was influenced by the British constitutional system and the political system of the United Provinces, plus the writings of Polybius, Locke, Montesquieu, and others. The document became a benchmark for republican and codified constitutions written thereafter and is commonly believed to be the oldest modern, national, codified constitution in the world.

6

Democracy

Democracy (literally "rule by the people", from the Greek demos, "people," and kratos, "rule") is a form of government. Today, the term democracy is often used to refer to liberal democracy, but there is no necessity that democracies be liberal (i.e. respectful of individual liberty and property) and in some cases may be illiberal democracies.

There are many other varieties and the methods used to govern differ. While the term democracy is typically used in the context of a political state, the principles are also applicable to other bodies such as intergovernmental organizations, non-governmental organizations, grassroot organizations, labor unions, industry trade groups, professional bodies, and learned societies.

VARIETIES

The definition of democracy is made complex by the varied concepts used at different periods of history in different contexts. Political systems, or proposed political systems, claiming or claimed to be democratic have ranged very broadly.

Aristotle

Aristotle contrasted rule by the many (democracy/polity), with rule by the few (oligarchy/aristocracy), and with rule by a single person (tyranny/monarchy or today autocracy). He also thought that there was a good and a bad variant of each system (he considered democracy to be degenerate counterpart to polity)..

Sortition

Sortition/Allotment have formed the basis of systems randomly selecting officers from the population: For example, Aristotle described the law courts in Athens which were selected by lot as democratic and described elections as oligarchic.

TRIBAL DEMOCRACY

Certain tribes organised themselves using forms of participatory democracy.

Consensus

Consensus democracy and deliberative democracy seek consensus among the people.

Direct

Direct democracy is largely referred to as a political system where the citizens vote on all major policy decisions. It is called direct because, in the classical forms, there are no intermediaries or representatives. All direct democracies to date have been relatively small communities, usually city-states. Although, some see the extensive use of referenda, as in California, as akin to direct democracy in a very large polity with over 20 million potential voters. Today, a limited direct democracy exists in some Swiss cantons. Other current examples include many small civic organizations (like college faculties) and town meetings in New England (usually in towns under 10,000 population).

Direct democracy obviously becomes difficult when the electorate is large. Modern direct democracy tries to accommodate this and sees a role for strictly controlled representatives. It is characterized by three pillars; referendums (initiated by governments or legislatures or by citizens responding to legislation), initiatives (initiated by citizens) and recall elections (on holders of public office).

Representative

Representative democracy is so named because the people select representatives to a governing body. Representatives may be chosen by the electorate as a whole (as in many proportional systems) or represent a particular district (or constituency), with some systems using a combination of the two. Some representative democracies also incorporate some elements of direct democracy, such as referenda.

Liberal Democracy

Liberal democracy is a representative democracy (with free and fair elections) along with the protection of minorities, the rule of law, a separation of powers, and protection of liberties (thus the name liberal) of speech, assembly, religion, and property. Conversely, an illiberal democracy is one where the protections that form a liberal democracy are either nonexistent, or not enforced. The experience in some post-Soviet states drew attention to the phenomenon, although it is not of recent origin. Napoleon III for example used plebiscites to ratify his imperial decisions.

Socialist

Socialism is a broad movement and has several different views on democracy. Social democracy, democratic socialism, Soviet democracy, and the dictatorship of the proletariat are some examples.

Anarchist

Some anarchists oppose democracy while others favor it. Pierre-Joseph Proudhon argued that the only acceptable form of direct democracy is one in which it is recognized that majority decisions are not binding on the minority. However, anarcho-communist Murray Bookchin criticizes individualist anarchists for opposing democracy, and says "majority rule" is consistent with anarchism, There are also some anarchists who expect society to operate by consensus. The notion of direct democracy, or participatory democracy, is very common to many anarchist movements, especially in libertarian communism, as a form of organizing and management based upon consensus, collective action, freedom and responsibility. This goes with the fundamental anarchist principle of denying authoritarian or alienating organizational structures.

HISTORY

Ancient Origins

The word democracy was coined in ancient Greece and used interchangeably with isonomia (equality of political rights). Although Athenian democracy is today considered by many to have been a form of direct democracy, originally it had two distinguishing features: firstly the allotment (selection by lot) of ordinary citizens to government offices and courts, and secondarily the assembly of all the citizens. In theory, all the Athenian citizens were eligible to speak and vote in the Assembly, which set the laws of the city-state, but neither political rights, nor citizenship, were granted to women, slaves, or metics. Of the 250,000 inhabitants only some 30,000 on average were citizens. Of those 30,000 perhaps 5,000 might regularly attend one or more meetings of the popular Assembly. Most of the officers & magistrates of Athenian government were allotted; only the generals (strategoi) and a few other officers were elected.

The seeds of representative democracy were arguably sown in the Roman Republic. Democratic principles and elements have also been argued for the Mahajanapadas of ancient India, and also in the local Sanghas, Ganas and Panchayats that existed throughout the centuries in India. However, political rights were to some extent a representative of social class and in particular the caste system. In these republics, power was typically vested in the hands of an elite class, and so the system would perhaps be better classified as an oligarchy. In the case of the village panchayats, the picture is somewhat more democratic. A panchayat in essence is a meeting of townspeople mediated by a group of village elders, and so it is an example of a direct democracy.

Democracy was also seen to a certain extent in bands and tribes such as the Iroquois Confederacy. However, in the Iroquois Confederacy only the males of certain clans could be leaders and some clans were excluded. Only the oldest females from the same clans could choose and remove the leaders. This excluded most of the population. An interesting detail is that there should be consensus among the leaders, not majority support decided by voting, when making decisions.

Middle Ages

During the Middle Ages, there were various systems involving elections or assemblies, although often only involving a minority of the population, such as the election of Gopala in Bengal, the Polish-Lithuanian Commonwealth, the Althing in Iceland, certain medieval Italian city-states such as Venice, the tuatha system in early medieval Ireland, the Veche in Slavic countries, and Scandinavian Things and Nayashu in Venice like autonomous merchant city of Sakai in the 16th century in Japan. Most regions during the middle-ages were ruled by clergy or feudal lords.

The Parliament of England had its roots in the restrictions on the power of kings written into Magna Carta. The first elected parliament was De Montfort's Parliament in England in 1265. However only a small minority actually had a voice; Parliament was elected by only a few percent of the population (less than 3% in 1780.), and the system had problematic features such as rotten boroughs. The power to call parliament was at the pleasure of the monarch. After the Glorious Revolution of 1688, the English Bill of Rights was enacted in 1689, which codified certain rights and increased the influence of the Parliament. The franchise was slowly increased and the Parliament gradually gained more power until the monarch became entirely a figurehead.

18th and 19th centuries

Although not described as a democracy by the founding fathers, the United States can be seen as the first liberal democracy. The United States Constitution, adopted in 1788, provided for an elected government and protected civil rights and liberties. Already in the colonial period before 1776 most adult white men could vote; there were still property requirements but most men owned their own farms and could pass the tests. On the American frontier, democracy became a way of life, with widespread social, economic and political equality. By 1840s almost all property restrictions were ended and nearly all white adult male citizens could vote; and turnout averaged 60-80% in frequent elections for local, state and national officials. The system gradually evolved, from

Jeffersonian Democracy to Jacksonian Democracy and beyond. In Reconstruction after the Civil War (late 1860s) the newly freed slaves became citizens and were given the right to vote. Some scholars, Judith Shklar for instance, argue that because America tolerated slavery, it could not be called a democracy until after the adoption of the Reconstruction Amendments at this time. In 1789, Revolutionary France adopted the Declaration of the Rights of Man and of the Citizen and, although short-lived, the National Convention was elected by all males.

Liberal democracies were few and often short-lived before the late nineteenth century. Various nations and territories have claimed to be the first with universal suffrage.

20th Century

20th century transitions to liberal democracy have come in successive "waves of democracy," variously resulting from wars, revolutions, decolonization, and economic circumstances. World War I and the dissolution of the Ottoman and Austro-Hungarian empires resulted in the creation of new nation-states in Europe, most of them nominally democratic. In the 1920s democracy flourished, but the Great Depression brought disenchantment, and most the countries of Europe, Latin America, and Asia turned to strong-man rule or dictatorships. Fascism and dictatorships flourished in Nazi Germany, Italy, Spain and Portugal, as well as nondemocratic regimes in Poland, the Baltics, the Balkans, Brazil, Cuba, China, and Japan, among others. Together with Stalin's regime in the Soviet Union, these made the 1930s the "Age of Dictators".

World War II brought a definitive reversal of this trend in western Europe. The successful democratization of the occupied Germany and the occupied Japan served as a model for the later theory of regime change. However, most of Eastern Europe was forced into the non-democratic Soviet bloc. The war was followed by decolonisation, and again most of the new independent states had nominally democratic constitutions. In the decades following World War II, most western democratic nations had mixed economies and developed a welfare state, reflecting a general consensus among their electorates and political parties. In the 1950s and 1960s, economic growth was high in both the western and Communist countries; it later declined in the state-controlled economies. By 1960, the vast majority of nation-states were nominally democracies, although the majority of the world's populations lived in nations that experienced sham elections, and other forms of subterfuge (particularly in Communist nations and the former colonies.)

A subsequent wave of democratisation brought substantial gains toward true liberal democracy for many nations. Several of the military dictatorships in South America became democratic in the late 1970s and early 1980s. This was followed by nations in East and South Asia by the mid-to late 1980s. Economic malaise in the 1980s, along with resentment of communist oppression, contributed to the collapse of the Soviet Union, the associated end of the Cold War, and the democratization and liberalisation of the former Eastern bloc countries. The most successful of the new democracies were those geographically and culturally closest to western Europe, and they are now members or candidate members of the European Union. The liberal trend spread to some nations in Africa in the 1990s, most prominently in South Africa. Some recent examples include the Indonesian Revolution of 1998, the Bulldozer Revolution in Yugoslavia, the Rose Revolution in Georgia, the Orange Revolution in Ukraine, the Cedar Revolution in Lebanon, and the Tulip Revolution in Kyrgyzstan.

The number of liberal democracies currently stands at an all-time high and has been growing without interruption for some time. As such, it has been speculated that this trend may continue in the future to the point where liberal democratic nation-states become the universal standard form of human society. This prediction forms the core of Francis Fukayama's "End of History" theory.

THEORY

Conceptions

Among political theorists, there are many contending conceptions of democracy.

- Aggregative democracy uses democratic processes to solicit citizens' preferences and then aggregate them together to determine what social policies society should adopt. Therefore, proponents of this view hold that democratic participation should primarily focus on voting, where the policy with the most votes gets implemented. There are different variants of this:

- o Under minimalism, democracy is a system of government in which citizens give teams of political leaders the right to rule in periodic elections. According to this minimalist conception, citizens cannot and should not "rule" because, for example, on most issues, most of the time, they have no clear views or their views are not well-founded. Joseph Schumpeter articulated this view most famously in his book Capitalism, Socialism, and Democracy. Contemporary proponents of minimalism include William H. Riker, Adam Przeworski, Richard Posner.
- o Direct democracy, on the other hand, holds that citizens should participate directly, not through their representatives, in making laws and policies. Proponents of direct democracy offer varied reasons to support this view. Political activity can be valuable in itself, it socializes and educates citizens, and popular participation can check powerful elites. Most importantly, citizens do not really rule themselves unless they directly decide laws and policies.
- o Government should produce laws and policies that are close to the views of the median voter -with half to his left and the other half to his right. Anthony Downs laid out this view in his 1957 book An Economic Theory of Democracy.
- o Robert A. Dahl argues that the fundamental democratic principle is that, when it comes to binding collective decisions, each person in a political community is entitled to have his/her interests be given equal consideration (not necessarily that all people are equally satisfied by the collective decision). He uses the term Polyarchy to refer to societies in which there exists a certain set of institutions and procedures which are perceived as leading to such

democracy. First and foremost among these institutions is the regular occurrence of free and open elections which are used to select representatives who then manage all or most of the public policy of the society. However, these polyarchic procedures may not create a full democracy if, for example, poverty prevents political participation. Some see a problem with the wealthy having more influence and therefore argue for reforms like campaign finance reform. Some may see it as a problem that the majority of the voters decide policy, as opposed to majority rule of the entire population. This can be used as an argument for making political participation mandatory, like compulsory voting.

- Deliberative democracy is based on the notion that democracy is government by discussion. Deliberative democrats contend that laws and policies should be based upon reasons that all citizens can accept. The political arena should be one in which leaders and citizens make arguments, listen, and change their minds. One modern proponents of this form of government are led by Jürgen Habermas.

"Democracy" and "Republic"

In historical usages and especially when considering the works of the Founding Fathers of the United States, the word "democracy" refers solely to direct democracy, while a representative democracy where representatives of the people are elected and whose power to govern is limited by laws enshrined in a constitution is referred to as a constitutional republic. Constitutional Republics are a deliberate attempt to diminish the threat of mobocracy thereby protecting minority groups from the tyranny of the majority by placing checks on the power of the majority of the population. The power of the majority of the people is checked by limiting that power to electing representatives who govern within limits of overarching constitutional law rather than the popular vote having legislative power itself. Moreover, the power of elected representatives is also checked by prohibitions against any single individual having legislative, judicial, and executive powers so that basic constitutional law is extremely difficult to change. John Adams defined a constitutional republic as "a government of laws, and not of men." Using the term "democracy" to refer solely to direct democracy, or to representative democracy without checks on the power of elected officials, retains some popularity in United States conservative and libertarian circles.

The original framers of the United States Constitution were notably cognizant of what they perceived as a danger of majority rule in oppressing freedom and liberty of the individual. For example, James Madison, in Federalist Paper No. 10, advocates a constitutional republic over a democracy to protect the individual from the majority. The framers carefully created the institutions within the Constitution and the United States Bill of Rights. They kept what they believed were the best elements of majority rule. But they were mitigated by a constitution with protections for individual liberty, a separation of powers, and a layered federal structure.

However, in contemporary usage, the term "democracy" refers to a government chosen by the people, whether it is direct or representative. The term "republic" has many different meanings but today often refers to a representative democracy with an elected head of state, such as a President, serving for a limited term, in contrast to states with a hereditary monarch as a head of state, even if these states also are representative democracies with an elected head of government such as a Prime Minister. Therefore, today the term is used by states which are quite different from the earlier use of the term, such as the Islamic Republic of Iran and the former German Democratic Republic.

Republicanism and Liberalism have complex relationships to democracy and republic.

CONSTITUTIONAL MONARCHS AND UPPER CHAMBERS

Initially after the American and French revolutions the question was open whether a democracy, in order to restrain unchecked majority rule, should have an elitist upper chamber, the members perhaps appointed meritorious experts or having lifetime tenures, or should have a constitutional monarch with limited but real powers. Some countries (as Britain, the

Netherlands, Belgium, Scandinavian countries and Japan) turned powerful monarchs into constitutional monarchs with limited or, often gradually, merely symbolic roles. Often the monarchy was abolished along with the aristocratic system (as in the U.S., France, China, Russia, Germany, Austria, Hungary, Italy, Greece and Egypt). Many nations had elite upper houses of legislatures which often had lifetime tenure, but eventually these senates lost power (as in Britain) or else became elective and remained powerful (as in the United States).

Democratic State

Though there remains some philosophical debate as to the applicability and legitimacy of criteria in defining democracy what follows may be a minimum of requirements for a state to be considered democratic (note that for example anarchists may support a form of democracy but not a state):

1. A demos-a group which makes political decisions by some form of collective procedure-must exist. Non-members of the demos do not participate. In modern democracies the demos is the adult portion of the nation, and adult citizenship is usually equivalent to membership.
2. A territory must be present, where the decisions apply, and where the demos is resident. In modern democracies, the territory is the nation-state, and since this corresponds (in theory) with the homeland of the nation, the demos and the reach of the democratic process neatly coincide. Colonies of democracies are not considered democratic by themselves, if they are governed from the colonial motherland: demos and territory do not coincide.
3. A decision-making procedure exists, which is either direct, in instances such as a referendum, or indirect, of which instances include the election of a parliament.
4. The procedure is regarded as legitimate by the demos, implying that its outcome will be accepted. Political legitimacy is the willingness of the population to accept decisions of the state, its government and courts, which go against personal choices or interests.

5. The procedure is effective in the minimal sense that it can be used to change the government, assuming there is sufficient support for that change. Showcase elections, pre-arranged to re-elect the existing regime, are not democratic.
6. In the case of nation-states, the state must be sovereign: democratic elections are pointless if an outside authority can overrule the result.

Advantages and Disadvantages of Liberal Democracy

It has been suggested that this article or section be merged with liberal democracy.

DIRECT DEMOCRACY

Some argue that "liberal democracy" does not respect absolute majority rule (except when electing representatives). The "liberty" of majority rule is restricted by the constitution or precedent decided by previous generations. Also, the real power is actually held by a relatively small representative body. Thus, the argument goes, "liberal democracy" is merely a decoration over an oligarchy. A system of direct democracy would be preferable. New technology, such as E-democracy, may make direct democracy easier to implement. Others would say that only a liberal democracy can guarantee the individual liberties of its citizens and prevent the development into a dictatorship. Unmoderated majority rule could, in this view, lead to an oppression of minorities. Another argument is that the elected leaders may be more interested and able than the average voter. A third that it takes much effort and time if everyone should gather information, discuss, and vote on most issues. Some liberal democracies have elements of direct democracy such as referenda and plebiscite. Switzerland and Uruguay are some examples; likewise several states of the United States. Many other countries have referenda to a lesser degree in their political system.

Democracy and Ethnic and Religious Conflicts

For historical reasons, many states are not culturally and ethnically homogeneous. There may be sharp ethnic, linguistic, religious and cultural divisions. In fact, some groups may be actively hostile to each other. A democracy, which by definition allows mass participation in decision-making theoretically also allows the use of the political process against 'enemy' groups. That may be especially visible during democratization, if the previous non-democratic government oppressed certain groups. It is also visible in established democracies, in the form of anti-immigrant populism. However, arguably the worst repressions have occurred in states without universal suffrage, like formerly apartheid South Africa and Nazi Germany.

Yale Law School professor Amy Chua claims that democratization can increase ethnic conflicts when an ethnic minority is disproportionately wealthy. "When free market democracy is pursued in the presence of a market-dominant minority, the almost invariable result is backlash. This backlash typically takes one of three forms. The first is a backlash against markets, targeting the market-dominant minority's wealth. The second is a backlash against democracy by forces favorable to the market-dominant minority. The third is violence, sometimes genocidal, directed against the market-dominant minority itself.". Also, "overnight democracy will empower the poor, indigenous majority. What happens is that under those circumstances, democracy doesn't do what we expect it to do --that is, reinforce markets. Instead, democracy leads to the emergence of manipulative politicians and demagogues who find that the best way to get votes is by scapegoating the minorities." Chua also states that she is "big fan of trying to promote markets and democracy globally", but that it should be accompanied by attempts to "redistribute the wealth, whether it's property title and giving poor people property, land reform.... Redistributive mechanisms are tough to have if you have so much corruption."

The collapse of the Soviet Union and the partial democratisation of Soviet bloc states was followed by wars and civil war in the former Yugoslavia, in the Caucasus, and in Moldova. Nevertheless, statistical research shows that the fall of Communism and the increase in the number of democratic states were accompanied by a sudden and dramatic decline in total warfare, interstate wars, ethnic wars, revolutionary wars, and the number of refugees and displaced people.

Bureaucracy

A persistent libertarian and monarchist critique of democracy is the claim that it encourages the elected representatives to change the law without necessity, and in particular to pour forth a flood of new laws. This is seen as pernicious in several ways. New laws constrict the scope of what were previously private liberties. Rapidly changing laws make it difficult for a willing non-specialist to remain law-abiding. This may be an invitation for law-enforcement agencies to misuse power. The claimed continual complication of the law may be contrary to a claimed simple and eternal natural law -although there is no consensus on what this natural law is, even among advocates. Supporters of democracy point to the complex bureaucracy and regulations that has occurred in dictatorships, like many of the former Communist states.

Liberal democracies are also criticized for a claimed slowness and complexity of their decision-making.

Short-term Focus

Modern liberal democracies, by definition, allow for regular changes of government. That has led to a common criticism of their short-term focus. In four or five years the government will face a new election, and it must think of how it will win that election. That would encourage a preference for policies that will bring short term benefits to the electorate (or to self-interested politicians) before the next election, rather than unpopular policy with longer term benefits. This criticism assumes that it is possible to make long term predictions for a society, something Karl Popper has criticized as historicism.

Besides the regular review of governing entities, short-term focus in a democracy could also be the result of collective short-term thinking. For example, consider a campaign for policies aimed at reducing environmental damage while causing temporary increase in unemployment. However, this risk applies also to other political systems.

Anarcho-capitalist Hans-Herman Hoppe explained short-termism of the democratic governments by the rational choice of currently ruling group to overexploit temporarily accessible resources, thus deriving maximal economic advantage to the members of this group. (He contrasted this with hereditary monarchy, in which a monarch has an interest in preserving the long-term capital value of his property (i.e. the country he owns) counter-balancing his desire to extract immediate revenue. He argues that the historical record of levels of taxation in certain monarchies (5-8%) and certain liberal democracies (40-60%) seems to confirm this contention. On the other hand, in hereditary autocracies like North Korea the state controls the whole economy while many liberal democratic states that score very high on rankings of economic freedom.

Public Choice Theory

Public choice theory is a branch of economics that studies the decision-making behavior of voters, politicians and government officials from the perspective of economic theory. One studied problem is that each voter has little influence and may therefore have a rational ignorance regarding political issues. This may allow special interest groups to gain subsidies and regulations beneficial to them but harmful to society. However, special interest groups may be equally or more influential in nondemocracies.

Plutocracy

Marxists, socialists and left-wing anarchists, argue that liberal democracy is an integral part of the capitalist system and is class-based and not fully democratic or participatory. It is bourgeois democracy where only the most financially powerful people rule. Because of this it is seen as fundamentally un-egalitarian, existing or operating in a way that facilitates economic exploitation. According to Marx, parliamentary elections are an opportunity citizens of a country get every few years to decide who among the ruling classes will misrepresent them in parliament.

The cost of political campaigning in representative democracies may mean that the system favors the rich, a form of plutocracy who may be a very small minority of the voters. In Athenian democracy, some public offices were randomly allocated to citizens, in order to inhibit the effects of plutocracy.

Modern democracy may also be regarded as a dishonest farce used to keep the masses from getting restless, or a conspiracy for making them restless for some political agenda. It may encourage candidates to make deals with wealthy supporters, offering favorable legislation if the candidate is elected - perpetuating conspiracies for monopolization of key areas. Campaign finance reform is an attempt to correct this perceived problem. However, United States economist Steven Levitt claims in his book Freakonomics, that campaign spending is no guarantee of electoral success. He compared electoral success of the same pair of candidates running against one another repeatedly for the same job, as often happens in United States Congressional elections, where spending levels varied. He concludes:

"A winning candidate can cut his spending in half and lose only 1 percent of the vote. Meanwhile, a losing candidate who doubles his spending can expect to shift the vote in his favor by only that same 1 percent."

Ownership of the media by the few may lead to more specific distortion of the electoral process, since the media are themselves a vital element of that process. Some critics argue that criticism of the status quo or a particular agenda tends to be suppressed by such media cartels, to protect their own self-interests. Proponents respond that constitutionally protected freedom of speech makes it possible for both for-profit and non-profit organizations to debate the issues. They argue that media coverage in democracies simply reflects public preferences, and does not entail censorship.

Limited Voter Turnout

Some see a problem with limited voter turnout since not all eligible voters participate in the political process. Get out the vote campaigns may increase voter turnout but may be advocated by special interest groups. Some therefore argue for compulsory voting and several nations have this system. Proponents argue that this increases the legitimacy of the elections and ensure political participation by all those affected by the political process. Also, political parties do not have to spend time and energy convincing voters that they should vote at all. Arguments against include restriction of freedom, economic costs of enforcing this, increased number of invalid and blank votes, and random voting.

Majoritarianism

The "tyranny of the majority" is the fear that a democratic government, reflecting the majority view, can take action that oppresses a particular minority. Theoretically, the majority could only be a majority of those who vote and not a majority of the citizens. In those cases, one minority tyrannizes another minority in the name of the majority. It can apply in both direct democracy or representative democracy. Possible examples include:

- those potentially subject to conscription are a minority.
- several European countries have introduced bans on personal religious symbols in public schools. Opponents see this as a violation of rights to freedom of religion. Supporters see it as following from the separation of state and religious activities.
- prohibition of pornography is typically determined by what the majority is prepared to accept.
- recreational drug use is also typically legalized (or at least tolerated) to the degree that the majority finds acceptable. Users may see themselves as an oppressed minority, victims of unjustifiable criminalisation.
- society's treatment of homosexuals is also cited in this context. Homosexual acts were widely criminalised in democracies until several decades ago; in some democracies they still are, reflecting the religious or sexual mores of the majority.
- the Athenian democracy and the early United States had slavery.
- the majority often taxes the minority who are wealthy at progressively higher rates, with the intention that the wealthy will incur a larger tax burden for social purposes. However, this is generally offset to some degree, by their better access to relevant expert advice (tax consultants and lawyers).

- in prosperous western democracies, the poor form a minority of the population, and may be disadvantaged by a majority who resent transfer taxation. Especially when they form a distinct underclass, the majority may use the democratic process to, in effect, withdraw the protection of the state.
- an often quoted example of the 'tyranny of the majority' is that Adolf Hitler came to power by legitimate democratic procedures. The Nazi party gained the largest share of votes in the democratic Weimar republic in 1933. Some might consider this an example of "tyranny of a minority" since he never gained a majority vote, but it is common for a plurality to exercise power in democracies, so the rise of Hitler can not be considered irrelevant. However, his regime's large-scale human rights violations took place after the democratic system had been abolished. Also, the Weimar constitution in an "emergency" allowed dictatorial powers and suspension of the essentials of the constitution itself without any vote or election, something not possible in most liberal democracies.

Proponents of democracy make a number of defenses concerning 'tyranny of the majority'. One is to argue that the presence of a constitution protecting the rights of all citizens in many democratic countries acts as a safeguard. Generally, changes in these constitutions require the agreement of a supermajority of the elected representatives, or require a judge and jury to agree that evidentiary and procedural standards have been fulfilled by the state, or two different votes by the representatives separated by an election, or, sometimes, a referendum. These requirements are often combined. The separation of powers into legislative branch, executive branch, judicial branch also makes it more difficult for a small majority to impose their will. This means a majority can still legitimately coerce a minority (which is still ethically questionable), but such a minority would be very small and, as a practical matter, it is harder to get a larger proportion of the people to agree to such actions. Another argument is that majorities and minorities can take a markedly different shape on different issues. People often agree with the majority view on some issues and agree with a minority view on other issues. One's view may also change. Thus, the members of a majority may limit oppression of a minority since they may well in the future themselves be in a minority.

A third common argument is that, despite the risks, majority rule is preferable to other systems, and the tyranny of the majority is in any case an improvement on a tyranny of a minority. All the possible problems mentioned above can also occur in nondemocracies with the added problem that a minority can oppress the majority. Proponents of democracy argue that empirical statistical evidence strongly shows that more democracy leads to less internal violence and mass murder by the government.. This is sometimes formulated as Rummel's Law, which states that the less democratic freedom a people have, the more likely their rulers are to murder them.

POLITICAL STABILITY

One argument for democracy is that by creating a system where the public can remove administrations, without changing the legal basis for government, democracy aims at reducing political uncertainty and instability, and assuring citizens that however much they may disagree with present policies, they will be given a regular chance to change those who are in power, or change policies with which they disagree. This is preferable to a system where political change takes place through violence.

Some think that political stability may be considered as excessive when the group in power remains the same for an extended period of time. On the other hand, this is more common in nondemocracies.

One notable feature of liberal democracies is that their opponents (those groups who wish to abolish liberal democracy) rarely win elections. Advocates use this as an argument to support their view that liberal democracy is inherently stable and can usually only be overthrown by external force, while opponents argue that the system is inherently stacked against them despite its claims to impartiality. In the past, it was feared that democracy could be easily exploited by leaders with dictatorial aspirations, who could get themselves elected into power. However, the actual number of liberal democracies that have elected dictators into power is low. When it has occurred, it is usually after a major crisis have caused many people to doubt the system or in young/poorly functioning democracies. Some possible examples include Adolf Hitler during the Great Depression and Napoleon III who become first President of the young Second French Republic and later Emperor.

Effective Response in Wartime

A liberal democracy, by definition, implies that power is not concentrated. One criticism is that this could be a disadvantage for a state in wartime, when a fast and unified response is necessary. The legislature usually must give consent before the start of an offensive military operation, although sometimes the executive can do this on its own while keeping the legislature informed. If the democracy is attacked, then no consent is usually required for defensive operations. The people may vote against a conscription army. Monarchies and dictatorships can in theory act immediately and forcefully.

However, actual research shows that democracies are more likely to win wars than non-democracies. One explanation attributes this primarily to "the transparency of the polities, and the stability of their preferences, once determined, democracies are better able to cooperate with their partners in the conduct of wars". Other research attributes this to superior mobilization of resources or selection of wars that the democratic states have a high chance of winning.

Stam and Reiter (2002, p. 64-70) also note that the emphasis on individuality within democratic societies means that their soldiers fight with greater initiative and superior leadership. Officers in dictatorships are often selected for political loyalty rather than ability. They may be exclusively selected from a small class or religious/ethnic group that support the regime. Also this may also exclude many able officers. The leaders in nondemocracies may respond violently to any perceived criticisms or disobedience. This may make the soldiers and officers afraid to raise any objections or do anything without explicit authorisation. The lack of initiative may be particularly detrimental in modern warfare. Enemy soldiers may more easily surrender to democracies since they can expect comparatively good treatment. Nazi Germany killed almost 2/3 of the captured Soviet soldiers. 38% of the American soldiers captured by North Korea in the Korean War were killed.

Better Information on and Corrections of Problems

A democratic system may provide better information for policy decisions. Undesirable information may more easily be ignored in dictatorships, even if this undesirable or contrarian information provides early warning of problems. The democratic system also provides a way to replace inefficient leaders and policies. Thus, problems may continue longer and crises of all kinds may be more common in autocracies.

Corruption

Research by the World Bank suggests that political institutions are extremely important in determining the prevalence of corruption: democracy, parliamentary systems, political stability, and freedom of the press are all associated with lower corruption. Freedom of information legislation is important for accountability and transparency. The Indian Right to Information Act "has already engendered mass movements in the country that is bringing the lethargic, often corrupt bureaucracy to its knees and changing power equations completely."

Terrorism

Several studies have concluded that terrorism is most common in nations with intermediate political freedom. The nations with the least terrorism are the most democratic nations. However, critics of Western democracy such as Noam Chomsky have argued that, according to official definitions of terrorism, liberal democratic states have committed many acts of terrorism against other nations.

Economic Growth and Financial Crises

Statistically, more democracy correlates with a higher gross domestic product (GDP) per capita. However, there is disagreement regarding how much credit the democratic system can take for this. One observation is that democracy became widespread only after the industrial revolution and the introduction of capitalism. On the other hand, the industrial revolution started in England which was one of the most democratic nations for its time within its own borders. (But this democracy was very limited and did not apply to the colonies which contributed significantly to the wealth.)

Several statistical studies support the theory that more capitalism, measured for example with one the several Indices of Economic Freedom which has been used in hundreds of studies by independent researchers, increases economic growth and that this in turn increases general prosperity, reduces poverty, and causes democratization. This is a statistical tendency, and there are individual exceptions like India, which is democratic but arguably not prosperous, or Brunei, which has a high GDP but has never been democratic. There are also other studies suggesting that more democracy increases economic freedom although a few find no or even a small negative effect. One objection might be that nations like Sweden and Canada today score just below nations like Chile and Estonia on economic freedom but that Sweden and Canada today have a higher GDP per capita. However, this is a misunderstanding, the studies indicate effect on economic growth and thus that future GDP per capita will be higher with higher economic freedom. It should also be noted that according to the index Sweden and Canada are among the world's most capitalist nations, due to factors such as strong rule of law, strong property rights, and few restrictions against free trade. Critics might argue that the Index of Economic Freedom and other methods used does not measure the degree of capitalism, preferring some other definition.

Some argue that economic growth due to its empowerment of citizens, will ensure a transition to democracy in countries such as China. However, other dispute this. Even if economic growth has caused democratization in the past, it may not do so in the future. Dictators may now have learned how to have economic growth without this causing more political freedom.

A high degree of oil or mineral exports is strongly associated with nondemocratic rule. This effect applies worldwide and not only to the Middle East. Dictators who have this form of wealth can spend more on their security apparatus and provide benefits which lessen public unrest. Also, such wealth is not followed by the social and cultural changes that may transform societies with ordinary economic growth.

A recent meta-analysis finds that democracy has no direct effect on economic growth. However, it has a strong and significant indirect effects which contribute to growth. Democracy is associated with higher human capital accumulation, lower inflation, lower political instability, and higher economic freedom. There is also some evidence that it is associated with larger governments and more restrictions on international trade. If leaving out East Asia, then during the last forty-five years poor democracies have grown their economies 50% more rapidly than nondemocracies. Poor democracies such as the Baltic countries, Botswana, Costa Rica, Ghana, and Senegal have grown more rapidly than nondemocracies such as Angola, Syria, Uzbekistan, and Zimbabwe.

Of the eighty worst financial catastrophes during the last four decades, only five were in democracies. Similarly, poor democracies are half likely as non-democracies to experience a 10 percent decline in GDP per capita over the course of a single year.

Famines and Refugees

A prominent economist, Amartya Sen, has noted that no functioning democracy has ever suffered a large scale famine. This includes democracies that have not been very prosperous historically, like India, which had its last great famine in 1943 and many other large scale famines before that in the late nineteenth century, all under British rule. However, some others ascribe the Bengal famine of 1943 to the effects of World War II. The government of India had been becoming progressively more democratic for years. Provincial government had been entirely so since the Government of India Act of 1935.

Refugee crises almost always occur in non-democracies. Looking at the volume of refugee flows for the last twenty years, the first eighty-seven cases occurred in autocracies.

Human Development

Democracy correlates with a higher score on the human development index and a lower score on the human poverty index.

Poor democracies have better education, longer life expectancy, lower infant mortality, access to drinking water, and better health care than poor dictatorships. This is not due to higher levels of foreign assistance or spending a larger percentage of GDP on health and education. Instead, the available resources are managed better.

Several health indicators (life expectancy and infant and maternal mortality) have a stronger and more significant association with democracy than they have with GDP per capita, size of the public sector, or income inequality.

In the post-Communist nations, after an initial decline, those most democratic have achieved the greatest gains in life expectancy.

DEMOCRATIC PEACE THEORY

Numerous studies using many different kinds of data, definitions, and statistical analyzes have found support for the democratic peace theory. The original finding was that liberal democracies have never made war with one another. More recent research has extended the theory and finds that democracies have few Militarized Interstate Disputes causing less than 1000 battle deaths with one another, that those MIDs that have occurred between democracies have caused few deaths, and that democracies have few civil wars.

There are various criticisms of the theory, including specific historic wars and that correlation is not causation.

Mass Murder by Government

Research shows that the more democratic nations have much less democide or murder by government. Similarly, they have less genocide and politicide.

Freedoms and Rights: The freedoms and rights of the citizens in liberal democracies are usually seen as beneficial.

Happiness: Democracies are more often associated with a higher average self-reported happiness in a nation.

Criticism: Some far right, theocratic, anarchist, and monarchist groups oppose all forms of democracy.

Beyond the Public Level

While this article deals mainly with democracy as a system to rule countries, voting and representation have been used to govern many other kinds of communities and organizations.

- Many non-governmental organisations decide policy and leadership by voting.
- In business, corporations elect their boards by votes weighed by the number of shares held by each owner.
- Trade unions sometimes choose their leadership through democratic elections. In the U.S. democratic elections were rare before Congress required them in the 1950s.
- Cooperatives are enterprises owned and democratically controlled by their customers or workers.

FEDERATION

A federation (Latin: foedus, covenant) is a union comprising a number of partially self-governing states or regions united by a central ("federal") government. In a federation, the self-governing status of the component states is typically constitutionally entrenched and may not be altered by a unilateral decision of the central government. The form of government or constitutional structure found in a federation is known as federalism (see also federalism as a political philosophy). It can be considered the opposite of another system, the unitary state. Federations may be multi-ethnic, or cover a large area of territory, although neither is necessarily the case. Federations are often founded on an original agreement between a number of sovereign states.

Federations and other Forms of State

In a federation the component states are regarded as in some sense sovereign, in so far as certain powers are reserved to them that may not be exercised by the central government. However a federation is more than a mere loose alliance of independent states. The component states of a federation usually possess no powers in relation to foreign policy and so they enjoy no independent status under international law.

Federations usually exhibit a single, two-tier structure of government across an entire jurisdiction. Exceptions may occur in which certain parts of the federation are under more direct control of the federal government, as is the case with the autonomous 'territories' of Canada and Australia, with Union Territories in India and with the United States District of Columbia. However it is not characteristic in a federation for small peripheral regions to be self-governing, while a central, much larger 'metropolis' region remains under the direct control of the central government.

Some federations are called assymmetric because some states have more autonomy than others, although they have the same constitutional status.

A federation often emerges from an initial agreement between a number of separate states to come together in order to solve mutual problems, or provide for mutual defence. This was the case with the United States, Switzerland, Canada and Australia. In other cases, like Brazil, the federation comes after a unitary state, as a new model in order to decentralize powers and functions.

Unitary States

A unitary state is sometimes one with only a single, centralised, national tier of government. However unitary states often also include one or more self-governing regions. The difference between a federation and this kind of unitary state is that in a unitary state the autonomous status of self-governing regions exists by the sufferance of the central government, and may be unilaterally revoked. While it is common for a federation to be brought into being by agreement between a number of formally independent states, in a unitary state self-governing regions are often created through a process of devolution, where a formerly centralised state agrees to grant autonomy to a region that was previously entirely subordinate. Thus federations are often established voluntarily from 'below' whereas devolution grants self-government from 'above'.

It is often part of the philosophy of a unitary state that, regardless of the actual status of any of its parts, its entire territory constitutes a single sovereign entity or nation-state, and that by virtue of this the central government exercises sovereignty over the whole territory as of right. In a federation, on the other hand, sovereignty is often regarded as residing notionally in the component states, or as being shared between these states and the central government.

DE FACTO FEDERATIONS

The distinction between a federation and a unitary state is often quite ambiguous. A unitary state may closely resemble a federation in structure and, while a central government may possess the theoretical right to revoke the autonomy of a self-governing region, it may be politically difficult for it to do so in practice. The self-governing regions of some unitary states also often enjoy greater autonomy than those of some federations. For these reasons, it is sometimes argued that some modern unitary states are de facto federations.

Spain is suggested as one possible de facto federation as it grants more self-government to its autonomous communities than most federations allow their constituent parts. For the Spanish parliament to revoke the autonomy of regions such as Galicia, Catalonia or the Basque Country, or for the United Kingdom government unilaterally to abolish the legislatures of Wales or Scotland, would be a near political impossibility. Additionally, some regions such as Navarra or the Basque Country have full control over taxation and spending, transferring a small payment to the central government for the common services (army, foreign relations, macroeconomic policy).

In the People's Republic of China, a form of de facto federation has evolved without formal legislation. This has occurred as largely informal grants of power to the provinces, to handle economic affairs and implement national policies. This has resulted in a system some have termed "de facto federalism with Chinese characteristics". Constitutionally, the power vested in the special administrative regions of the People's Republic is granted from the Central People's Government, through decision by the National People's Congress. Special administrative regions are not constitutionally stated to be administrative divisions. It is also not stated that special administrative regions are incorporated territories.

OTHER FORMS OF STATE

While distinct from a unitary state, a federation is also to be distinguished from a confederation. By connotation, a confederation is similar in structure to a federation but with a weaker central government. Over time these terms acquired distinct connotations leading to the present difference in definition. An example of this is the United States under the Articles of Confederation. The Articles established a national government under what today would be defined as a federal system (albeit with a comparatively weaker federal government).

Empire

An empire is a multi-ethnic state or group of nations with a central government established usually through coercion (on the model of the Roman Empire). An empire will often include self-governing regions but these will possess autonomy only at the sufferance of the central government. The term empire, except where used metaphorically, is usually reserved for an entity headed by an emperor, although his or her constitutional role may be purely ceremonial. An empire may, in some cases, also consist of multiple kingdoms organised together with a high king designated as an emperor. One example of this was Imperial Germany.

European Union

The European Union (EU) possesses some of the attributes of a federal state. However, its central government is far weaker than that of most federations so it is usually characterised as an unprecedented form of supra-national union or confederation. The EU has responsibility for important areas such as trade and monetary union, and today around sixty per cent of the legislation in member-states originates in the institutions of the Union. Nonetheless, EU member-states retain the right to act independently in matters of foreign policy and defence, and also enjoy a near monopoly over other major policy areas such as criminal justice and taxation. Furthermore, member-states are separate, sovereign entities under international law and, currently at least, possess a de facto if not explicit de jure right of secession. The proposed Constitutional Treaty would codify the Member States' right to leave the Union, but would at the same time also provide the European Union with more powers in some areas. Whether or not this would move the European Union closer to a federal state than an international organisation is currently the subject of heated political debate.

Russian Federation

An interesting example is provided by the Russian Federation. It has inherited its structure from the Russian Soviet Federative Socialist Republic that was one of the 15 republics of the Soviet Union and itself was considered a federation. The RSFSR, however, consisted of "autonomous republics" which had a certain degree of autonomy, at least de jure, and of other types of administrative units (mostly oblasts and krays) whose status was the same as that of oblasts in other -unitary -Soviet republics. In today's Russia, republics, oblasts and krays, as well as one "autonomous oblast" and "autonomous districts" are equal in legal terms, save some symbolic features of a republic (constitution, president, citizenship, national language). Some regions have concluded agreements with the Federation so as to modify the degree of their autonomy. It is also to be noted that several "autonomous districts" are part of the territory of a kray, a complicated system that is now being gradually abolished through referendums on merging certain regions.

Since 2004, governors of each region, who were previously elected by popular vote, have been directly appointed by the President of Russia. Local parliaments theoretically have authority to veto an appointment, but if this occurs the parliament must be dissolved and new elections held. This lets some argue that the Russian Federation is not a federation in the strictest sense.

Soviet Union (USSR)

The constitution of the 1922-1991 Soviet Union (USSR) theoretically provided for a voluntary federation or confederation of 'soviet socialist republics'. Each was notionally governed by its own supreme council and had the right to secede. Furthermore, some republics themselves possessed further nominally self-governing units. Two of them, Belarus and Ukraine, were even members of the United Nations, some other republics had their own foreign ministries. In practice, the system of one-party government found in the USSR meant that governance of the Union was highly centralised, with important decisions taken by the leaders of the Communist Party in Moscow and merely 'rubber stamped' by local institutions. Nonetheless, with the introduction of free, competitive elections in the final days of the USSR, the Union's theoretically federal structure became a reality in practice; this occurred only for a brief interim period, as the elected governments of many republics demanded their right to secede and became independent states. Thus the USSR's de jure federal structure played a key role in its dissolution.

Myanmar

Myanmar (formerly Burma) is claimed to have adopted federation status (the country's official name is "Union of Myanmar"). However, after General Ne Win seized power Burma in 1962 and abolished the Constitution of the Union of Burma, the country adopted a unitary system under his military dictatorship.

7

Constitutional Structure

DIVISION OF POWERS

In a federation, the division of power between federal and regional governments is usually outlined in the constitution. It is in this way that the right to self-government of the component states is usually constitutionally entrenched. Component states often also possess their own constitutions which they may amend as they see fit, although in the event of conflict the federal constitution usually takes precedence.

In almost all federations the central government enjoys the powers of foreign policy and national defence. Were this not the case a federation would not be a single sovereign state. Beyond this the precise division of power varies from one nation to another. The United States Constitution provides that all powers not specifically granted to the federal government are retained by the states. The Constitution of Canada, on the other hand, provides the opposite: that powers not explicitly granted to the provincial governments are retained by the centre. In Germany, the division of powers is less one of content than of administration: the federal government often merely issues broad directives to the Länder (self-governing regions), which then have broad discretion as to how to implement them. In the People's Republic of China, regarded by some as a de facto although not de jure federation, the central government sets up general economic policy and goals, and leaves the implementation to provincial governments. Much like the Canadian system, the Australian Division of Powers serperates some powers which were considered too difficult for the states to manage so that the Federal Government takes on that responsibility.

Where every component state of a federation possesses the same powers, we are said to find 'symmetric federalism'. Asymmetric federalism exists where states are granted different powers, or some possess greater autonomy than others do. This is often done in recognition of the existence of a distinct culture in a particular region or regions. In Spain, "historical communities" such as Navarre, Galicia, Catalonia, and the Basque Country have more powers than other autonomous communities, partly to deal with their distinctness and to appease nationalist leanings, partly out of respect of privileges granted earlier in history.

It is common that during the historical evolution of a federation there is a gradual movement of power from the component states to the centre, as the federal government acquires additional powers, sometimes to deal with unforeseen circumstances. The acquisition of new powers by a federal government may occur through formal constitutional amendment or simply through a broadening of the interpretation of a government's existing constitutional powers given by the courts.

Usually, a federation is formed at two levels: the central government and the regions (states, provinces, territories). Brazil is an exception, because the 1988's Constitution has included the municipalities as autonomous political entities making the federation tripartite: encompassing the Union, the States, and the municipalities. Each state is divided into municipalities (municípios) with their own legislative council (câmara de vereadores) and a mayor (prefeito), which are autonomous and hierarchically independent from both Federal and State Government. Each municipality has a "little constitution", called "organic law" (lei orgânica).

Federations often employ the paradox of being a union of states, while still being states (or having aspects of statehood) in themselves. For example, James Madison (author of the US Constitution) wrote in Federalist Paper No. 39 that the US Constitution "is in strictness neither a national nor a federal constitution; but a composition of both. In its foundation, it is federal, not national; in the sources from which the ordinary powers of the Government are drawn, it is partly federal, and partly national...." This paradox stems from the fact that states in a federation maintain all sovereignty that they do not yield to the federation by their own consent. The sharing of sovereignty between a federation and its constituent states sometimes makes it difficult to differentiate between a sovereign state and a non-sovereign state.

ORGANS OF GOVERNMENT

The structures of most federal governments incorporate mechanisms to protect the rights of component states. One method, known as 'intrastate federalism', is to directly represent the governments of component states in federal political institutions. Where a federation has a bicameral legislature the upper house is often used to represent the component states while the lower house represents the people of the nation as a whole. A federal upper house may be based on a special scheme of apportionment, as is the case in the senates of the United States and Australia, where each state is represented by an equal number of senators irrespective of the size of its population.

Alternatively, or in addition to this practice, the members of an upper house may be indirectly elected by the government or legislature of the component states, as occurred in the United States prior to 1913, or be actual members or delegates of the state governments, as, for example, is the case in the German Bundesrat. The lower house of a federal legislature is usually directly elected, with apportionment in proportion to population, although states may sometimes still be guaranteed a certain minimum number of seats. In Canada, the provincial governments represent regional interests and negotiate directly with the central government. A First Ministers conference of the prime minister and the provincial premiers is the de facto highest political forum in the land, although it is not mentioned in the constitution.

Federations often have special procedures for amendment of the federal constitution. As well as reflecting the federal structure of the state this may guarantee that the self-governing status of the component states cannot be abolished without their consent. An amendment to the constitution of the United States must be ratified by three-quarters of either the state legislatures, or of constitutional conventions specially elected in each of the states, before it can come into effect. In referenda to amend the constitutions of Australia and Switzerland it is required that a proposal be endorsed not just by an overall majority of the electorate in the nation as a whole, but also by separate majorities in each of a majority of the states or cantons. In Australia, this latter requirement is known as a double majority.

Some federal constitutions also provide that certain constitutional amendments cannot occur without the unanimous consent of all states or of a particular state. The US constitution provides that no state may be deprived of equal representation in the senate without its consent. In Australia, if a proposed amendment will specifically impact one or more states than it must be endorsed in the referendum held in each of those states. Any amendment to the Canadian constitution that would modify the role of the monarchy would require unanimous consent of the provinces. The German Basic Law provides that no amendment is admissible at all that would completely abolish the federal system.

OTHER TECHNICAL TERMS

- Fiscal federalism -federalism involving the transfer of funds between different levels of government.
- Formal federalism (or 'constitutional federalism') -the delineation of powers is specified in a written constitution.
- Executive federalism (also known as 'administrative federalism').

Federalism as a Political Philosophy

The meaning of federalism, as a political movement, and of what constitutes a 'federalist', varies with country and historical context. Movements associated with the establishment or development of federations can be either centralising or decentralising. For example, at the time those nations were being established, 'federalists' in the United States and Australia were those who advocated the creation of strong central government. Similarly, in European Union politics, federalists are mostly those who seek greater EU integration. In contrast, in Spain and post-war Germany, federal movements have sought decentralisation: the transfer of power from central authorities to local units. In Canada, where Quebec separatism has been a political force for several decades, the 'federalist' force is dedicated to keeping the federation intact and adapting the federal structure to better suit Quebec interests.

Internal Controversy and Conflict

Certain forms of political and constitutional dispute are common to federations. One issue is that the exact division of power and responsibility between federal and regional governments is often a source of controversy. Often, as is the case with the United States, such conflicts are resolved through the judicial system, which delimits the powers of federal and local governments. The relationship between federal and local courts varies from nation to nation and can be a controversial and complex issue in itself.

Another common issue in federal systems is the conflict between regional and national interests, or between the interests and aspirations of different ethnic groups. In some federations the entire jurisdiction is relatively homogeneous and each constituent state resembles a miniature version of the whole; this is known as 'congruent federalism'. On the other hand, incongruent federalism exists where different states or regions possess distinct ethnic groups.

The ability of a federal government to create national institutions that can mediate differences that arise because of linguistic, ethnic, religious, or other regional differences is an important challenge. The inability to meet this challenge may lead to the secession of parts of a federation or to civil war, as occurred in United States and Switzerland. In case of Malaysia, Singapore was expelled from the federation because of rising racial tension. In some cases internal conflict may lead a federation to collapse entirely, as occurred in Nigeria, the

Federation of Rhodesia and Nyasaland, the United Provinces of Central America and the West Indies Federation.

POLITICAL POWER

Political power (imperium in Latin) is a type of power held by a person or group in a society. There are many ways to hold such power. Officially, political power is held by the holders of the sovereignty. Political powers are not limited to heads of states, however, and the extent to which a person or group holds such power is related to the amount of societal influence they can wield, formally or informally. In many cases this influence is not contained within a single state and it refers to international power.

Political scientists have frequently defined power as "the ability to influence the behaviour of others" with or without resistance.

For analytical reasons, MacMillan separates the concepts power

Power is the capacity to restructure actual situations.
—I.C. Macmillan

and influence

Influence is the capacity to control and modify the perceptions of others. —I.C. Macmillan

Abuse of Power

Throughout history there have been many examples of the destructive or senseless use of political power. This has happened most frequently when too much power has been concentrated in too few hands, without enough room for political debate, public criticism, and other types of correctives. Examples of such regimes are despotism, tyranny, and dictatorship. To counter these potential problems, people have devised and practised different solutions, most of them related to the sharing of power (as in democracy), the placing of limitations on the extent of power one individual or group can have, and the creation of protective rights for individuals through legislation or charters (such as human rights).

Separation of Powers

Charles de Montesquieu claimed that without following a principle of containing and balancing legislative, executive and judiciary powers, there is no freedom and no protection against abuse of power. This is the separation of powers principle.

Division of Power

A similar concept, termed Division of Power, also consists of differentiated legislative, executive and judiciary powers. However, while Separation of Power prohibits one branch from interfering with another, Division of Power permits such interference. For example, in Indonesia, the President (who wields executive power) can introduce a new bill, but the People's Consultative Assembly (holding legislative power) chooses to either legalize or reject the bill.

POLITICAL SCIENCE PERSPECTIVES

Within normative political analysis, there are also various levels of power as described by academics that add depth into the understanding of the notion of power and its political implications. Robert Dahl, a prominent American political scientist, first ascribed to political power the trait of decision-making as the source and main indicator of power. Later, two other political scientists, Peter Bachrach and Morton Baratz, decided that simply ascribing decision-making as the basis of power was too simplistic and they added what they termed a 2nd dimension of power, agenda-setting by elites who worked in the backrooms and away from public scrutiny in order to exert their power upon society. Lastly, British academic Steven Lukes added a 3rd dimension of power, preference-shaping, which he claimed was another important aspect of normative power in politics which entails theoretical views similar to notions of cultural hegemony. These 3 dimensions of power are today often considered defining aspects of political power by political researchers.

A radical alternative view of the source of political power follows the formula: information plus authority permits the exercise of power. Political power is intimately related to information. Sir Francis Bacon's statement: "Nam et ipsa scientia potestas est" for knowledge itself is power, assumed authority as given. Many will know that unless someone with authority listens and acts, there is no political power.

It is said democracy is the best method of informing those entrusted with authority. They are best able to use authority without ignorance to maximize political power. Those who exercise authority in ignorance are not powerful, because they do not realize their intentions and have little control over the effects of using their authority.

Post-modernism has debated over how to define political power. Perhaps, the best known definition comes from the late Michel Foucault, whose work in Discipline and Punish (and other writings) conveys a view of power that is organic within society. This view holds that political power is more subtle and is part of a series of societal controls and 'normalizing' influences through historical institutions and definitions of normal vs. abnormal. Foucault once characterized power as "an action over actions" (une action sur des actions), arguing that power was essentially a relation between several dots, in continuous transformation as in Nietzsche's philosophy. His view of power lent credence to the view that power in human society was part of a training process in which everyone, from a Prime Minister to a homeless person, played their role within the power structure of society. Jürgen Habermas opposed himself to Foucault's conception of discourse as a battlefield for power relations, arguing that it should be possible to achieve consensus on the fundamentals rules of discourse, in order to establish a transparent and democratic dialogue. Thenceforth, he argued against Foucault and Althusser that power was not immanent to discourse, and that philosophy could be completely distinguished from ideology.

More recently, there has been a move among academics to differentiate power from a new concept of luck. Under some conditions (particularly the when examining the third dimension of power) it becomes necessary to determine who obtains a favourable result through the wielding of genuine power and who is simply "lucky". An example might be an ethnic minority who receive favourable treatment while not intentionally seeking it. A person promoted through positive discrimination would be considered "lucky" rather than "powerful". The eventual aim of such discrimination would be to eventually convert some (or all) of that luck into power. Some groups remain serially lucky without ever obtaining power.

ANARCHY IN INTERNATIONAL RELATIONS

Anarchy in international relations posits that the world system is leaderless: there is no universal sovereign or worldwide government. There is thus no hierarchically superior, coercive power that can resolve disputes or order the system. Political scientists do not use the term "anarchy" to signify a world in chaos, in disorder, or in conflict. It simply reflects the order of the international system: independent states with no central authority above them. The concept of anarchy is the foundation for realist, liberal, neorealist, and neoliberal international relations theories. Constructivist theory disputes that anarchy is a fundamental condition of the international system, saying that "anarchy is what states make of it" (Alexander Wendt).

REALISM AND INTERNATIONAL RELATIONS

Realism, also known as political realism, in the context of international relations, encompasses a variety of theories and approaches, all of which share a belief that states are primarily motivated by the desire for military and economic power or security, rather than ideals or ethics. This term is often synonymous with power politics.

The term realism can, instead of referring to the broad family of realist theories, refer specifically to classical realism, the common ancestor and original form of realism.

Common Assumptions

Realist theories share the following key assumptions:

- The international system is anarchic. There is no authority above states capable of regulating their interactions; states must arrive at relations with other states on their own, rather than it being dictated to them by some higher controlling entity (that is, no true authoritative world government exists).

- Sovereign states are the principal actors in the international system. International institutions, non-governmental organizations, multinational corporations and other sub-state or trans-state actors are viewed as having little independent influence.
- States are rational unitary actors each moving towards their own national interest. There is a general distrust of long-term cooperation or alliance.
- The overriding 'national interest' of each state is its national security and survival.
- In pursuit of national security, states strive to amass resources.
- Relations between states are determined by their comparative level of power derived primarily from their military and economic capabilities.

In summary, realists believe that mankind is not inherently benevolent but rather self-centered and competitive. This Hobbesian perspective contrasts with the liberalism approach to international relations which views human nature as selfish and conflictual unless given appropriate conditions under which to cooperate. Further, they believe that states are inherently aggressive (offensive realism) and/or obsessed with security (defensive realism); and that territorial expansion is only constrained by opposing power(s). This aggressive build-up, however, leads to a security dilemma where increasing one's own security can bring along greater instability as the opponent(s) builds up its own arms. Thus, security is a zero-sum game where only relative gains can be made.

HISTORY AND BRANCHES

Historic Antecedents

While Realism as a formal discipline in international relations didn't arrive until World War II, its primary assumptions have been expressed in earlier writings:

- Sun Tzu (or Sunzi), an ancient Chinese military strategist who wrote the Art of War.
- Chanakya early Indian statesman, and writer on the Arthashastra.

- Thucydides, an ancient Greek historian who wrote the History of the Peloponnesian War and is also cited as an intellectual forebearer of realpolitik.
- Hanfeizi, Chinese scholar who theorised Legalism (or Legism) and who served in the court of the King of Qin -later unifier of China ending the Warring States Period. His writings include The Two Handles (about punishments and rewards as tools of governance). He theorised about a neutral, manipulative ruler who would act as Head of State while secretly controlling the executive through his ministers -the ones to take real responsibility for any policy.
- Niccolò Machiavelli, a Florentine political philosopher, who wrote II Principe (The Prince) in which he held that the sole aim of a prince (politician) was to seek power, regardless of religious or ethical considerations.
- Thomas Hobbes, an English philosopher who wrote Leviathan in which he stated that in anarchy there is a "war of all against all".
- Otto von Bismarck, a Prussian statesman coined the term balance of power. Balancing power meant keeping the peace and careful realpolitik practitioners tried to avoid arms races.
- Carl von Clausewitz was a 19th century Prussian general and military theorist who wrote Vom Kriege (On War).

"Classical Realism"

Modern realism began as a serious field of research in the United States during and after World War II. This evolution was partly fueled by European war migrants like Hans Morgenthau who had a negative view of human nature, thought by some to be due to their experiences in war.

Prominent classical realists:

- George F. Kennan -Containment
- Nicholas Spykman -Geostrategy, Containment
- Herman Kahn -Nuclear strategy

- E. H. Carr
- Reinhold Niebuhr
- Hans Morgenthau
- Arnold Wolfers
- Charles Beard
- Walter Lippmann

"Liberal Realism" or the "English School" or "Rationalism"

The English School holds that while the international system is anarchical, order can be promoted through diplomacy, international law and society. This school thus gives credence to establishing IGOs such as the United Nations.

Prominent liberal realists:

- Hedley Bull -Liberal realism (sometimes called the "English School" or "Rationalism")

Hedley Bull argued for both the existence of international society of states and its perseverance even in times of great systemic upheaval, meaning regional or so-called "world wars."

- Martin Wight

This section is a stub. You can help by expanding it.

"Neorealism" or "Structural Realism"

Neorealism derives from classical realism except that instead of human nature, its focus is predominantly on the international system. While states remain the principal actors, greater attention is given to the forces above and below the states through a levels of analysis or structure-agency debate. The international system is seen as a structure acting on the state with individuals below the level of the state acting as agency on the state as a whole.

While neorealism shares a focus on the international system with the English School, neorealism differs in the emphasis it places on the permanence of conflict. To ensure state security, states must be on constant preparation for conflict through economic and military build-up.

Prominent neorealists:

- Robert Jervis -Defensive realism
- Kenneth Waltz -Defensive realism
- Stephen Walt -Defensive realism
- John Mearsheimer -Offensive realism
- Robert Gilpin -Hegemonic theory

"Neoclassical Realism"

Neoclassical Realism can be seen as the third generation of realism, coming after the classical authors of the first wave (Thucydides, Machiavelli, Hobbes, Morgenthau), and the neorealists (esp. Kenneth Waltz). Its designation of "neoclassical", then, has a double meaning: 1) It offers the classics a renaissance; 2) It is a synthesis of the neorealist and the classical realist approaches.

Gideon Rose is responsible for coining the term in a book review he wrote.

The primarily motivation underlying the development of neoclassical realism was the fact that neorealism was only useful to explain political outcomes (classified as being 'theories of international politics'), but had nothing to offer about particular states' behavior (or 'theories of foreign policy'). The basic approach, then, was for these authors to "refine, not refute, Kenneth Waltz", by adding domestic intervening variables between systemic incentives and a state's foreign policy decision. Thus, the basic theoretical architecture of Neoclassical Realism is:

Distribution of power in the international system (Independent Variable) >>> Domestic perception of the system and/or domestic incentives (Intervening Variable) >>> Foreign Policy decision (Dependent Variable)

While neoclassical realism has only been used for theories of foreign policy so far, Randall Schweller notes that it could be useful to explain certain types of political outcomes as well..

Neoclassical realism is particularly appealing from a research standpoint because it still retains a lot of the theoretical rigor that Waltz has brought to realism, but at the same time can easily incorporate a content-rich analysis, since its main method for testing theories is the process-tracing of case studies.

NEOREALISM

Neorealism or structural realism is a theory of international relations, outlined by Kenneth Waltz in his 1979 book, Theory of International Politics. Waltz argues in favor of a systemic approach: the internationai structure acts as a constraint on state behavior, so that different states behave in a similar rational manner, and outcomes fall within an expected range.

Neorealism, developed largely within the American political science tradition, seeks to reformulate the classical realism tradition of E.H. Carr, Hans Morgenthau, and Reinhold Niebuhr into a rigorous and positivistic social science.

Theory

Neorealism shuns classical realism's use of often essentialist concepts such as "human nature" to explain international politics. Instead, neorealist thinkers developed a theory that privileges structural constraints over agents' strategies and motivations.

Neorealism holds that the international structure is defined by its ordering principle, anarchy, and by the distribution of capabilities, measured by the number of great powers within the international system. The anarchic ordering principle of the international structure is decentralized, having no formal central authority, and is composed of formally equal sovereign states. These states act according to the logic of self-help-- states seek their own interest and will not subordinate their interest to another's.

States are assumed at a minimum to want to ensure their own survival as this is a prerequisite to pursue other goals. This driving force of survival is the primary factor influencing their behaviour and in turn ensures states develop offensive military capabilities, as a means to increase their relative power. Because states can never be certain of other states' future intentions, there is a lack of trust between states which requires states to be on guard against relative losses of power which could enable other states to threaten their survival. This lack of trust, based on uncertainty, is called the security dilemma.

States are deemed similar in terms of needs but not in capabilities for achieving them. The positional placement of states in terms of abilities determines the distribution of capabilities. The structural distribution of capabilities then limits cooperation among states through fears of relative gains made by other states, and the possibility of dependence on other states.

The desire and relative abilities of each state to maximize relative power constrain each other, resulting in a 'balance of power', which shapes international relations. It also gives rise to the 'security dilemma' that all nations face. There are two ways in which states balance power: internal balancing and external balancing. Internal balancing occurs as states grow their own capabilities by increasing economic growth and/or increasing military spending. External balancing occurs as states enter into alliances to check the power of more powerful states or alliances.

Neorealists contend that there are essentially three possible systems according to changes in the distribution of capabilities, defined by the number of great powers within the international system. A unipolar system contains only one great power (this is often referred to as hegemony), a bipolar system contains two great powers, and a multipolar system contains more than two great powers. Neorealists conclude that a bipolar system is more stable (less prone to great power war and systemic change) than a unipolar system because balancing can only occur through internal balancing as there are no extra great powers with which to form alliances. Because there is only internal balancing in a bipolar system, rather than external balancing and internal balancing, there is less opportunity for miscalculations and therefore less chance of great power war.

Neorealists conclude that because war is an effect of the anarchic structure of the international system, it is likely to continue in the future. Indeed, neorealists often argue that the ordering principle of the international system has not fundamentally changed from the time of Thucydides to the advent of nuclear warfare. The view that long-lasting peace is not likely to be achieved is described by other theorists as a largely pessimistic view of international relations. One of the main challenges to neorealist theory is the democratic peace theory and supporting research such as the book Never at War. Neorealists answer this challenge by arguing that democratic peace theorists tend to pick and choose the definition of democracy to get the wanted empirical result. For example, Germany of Kaiser Wilhem II, the Dominican Republic of Juan Bosch, or Chile of Salvador Allende are not considered to be democratic or the conflicts do not qualify as wars according to these theorists. Furthermore they claim several wars between democratic states have been averted only by causes other than ones covered by democratic peace theory.

Criticism

Neorealism has been criticized from the point of view of the philosophy of science. John Vasquez uses the Lakatosian criteria of the Methodology of Scientific Research Programs in an attempt to prove the degenerative nature of the neorealist research program. Thus, Waltz's theory of neorealism explains international behaviour through the balance-of-power concept, according to which states in almost all cases balance each other in order to survive. Stephen Walt, on the other hand, argues that states do not balance power, but there is a so-called balance-of-threat, thus always balancing states which seem to be the most threatening, not necessarily the most powerful. Randall Schweller introduces the concept of balance-of-interests, better known as bandwagoning.

Thomas J. Christensen and Jack Snyder try to correct gaps in Waltz's original theory by using the concepts of buck-passing and chain-ganging. However these similar theories contradict each other, at least partially: for example balancing versus bandwagoning. Vasquez considers them as theory shifts which explain away discrepant evidence. These contradictory hypotheses increase the probability that at least one passes an empirical test, thus the whole neorealist research program showing signs of degeneration.

IDEALISM AND INTERNATIONAL RELATIONS

Idealism in international relations usually refers to the school of thought personified in American diplomatic history by Woodrow Wilson, such that it is sometimes referred to as Wilsonianism. Idealism holds that a state should make its internal political philosophy the goal of its foreign policy. For example, an idealist might believe that ending poverty at home should be coupled with tackling poverty abroad. Wilson's idealism was a precursor to liberal international relations theory, which would arise amongst the "institution-builders" after World War II.

Idealism is also marked by the prominent role played by international law and international organizations in its conception of policy formation. One of the most well-known tenets of modern idealist thinking is democratic peace theory, which holds that states with similar modes of democratic governance do not fight one another. Wilson's idealistic thought was embodied in his Fourteen points speech, and in the creation of the League of Nations.

Idealism transcends the left-right political spectrum. Idealists can include both human rights campaigners (traditionally, but not always, associated with the left) and American neoconservatism which is usually associated with the right.

Idealism may find itself in opposition to Realism, a worldview which argues that a nation's national interest is more important than ethical or moral considerations; however, there need be no conflict between the two. Realist thinkers include Hans Morgenthau, Niccolò Machiavelli, Otto von Bismarck, George F. Kennan and others.

Descendant Theories

Idealism proper was a relatively short lived school of thought, and suffered a crisis of confidence following the failure of the League of Nations and the outbreak of World War II. However, subsequent theories of international relations would draw elements from Wilsonian Idealism when constructing their world views.

Liberalism

Liberalism manifested a tempered version of Wilson's idealism in the wake of World War II. Cognizant of the failures of Idealism to prevent renewed isolationism following World War I, and its inability to manage the balance of power in Europe to prevent the outbreak of a new war, liberal thinkers devised a set of international institutions based on rule of law and regularized interaction. These international regimes, such as the United Nations, NATO, the Bretton Woods system, and the GATT, were calculated both to maintain a balance of power as well as regularize cooperation between nations.

Neoconservatism

Neoconservatism drew from Liberalism its intense focus on the promotion of "universal values", in this case democracy, human rights, free trade, women's rights and minority protections. However, it differs in that instead of building institutions or negotiating treaties, neoconservatism is less wedded to the importance of preserving international institutions and treaties while pursuing assertive or aggressive stances which it deems morally worthy, and is willing to use force or the threat of force, unilaterally if necessary, to push for its goals.

IDEALISM

Idealism is a class of positions in ontology and epistemology. Idealism as an epistemological position asserts that everything we experience is of a mental nature. That is, we can only have direct, immediate knowledge of the contents of our mind. We can never directly know or experience an external object itself. As an ontological position Idealism asserts either that only minds and the objects of mind exist, or that everything is composed of mental realities (e.g., thoughts, feelings, perceptions, ideas, or will). As a foundation for cosmology, or an approach to understanding the nature of existence, idealism is often contrasted with materialism, both belonging to the class of monist as opposed to dualist or pluralist ontologies. (Note that this contrast between idealism and materialism is approximately as to whether the substance of the world is at base mental or physical -it has nothing to do with thinking that things should be idealized, or with coveting goods.) Subjective Idealists and Phenomenalists (such as George Berkeley) hold that minds and their experiences constitute existence. Objective Idealists hold either that all of reality is included in a Universal Thought or Experience (Absolute Idealism), or hold that the world is composed of mental realities. Panpsychists (such as Leibniz) hold that all objects of experience are also subjects.

That is, plants and minerals have subjective experiences--though very different from the consciousness of animals. Most Idealists tend to reject representationalist views of experience and instead hold that the world of experience is the same as the world of reality. The approach to idealism by Western philosophers has been different from that of Eastern thinkers. In much of Western thought (though not in such major Western thinkers as Plato and Hegel) the ideal relates to direct knowledge of subjective mental ideas, or images. It is then usually juxtaposed with realism in which the real is said to have absolute existence prior to and independent of our knowledge. Epistemological idealists (such as Kant) might insist that the only things which can be directly known for certain are ideas. In Eastern thought, as reflected in Hindu idealism, the concept of idealism takes on the meaning of consciousness, essentially the living consciousness of an all-pervading God, as the basis of all phenomena. A type of Asian idealism is Buddhist idealism.

History

Idealism names a number of philosophical positions with quite different tendencies and implications.

Idealism in the East

Several Hindu traditions and schools of Buddhism can be accurately characterized as idealist. Some of the Buddhist schools are called "Consciousness-only" schools as they focus on consciousness without an omnipotent deity or soul.

Idealism in the West

In his chief work Truth, Antiphon wrote: "Time is a thought or a measure, not a substance". This presents time as an ideational, internal, mental operation, rather than a real, external object.

Plato

Plato proposed an idealist theory as a solution to the problem of universals. A universal is that which all things share in virtue of having some particular property. So for example the wall, the moon and a blank sheet of paper are all white; white is the universal that all white things share. Plato argued that it is universals, The Forms, or Platonic Ideals that are real, not specific individual things. Confusingly, because this idea asserts that these mental entities are real, it is also called Platonic realism; in this sense realism contrasts with nominalism, the notion that mental abstractions are merely names without an independent existence. Nevertheless, it is a form of idealism because it asserts the primacy of the idea of universals over material things.

Plato's Allegory of the Cave relates to epistemological idealism. The mental images, or ideas, that are immediately and directly known are not the same as the exterior objects in the real world.

This world that appears to the senses has no true being, but only a ceaseless becoming; it is, and it also is not; and its comprehension is not so much a knowledge as an illusion. This is what he expresses in a myth at the beginning of the seventh book of the Republic, the most important passage in all his works .... He says that men, firmly chained in a dark cave, see neither the genuine original light nor actual things, but only the inadequate light of the fire in the cave, and the shadows of actual things passing by the fire behind their backs. Yet they imagine that the shadows are the reality, and that determining the succession of these shadows is true wisdom. - Schopenhauer, The World as Will and Representation, Vol. I, Appendix

Plotinus

Schopenhauer wrote of this Neoplatonist philosopher: "With Plotinus there even appears, probably for the first time in Western philosophy, idealism that had long been current in the

East even at that time, for it taught (Enneads, iii, lib. vii, c.10) that the soul has made the world by stepping from eternity into time, with the explanation: 'For there is for this universe no other place than the soul or mind' (neque est alter hujus universi locus quam anima), indeed the ideality of time is expressed in the words: 'We should not accept time outside the soul or mind' (oportet autem nequaquam extra animam tempus accipere)." (Parerga and Paralipomena, Volume I, "Fragments for the History of Philosophy."

Descartes

Writing about Descartes, Schopenhauer claimed, "... he was the first to bring to our consciousness the problem whereon all philosophy has since mainly turned, namely that of the ideal and the real. This is the question concerning what in our knowledge is objective and what subjective, and hence what eventually is to be ascribed by us to things different from us and what is to be attributed to ourselves." (Parerga and Paralipomena, Vol. I, "Sketch of a History of the Doctrine of the Ideal and the Real") According to Descartes, we really know only what is in our own consciousnesses. We are immediately and directly aware of only our own states of mind. The whole external world is merely an idea or picture in our minds. Therefore, it is possible to doubt the reality of the external world as consisting of real objects. "I think, therefore I am" is the only assertion that can't be doubted. This is because self-consciousness and thinking are the only things that are unconditionally experienced for certain as being real. In this way, Descartes clearly presented the main problem of philosophical idealism, which is awareness of the difference between the world as an ideational mental picture and the world as a system of external objects.

Malebranche

Malebranche a student of the Cartesian School of Rationalism disagreed that if the only things that we know for certain are the ideas within our mind, then the existence of the external world would be dubious and known only indirectly. He declared instead that the real external world is actually God. All activity only appears to occur in the external world. In actuality, it is the activity of God. For Malebranche, we directly know internally the ideas in our mind. Externally, we directly know God's operations. This kind of idealism led to the pantheism of Spinoza.

Leibniz

Leibniz expressed a form of Idealism known as Panpsychism in his theory of monads, as exposited in his Monadologie. He held Monads are the true atoms of the universe, and are also entities having sensation. The monads are "substantial forms of being" They are indecomposable, individual, subject to their own laws, un-interacting, and each reflecting the entire universe. Monads are centers of force; substance is force, while space, matter, and motion are phenomenal. For Leibniz, there is an exact pre-established harmony or parallel between the world in the minds of the alert monads and the external world of objects. God, who is the central monad, established this harmony and the resulting world is an idea of the monads' perception. In this way, the external world is ideal in that it is a spiritual phenomenon whose motion is the result of a dynamic force. Space and time are ideal or phenomenal and their form and existence is dependent on the simple and immaterial monads. Leibniz's cosmology, with its central monad, embraced a traditional Christian Theism and was more of a Personalism than the naturalistic Pantheism of Spinoza.

George Berkeley

Bishop Berkeley, in seeking to find out what we could know with certainty, decided that our knowledge must be based on our perceptions. This led him to conclude that there was indeed no "real" knowable object behind one's perception, that what was "real" was the perception itself. This is characterised by Berkeley's slogan: "Their esse est aut percipi aut percipere" or "To be is to be perceived or to perceive", meaning that something only exists, in the particular way that it is seen to exist, when it is being perceived (seen, felt etc.) by an observing subject.

This subjective idealism or dogmatic idealism led to his placing the full weight of justification on our perceptions. This left Berkeley with the problem, common to other forms of idealism, of explaining how it is that each of us apparently has much the same sort of perceptions of an object. He solved this problem by having God intercede, as the immediate cause of all of our perceptions. Schopenhauer wrote: "Berkeley was, therefore, the first to treat the subjective starting-point really seriously and to demonstrate irrefutably its absolute necessity. He is the father of idealism...." (Parerga and Paralipomena, Vol. I, "Fragments for the History of Philosophy," § 12)

Arthur Collier

Arthur Collier published the same assertions that were made by Berkeley. However, there seemed to have been no influence between the two contemporary writers. Collier claimed that the represented image of an external object is the only knowable reality. Matter, as a cause of the representative image, is unthinkable and therefore nothing to us. An external world, as absolute matter, unrelated to an observer, does not exist for human perceivers. As an appearance in a mind, the universe cannot exist as it appears if there is no perceiving mind.

Collier was influenced by John Norris's (1701) An Essay Towards the Theory of the Ideal or Intelligible World. The idealist statements by Collier were generally dismissed by readers who were not able to reflect on the distinction between a mental idea or image and the object that it represents.

Jonathan Edwards

Jonathan Edwards, an American theologian, went to Yale University in 1716 at the age of thirteen. After reading Locke's doctrine of ideas, he kept a notebook entitled "Mind." In it, he wrote, at the age of fourteen, that the only things that are real are minds. He contended that matter exists only as an idea in a mind. Due to his theological manner of thinking, he asserted that space is God, due to its infinity. After adolescence, he never elaborated on these early idealistic notes.

Immanuel Kant

Immanuel Kant held that the mind shapes the world as we perceive it to take the form of space-and-time. Kant focused on the idea drawn from British empiricism (and its philosophers such as Locke, Berkeley, and Hume) that all we can know is the mental impressions, or phenomena, that an outside world which may or may not exist independently creates in our minds; our minds can never perceive that outside world directly.

> ... if I remove the thinking subject, the whole material world must at once vanish because it is nothing but a phenomenal appearance in the sensibility of ourselves as a subject, and a manner or species of representation.
>
> –Critique of Pure Reason A383

Kant's postscript to this added that the mind is not a blank slate (contra John Locke), but rather comes equipped with categories for organising our sense impressions. This Kantian sort of idealism opens up a world of abstractions (i.e., the universal categories minds use to understand phenomena) to be explored by reason, but in sharp contrast to Plato's, confirms uncertainties about a (un)knowable world outside our own minds. We cannot approach the noumenon, the "Thing in Itself" (German: Ding an Sich) outside our own mental world. (Kant's idealism goes by the counterintuitive name of transcendental idealism.)

Kant distinguished his transcendental or critical idealism from previous varieties: The dictum of all genuine idealists, from the Eleatic school to Bishop Berkeley, is contained in this formula: "All knowledge through the senses and experience is nothing but sheer illusion, and only in the ideas of the pure understanding and reason is there truth." The principle that throughout dominates and determines my idealism is, on the contrary,: "All knowledge of things merely from pure understanding or pure reason is nothing but sheer illusion, and only in experience is there truth." —Prolegomena, 374

Fichte

Johann Fichte denied Kant's noumenon, and made the claim that consciousness made its own foundation, that the mental ego of the self relied on no external, and that an external of any kind would be the same as admitting a real material. He was the first to make the attempt at a presuppositionless theory of knowledge, wherein nothing outside of thinking would be assumed to exist outside the initial analysis of concept. So that conception could be solely grounded in itself, and assume nothing without deduction from there first, what he called a Wissenschaftslehre. (This stand is very similar to Giovanni Gentile's Actual Idealism, except that Gentile's theory goes further by denying a ground for even an ego or self made from thinking.)

Hegel

Hegel, another philosopher whose system has been called idealism, argued in his Science of Logic (1812-1814) that finite qualities are not fully "real," because they depend on other finite qualities to determine them. Qualitative infinity, on the other hand, would be more self-determining, and hence would have a better claim to be called fully real. Similarly, finite natural things are less "real"--because they're less self-determining--than spiritual things like morally responsible people, ethical communities, and God. So any doctrine, such as materialism, that asserts that finite qualities or merely natural objects are fully real, is mistaken. Hegel called his philosophy absolute idealism, in contrast to the "subjective idealism" of Berkeley and the "transcendental idealism" of Kant and Fichte, which were not based (like Hegel's idealism) on a critique of the finite. The "idealists" listed above whose philosophy Hegel's philosophy most closely resembles are Plato and Plotinus. None of these three thinkers associates their idealism with the epistemological thesis that what we know are "ideas" in our minds.

Schopenhauer

In the first volume of his Parerga and Paralipomena, Schopenhauer wrote his "Sketch of a History of the Doctrine of the Ideal and the Real". He defined the ideal as being mental pictures that constitute subjective knowledge. The ideal, for him, is what can be attributed to our own minds. The images in our head are what comprise the ideal. Schopenhauer emphasized that we are restricted to our own consciousness. The world that appears there is only a representation or mental picture of objects. We directly and immediately know only representations. All objects that are external to the mind are known indirectly through the mediation of our mind. Schopenhauer's history is an account of the concept of the "ideal" in its meaning as "ideas in a subject's mind." In this sense, "ideal" means "ideational" or "existing in the mind as an image." He does not refer to the other meaning of "ideal" as being qualities of the highest perfection and excellence. In his On the Freedom of the Will, Schopenhauer noted the ambiguity of the word "idealism" by calling it a "term with multiple meanings."

True philosophy must at all costs be idealistic; indeed, it must be so merely to be honest. For nothing is more certain than that no one ever came out of himself in order to identify himself immediately with things different from him; but everything of which he has certain, sure, and therefore immediate knowledge, lies within his consciousness. Beyond this consciousness, therefore, there can be no immediate certainty .... There can never be an existence that is objective absolutely and in itself; such an existence, indeed, is positively inconceivable. For the objective, as such, always and essentially has its existence in the consciousness of a subject; it is therefore the subject's representation, and consequently is conditioned by the subject, and moreover by the subject's forms of representation, which belong to the subject and not to the object.-The World as Will and Representation, Vol. II, Ch. 1

British Idealism

British idealism enjoyed ascendancy in English-speaking philosophy in the later part of the 19th century. F. H. Bradley of Merton College, Oxford, saw reality as a monistic whole, which is apprehended through "feeling", a state in which there is no distinction between the perception and the thing perceived. Bradley was the apparent target of G. E. Moore's radical rejection of idealism.

J. M. E. McTaggart of Cambridge University, argued that minds alone exist, and that they only relate to each other through love. Space, time and material objects are for McTaggart unreal. He argued, for instance, in The Unreality of Time that it was not possible to produce a coherent account of a sequence of events in time, and that therefore time is an illusion.

American philosopher Josiah Royce described himself as an objective idealist.

Karl Pearson

In The Grammar of Science, Preface to the 2nd Edition, 1900, Karl Pearson wrote, "There are many signs that a sound idealism is surely replacing, as a basis for natural philosophy, the crude materialism of the older physicists." This book influenced Einstein's regard for the importance of the observer in scientific measurements. In § 5 of that book, Pearson asserted that "...science is in reality a classification and analysis of the contents of the mind...." Also, "...the field of science is much more consciousness than an external world."

CRITICISM OF IDEALISM

Immanuel Kant

In the 1st edition (1781) of his Critique of Pure Reason, Kant described Idealism as such.

We are perfectly justified in maintaining that only what is within ourselves can be immediately and directly perceived, and that only my own existence can be the object of a mere perception. Thus the existence of a real object outside me can never be given immediately and directly in perception, but can only be added in thought to the perception, which is a modification of the internal sense, and thus inferred as its external cause .... In the true sense of the word, therefore, I can never perceive external things, but I can only infer their existence from my own internal perception, regarding the perception as an effect of something external that must be the proximate cause .... It must not be supposed, therefore, that an idealist is someone who denies the existence of external objects of the senses; all he does is to deny that they are known by immediate and direct perception ....

—Critique of Pure Reason, A367 f.

In the 2nd edition (1787) of his Critique of Pure Reason, he wrote a section called Refutation of Idealism to distinguish his transcendental idealism from Descartes's Sceptical Idealism and Berkeley's Dogmatic Idealism. In addition to this refutation in both the 1781 & 1787 editions the section "Paralogisms of Pure Reason" is an implicit critique of Descartes Problematic Idealism, namely the Cogito. He says that just from "the spontaneity of thought" (cf. Descartes' Cogito) it is not possible to infer the 'I' as an object.

Søren Kierkegaard

Kierkegaard attacked Hegel's idealist philosophy in several of his works, but most succinctly in Concluding Unscientific Postscript (1846). In the Postscript, Kierkegaard, as the pseudonymous philosopher Johannes Climacus, argues that a logical system is possible but an existential system is impossible. Hegel argues that once one has reached an ultimate understanding of the logical structure of the world, one has also reached an understanding of the logical structure of God's mind. Climacus claims Hegel's absolute idealism mistakenly blurs the distinction between existence and thought. Climacus also argues that our mortal nature places limits on our understanding of reality. As Climacus argues: "So-called systems have often been characterized and challenged in the assertion that they abrogate the distinction between good and evil, and destroy freedom. Perhaps one would express oneself quite as definitely, if one said that every such system fantastically dissipates the concept existence.... Being an individual man is a thing that has been abolished, and every speculative philosopher confuses himself with humanity at large; whereby he becomes something infinitely great, and at the same time nothing at all."

Friedrich Nietzsche

Friedrich Nietzsche was the first to mount a logically serious criticism of Idealism that has been popularised by David Stove. He pre-empts Stove's GEM by arguing that Kant's argument for his transcendental idealism rests on a tautology and/or begging the question, and therefore is an invalid, improper argument.

In his book Beyond Good and Evil, Part 1 On the Prejudice of Philosophers Section 11, he ridicules Kant for admiring himself because he had undertaken and (thought he) succeeded in tackling "the most difficult thing that could ever be undertaken on behalf of metaphysics."

Quoting Nietzsche's prose: "But let us reflect; it is high time to do so. 'How are synthetic judgements a priori possible?' Kant asked himself-and what really is his answer? 'By virtue of a faculty' -but unfortunately not in five words,...The honeymoon of German philosophy arrived. All the young theologians of the Tübingen seminary went into the bushes all looking for 'faculties.'...'By virtue of a faculty' -he had said, or at least meant. But is that an answer? An explanation? Or is it not rather merely a repetition of the question? How does opium induce sleep? 'By virtue of a faculty,' namely the virtus dormitiva, replies the doctor in Moliére."

In addition to the Idealism of Kant, Nietzsche in the same book attacks the idealism of Schopenhauer and Descartes via a similar argument to Kant's original critique of Descartes. Quoting Nietzsche: There are still harmless self-observers who believe that there are "immediate certainties"; for example, "I think," or as the superstition of Schopenhauer put it, "I will"; as though knowledge here got hold of its objects purely and nakedly as "the thing in itself," without any falsification on the part of either the subject or the object. But that "immediate certainty," as well as "absolute knowledge" and the "thing in itself," involved a contradictio in adjecto, (contradiction between the noun and the adjective) I shall repeat a hundred times; we really ought to free ourselves from the seduction of words!

G. E. Moore

The first criticism of Idealism that falls within the analytic philosophical framework is by one of its cofounders Moore. This 1903 seminal article, The Refutation of Idealism. This one of the first demonstrations of Moore's commitment to analysis as the proper philosophical method.

Moore proceeds by examining the Berkeleian aphorism esse est percipi: "to be is to be perceived". He examines in detail each of the three terms in the aphorism, finding that it must mean that the object and the subject are necessarily connected. So, he argues, for the idealist, "yellow" and "the sensation of yellow" are necessarily identical -to be yellow is necessarily to be experienced as yellow. But, in a move similar to the open question argument, it also seems clear that there is a difference between "yellow" and "the sensation of yellow". For Moore, the idealist is in error because "that esse is held to be percipi, solely because what is experienced is held to be identical with the experience of it".

Though this refutation of idealism was the first strong statement by analytic philosophy against its idealist predecessors this argument did not show that the GEM is logically invalid. Arguments advanced by Nietzsche (prior to Moore), Russell (just after Moore) & 80 years later Stove put a nail in the coffin for the "master" argument supporting idealism.

Bertrand Russell

Despite his hugely popular book The Problems of Philosophy (this book was in its 17th printing by 1943) which was written for a general audience rather than academia; few ever mention Russell's critique even though he completely anticipates David Stove's GEM both in form and content. In chapter 4 (Idealism) highlights Berkeley's tautological premise for advancing idealism.

Quoting Russell's prose (1912:42-43): "If we say that the things known must be in the mind, we are either un-duly limiting the mind's power of knowing, or we are uttering a mere tautology. We are uttering a mere tautology if we mean by 'in the mind' the same as by 'before the mind', i.e. if we mean merely being apprehended by the mind. But if we mean this, we shall have to admit that what, in this sense, is in the mind, may nevertheless be not mental. Thus when we realize the nature of knowledge, Berkeley's argument is seen to be wrong in substance as well as in form, and his grounds for supposing that 'idea'-i.e. the objects apprehended-must be mental, are found to have no validity whatever. Hence his grounds in favour of the idealism may be dismissed."

A.C. Ewing

Published in 1933 A.C. Ewing according to David Stove mounted the first full length book critique of Idealism, entitled

Idealism; a critical survey. Stove does not mention that Ewing anticipated his GEM.

David Stove

The Australian philosopher David Stove argued in typically acerbic style that idealism rested on what he called "the worst argument in the world". His critique of Idealism is perhaps the most devastating critique of subjective idealism in philosophy. From a logical point of view his critique is no different from Russell or Nietzsche's but Stove has been more widely cited and most clearly highlighted the mistake of idealist proponents.

He named the form of this argument -invented by Berkeley "the GEM". Berkeley claimed that "[the mind] is deluded to think it can and does conceive of bodies existing unthought of, or without the mind, though at the same time they are apprehended by, or exist in, itself". Stove argued that this claim proceeds from the tautology that nothing can be thought of without its being thought of, to the conclusion that nothing can exist without its being thought of.

The following is Stove's homely version of Berkeley's GEM (1991:139):

(1) You cannot have trees-without-the-mind in mind, without having them in mind.

(2) Therefore, you cannot have trees-without-the-mind in mind.

 (i) Is a tautology (self-referential statement); therefore the premise of this argument is trivially true.

 (ii) Is not a trivially true conclusion. The logic flowing from 1) to 2) is valid (as this premise cannot lead to a false conclusion), but unsound because tautological premises can bring only tautological conclusions.

Refer to Stove's 1991 book The Plato Cult & Other Philosophical Follies chapter 6 Idealism: A Victorian Horror Story for numerous elucidations and numerous GEM's quoted from the history of philosophy and GEM's reconstructed in syllogistic form.

For readers familiar with Nietzsche, Russell and Stove's criticism of Idealism it is clear that Stove's GEM merely repackages Russell's precise points and borrowing Nietzsche's polemics against idealism.

John Searle

In The Construction of Social Reality John Searle offers an attack on some versions of idealism. Searle conveniently summarises two important arguments for idealism. The first is based on our perception of reality:

1. All we have access to in perception are the contents of our own experiences
2. The only epistemic basis we can have for claims about the external world are our perceptual experiences therefore,
3. the only reality we can meaningfully speak of is the reality of perceptual experiences (The Construction of Social Reality p. 172)

Whilst agreeing with (2), Searle argues that (1) is false, and points out that (3) does not follow from (1) and (2).

The second argument for idealism runs as follows:

Premise: Any cognitive state occurs as part of a set of cognitive states and within a cognitive system

Conclusion 1: It is impossible to get outside of all cognitive states and systems to survey the relationships between them and the reality they are used to cognize

Conclusion 2: No cognition is ever of a reality that exists independently of cognition (The Construction of Social Reality p. 174)

Searle goes on to point out that conclusion 2 simply does not follow from its precedents.

Alan Musgrave

Alan Musgrave in an article titled Realism and Antirealism in R. Klee (ed), Scientific Inquiry: Readings in the Philosophy of Science, Oxford, 1998, 344-352 -later re-titled to Conceptual

Idealism and Stove's GEM in A. Musgrave, Essays on Realism and Rationalism, Rodopi, 1999 also in M.L. Dalla Chiara et. al. (eds), Language, Quantum, Music, Kluwer, 1999, 25-35 -Alan Musgrave argues in addition to Stove's GEM, Conceptual Idealists compound their mistakes with use/mention confusions and proliferation of unnecessary hyphenated entities.

Stock examples of use/mention confusions:

Santa Claus (the person) does not exist.

'Santa Claus' (the name/concept/fairy tale) does exist; because adults tell children this every Christmas season.

The distinction in philosophical circles is highlighted by putting quotations around the word when we want to refer only to the name and not the object.

Stock examples of hyphenated entities:

things-in-itself (Immanuel Kant)

things-as-interacted-by-us (Arthur Fine)

Table-of-commonsense (Sir Arthur Eddington)

Table-of-physics (sir Arthur Eddington)

Moon-in-itself

Moon-as-howled-by-wolves

Moon-as-conceived-by-Aristotelians

Moon-as-conceived-by-Galileans

Hyphenated entities are "warning signs" for conceptual idealism according to Musgrave is because they over emphasis the epistemic (ways on how people come to learn about the world) activities and will more likely commit errors in use/ mention. These entities do not exist (strictly speaking and are ersatz entities) but highlight the numerous ways in which people come to know the world.

In Sir Arthur Eddington's case use/mention confusions compounded his problem when he thought he was sitting at two different tables in his study (table-of-commonsense and table-of-physics). In fact Eddington was sitting at one table but had two different perspectives or ways of knowing about that one table. Richard Rorty and Postmodernist Philosophy in general have been attacked by Musgrave for committing use/mention confusions. Musgrave argues that these confusions help proliferate GEM's in our thinking and serious thought should avoid GEM's.

Philip J. Neujahr

"Although it would be hard to legislate about such matters, it would perhaps be well to restrict the idealist label to theories which hold that the world, or its material aspects, are dependent upon the specifically cognitive activities of the mind or Mind in perceiving or thinking about (or 'experiencing') the object of its awareness." (Kant's Idealism, Ch. 1)

Idealism in Religious Thought

A broad enough definition of idealism could include most religious viewpoints. The belief that personal beings (e.g., God and the angels) preceded the existence of insentient matter seems to suggest that an experiencing subject is a necessary reality. Also, the existence of an omniscient God suggests, regardless of the actual nature of matter, that all of nature is the object of at least one consciousness. Materialism sees no incoherence in a scenario of there being a cosmos where no sentient subject ever develops; a wholly unknown universe where neither any subject, nor any object of a subject's experience ever exists. Historically, Mechanistic Materialism has been the favorite viewpoint of Atheist philosophers. Still, idealistic viewpoints that have not included God, supernatural beings, or a post-mortem existence have sometimes been advanced.

While many religious philosophies are indeed specifically idealist, for example, some Hindu denominations view regarding the nature of Brahman, souls, and the world are idealistic, some have favored a form of substance dualism. Mahayana Buddhist denominations have usually embraced some form of idealism, while some Christian theologians have held idealist views, substance dualism has been the more common view of Christian authors, especially with the strong influence of the philosophy of Aristotle among the Scholastics. Several modern religious movements, for example the organizations within the

New Thought Movement and the Unity Church, may be said to have a particularly idealist orientation.

The theology of Christian Science includes a form of subjective idealism: it teaches that all that exists is God and God's ideas; that the world as it appears to the senses is a distortion of the underlying spiritual reality.

To meet Wikipedia's quality standards, this section may require cleanup.

Please discuss this issue on the talk page, and/or replace this tag with a more specific message. Editing help is available.

This section has been tagged since September 2006.

A Course in Miracles, a spiritual self-study course published in 1976, represents an explicitly idealist, pure non-dualistic thought system. In the Course, only God and His Creation, which is Spirit and has nothing to do with the world, are real. The physical universe is an illusion and does not exist. The Course compares the world of perception with a dream. It arises from the projection of the dreamer, i.e. the mind ("projection makes perception," T-21.in.1:5), according to its wishes (perception "is the outward picture of a wish; an image that you wanted to be true," T-24.VII.8:10). The purpose of the perceptual world is to ensure our separate, individual existence apart from God but avoid the responsibility and project the guilt onto others. As we learn to give the world another purpose and recognize our perceptual errors, we also learn to look past them or "forgive," as a way to awaken gradually from the dream and finally remember our true Identity in God. The Course's non-dualistic metaphysics is similar to Advaita Vedanta. What A Course in Miracles adds, is that it gives a motivation for the seeming though illusory existence of the perceptual world.

The West is inundated with physicalistic monism. There is widespread belief that everything will be explained in terms of matter/energy by science. Since we are constantly taught this it may make the idea of mentalistic monism hard to grasp. One way to begin to grasp the idea is through analogy. One analogy is the movie screen. If we next consider "Star Trek's holodeck" it takes us a step further as what appear to be physical objects are not. Next consider the movie "The Matrix". In "The Matrix" even people's bodies and identities are projected. Then replace the machine with a vast and powerful mind. A last analogy is our dreams at night. We seem to be in a world filled with other objects and other people and yet nothing of it is real. Although this is not a strict philosophical argument it does allow us to begin to think along these lines.

Idealism is based on the root word "Ideal," meaning a perfect form of, and is also described as a belief in perfect forms of virtue, truth, and the absolute. (i.e., Webster's Dictionary says "conforming exactly to an ideal, law, or standard: perfect."). idealism in comparison to pragmatism

OTHER USES

In general parlance, "idealism" or "idealist" is also used to describe a person having high ideals, sometimes with the connotation that those ideals are unrealisable or at odds with "practical" life.

The word "ideal" is commonly used as an adjective to designate qualities of perfection, desirability, and excellence. This is foreign to the epistemological use of the word "idealism" which pertains to internal mental representations. These internal ideas represent objects that are assumed to exist outside of the mind.

HUMAN RIGHTS

Human rights refers to inherent, universal rights of human beings regardless of jurisdiction or other factors, such as ethnicity, nationality, or sex.

The idea of human rights descended from the philosophical idea of natural rights; some recognize no difference between the two and regard both as labels for the same thing while others choose to keep the terms separate to eliminate association with some features traditionally associated with natural rights.

As is evident in the United Nations Universal Declaration of Human Rights, human rights, at least in the post-war period, are conceptualized as based on inherent human dignity, retaining their universal and inalienable character.

The existence, validity and the content of human rights continue to be the subject to debate in philosophy and political science and many other forms. Legally, human rights are defined in international law and covenants, and further, in the domestic laws of many states. However, for many people the doctrine of human rights goes beyond law and forms a fundamental moral basis for regulating the contemporary geo-political order. For them, they are democratic ideals.

Human Rights Legislation

Where it has been adopted, legislation commonly contains:

- security rights that protect people against crimes such as murder, massacre, torture and rape
- liberty rights that protect freedoms in areas such as belief and religion, association, assembling and movement
- political rights that protect the liberty to participate in politics by expressing themselves, protesting, participating in a republic
- due process rights that protect against abuses of the legal system such as imprisonment without trial, secret trials and excessive punishments
- equality rights that guarantee equal citizenship, equality before the law and nondiscrimination
- welfare rights (also known as economic rights) that require the provision of education and protections against severe poverty and starvation
- group rights that provide protection for groups against ethnic genocide and for the ownership by countries of their national territories and resources

History

Appalled by the barbarism of the Second World War, the United Nations General Assembly adopted the Universal Declaration of Human Rights in 1948. While not legally binding, it urged member nations to promote a number of human, civil, economic and social rights, asserting these rights are part of the "foundation of freedom, justice and peace in the world". The declaration was the first international legal effort to limit the behavior of states and press upon them duties to their citizens following the model of the rights-duty duality.

Many states wanted to go beyond the declaration of rights and create legal covenants which would put greater pressure on states to follow human rights norms. Because some states disagreed over whether this international covenant should contain economic and social rights (which usually require a greater effort to fulfill on the part of individual states), two treaties were prepared.

In 1966 and 1976 respectively, the International Covenant on Civil and Political Rights and the International Covenant on Economic, Social and Cultural Rights came into force. With the Universal Declaration of Human Rights these documents form the International bill of rights.

- ...recognition of the inherent dignity and of the equal and inalienable rights of all members of the human family is the foundation of freedom, justice and peace in the world" -Preamble to the Universal Declaration of Human Rights, 1948

Since then several other pieces of legislation have been introduced at the international level:

- Convention on the Prevention and Punishment of the Crime of Genocide (entry into force: 1951)
- Convention against Torture (entry into force: 1984)
- Convention on the Elimination of All Forms of Racial Discrimination (entry into force: 1969)
- Convention on the Elimination of All Forms of Discrimination Against Women (entry into force: 1981)
- Convention on the Rights of the Child (entry into force: 1989)
- Rome Statute of the International Criminal Court (entry into force: 2002)

With the exception of the non-deformable human rights (the four most important are the right to life, the right to be free from slavery, the right to be free from torture and the right to be free from retroactive application of penal laws), the UN recognises that human rights can be limited or even pushed aside during times of national emergency -although "the emergency must be actual, affect the whole population and the threat must be to the very existence of the nation. The declaration of emergency must also be a last resort and a temporary measure". Conduct in war is governed by International Humanitarian Law.

INTERNATIONAL BODIES

The International Covenant on Civil and Political Rights created an agency, the Human Rights Committee to promote compliance with its norms. The 18 members of the committee express opinions as to whether a particular practice is a human rights violation, although its reports are not legally binding.

A modern interpretation of the original Declaration of Human Rights was made in the Vienna Declaration and Programme of Action adopted by the World Conference on Human Rights in 1993. The degree of unanimity over these conventions, in terms of how many and which countries have ratified them varies, as does the degree to which they are respected by various states. The UN has set up a number of bodies to monitor and study human rights, under the leadership of the UN High Commissioner for Human Rights (UNHCHR).

Regional Legislation

There are also many regional agreements and organisations governing human rights including the European Court of Human Rights, which is the only international court with jurisdiction to deal with cases brought by individuals (rather than states); the African Commission on Human and Peoples' Rights; Inter-American Commission on Human Rights; Cairo Declaration on Human Rights in Islam; Inter-American Court of Human Rights; and Iran's Defenders of Human Rights Center.

History of Human Rights

Ur-Nammu, the king of Ur created what was arguably the first legal codex in ca. 2050 BC. Several other sets of laws were created in Mesopotamia including the Code of Hammurabi, (ca. 1780 BC) which is one of the best preserved examples of this type of document. It shows rules and punishments if those rules are broken on a variety of matters including women's rights, children's rights and slave rights.

The Persian Empire (Iran) established unprecedented principles of human rights in the 6th century BC under the reign of Cyrus the Great. After his conquest of Babylon in 539 BC, tne king issued tne Cyrus Cylinder, dıscovered in 1879 and recognized by many today as the first human rights document. The cylinder declared that citizens of the empire would be allowed to practice their religious beliefs freely. It also abolished slavery, so all the palaces of the kings of Persia were built by paid workers in an era where slaves typically did such work. These two reforms were reflected in the biblical books of Chronicles and Ezra, which state that Cyrus released the followers of Judaism from slavery and allowed them to migrate back to their land. The cylinder now lies in the British Museum, and a replica is kept at the United Nations headquarters.

Three centuries later, the Mauryan Empire of ancient India established unprecedented principles of civil rights in the 3rd century BC under the reign of Ashoka the Great. After his brutal conquest of Kalinga in circa 265 BC, he felt remorse for what he had done, and as a result, adopted Buddhism. From then, Ashoka, who had been described as "the cruel Ashoka" eventually came to be known as "the pious Ashoka". During his reign, he pursued an official policy of nonviolence (ahimsa). The unnecessary slaughter or mutilation of animals was immediately abolished, such as sport hunting and branding. Ashoka also showed mercy to those imprisoned, allowing them outside one day each year, and offered common citizens free education at universities. He treated his subjects as equals regardless of their religion, politics or caste, and constructed free hospitals for both humans and animals. Ashoka defined the main principles of nonviolence, tolerance of all sects and opinions, obedience to parents, respect for teachers and priests, being liberal towards friends, humane treatment of servants (slavery was non-existent in India at the time), and generosity towards all. These reforms are described in the Edicts of Ashoka.

Elsewhere societies have located the beginnings of human rights in religious documents. The Vedas, the Bible, the Qur'an and the Analects of Confucius are some of the oldest written sources which address questions of people's duties, rights, and responsibilities.

In 1215 King John of England issued the Magna Carta, a document forced upon him by the Pope and English barons, which required him to renounce certain rights, respect certain legal procedures and accept that the will of the king could be bound by law. Although the document did not itself limit the power of the king in the Middle Ages, its later reinterpretation in the Elizabethean and Stuart periods established it as a powerful document on which constitutional law was founded in Britain and elsewhere.

In 1222, the Manden Charter in Mali was a declaration of essential human rights, including the right to life, and opposed the practice of slavery.

Several 17th and 18th century European philosophers, most notably John Locke, developed the concept of natural rights, the notion that people possess certain rights by virtue of being human. Though Locke believed natural rights were derived from divinity since humans were creations of God, his ideas were important in the development of the modern notion of rights. Lockean natural rights did not rely on citizenship nor any law of the state, nor were they necessarily limited to one particular ethnic, cultural or religious group.

Two major revolutions occurred that century in the United States (1776) and in France (1789). The United States Declaration of Independence includes concepts of natural rights and famously states "that all men are created equal, that they are endowed by their creator with certain unalienable rights, that among these are life, liberty and the pursuit of happiness."

Similarly, the Declaration of the Rights of Man and of the Citizen defines a set of individual and collective rights of the people. These are held to be universal -not only to French citizens but to all men without exception.

Philosophers such as Thomas Paine, John Stuart Mill and Hegel expanded on the theme of universality during the 18th and 19th centuries. In 1831 William Lloyd Garrison wrote in a newspaper called The Liberator that he was trying to enlist his readers in "the great cause of human rights" so the term human rights probably came into use sometime between Paine's The Rights of Man and Garrison's publication. In 1849 a contemporary, Henry David Thoreau, wrote about human rights in his treatise On the Duty of Civil Disobedience which was later influential on human rights and civil rights thinkers. United States Supreme Court Justice Davis Davis, in his 1867 opinion for Ex Parte Milligan, wrote "By the protection of the law, human rights are secured; withdraw that protection and they are at the mercy of wicked rulers or the clamor of an excited people."

Many groups and movements have managed to achieve profound social changes over the course of the 20th century in the name of human rights. In Western Europe and North America, labour unions brought about laws granting workers the right to strike, establishing minimum work conditions and forbidding or regulating child labour. The women's rights movement succeeded in gaining for many women the right to vote. National liberation movements in many countries succeeded in driving out colonial powers. One of the most influential was Mahatma Gandhi's movement to free his native India from British rule. Movements by long-oppressed racial and religious minorities succeeded in many parts of the world, among them the civil rights movement, and more recent diverse identity politics movements, on behalf of women and minorities in the United States.

Bibliography

Ahmad, Imtiaz: *State and Foreign Policy: India's Role in South Asia*, New Delhi, Vikas, 1993.

Alte, I.D.: *Rural Employment of Scheduled Castes*, New Delhi, Deep & Deep, 1992

Appleby, Paul H.: *Policy and Administration*, Birmingham, AL: University of Alabama Press, 1949.

Augustine, P.A.: *Social Equality in Indian Society*, New Delhi, Concept, 1991

Austin, Granville: *The Indian Constitution: Cornerstone of a Nation*, Oxford, Clarendon Press, 1966.

Bailey, F.G.: *Caste and the Economic Frontier*, Manchester, MUP, 1957.

Barill, C.: *Social and Political Ideas of B.R. Ambedkar*, Jaipur, Aalekh Publishers, 1977.

Basu, Prahlad K.: *Governance and Public Administration for Poverty Reduction*, Salvador, Brazil, 1997.

Baxi, Upendra: *The Crisis of the Indian Legal System*, New Delhi, Vikas, 1982.

Bhai, N.: *Harijan Women in Independent India*, Delhi, BR Publishing, 1986.

Bhatia, B.M.: *Indian Agriculture: A Policy Perspective*, New Delhi, Sage, 1988.

Brecher, Michael: *The Politics of Succession in India*, Connecticut, Greenwood, 1976.

Brierly, L.: *The Law of Nations*, New York, Oxford University Press, 1955.

Calman, J.: *Toward Empowerment: Women and Politics in India*, Colorado, Westview Press, 1992.

Carl J. Friedrich: *Constitutional Government and Democracy*, Boston, Ginn, 1950.

Chandel, M.P.S.: *A Social Force in Politics: Study of Scheduled Castes of UP*, New Delhi, Mittal, 1990.

Chandra, R.: *Judicial System in India*, Lucknow, Print House (India), 1992.

Charles Howard McIlwain: *Constitutionalism: Ancient and Modern*, N.Y., Cornell University Press, 1958.

Conway, Margaret : *Political Analysis: An Introduction*, Boston, Allyn and Bacon, 1972.

David H.: *Public Administration: Understanding Management, Politics, and Law in the Public Sector*, New York, McGraw-Hill, 1993.

Deaton, Angus, and Valerie Kozel: *The Great Indian Poverty Debate*, Delhi, MacMillan India Ltd., 2005.

Dennis, L.: *Public Policy Management and Public Policy*, New York, Longman, 1999.

Derrett, J. : *Religion, Law, and the State in India*, London, Faber, 1968.

Dunner, Joseph: *Dictionary of Political Science*, New York, Philosophical Library, 1964.

Dwight Waldo: *Study of Public Administration*, New York, Random House, 1955.

Eldridge, P.J.: *The Politics of Foreign Aid in India*, New York, Schocken, 1970.

Ezra, N.: *Bureaucrats and Policy Making*, New York, Holmes & Meier, 1984.

Francis, E.: *Bureaucratic Power in National Politics*, Boston, Little Brown and Company, 1978.

Freeman, J.M.: *Untouchable. An Indian Life History*, London, Allen & Unwin, 1979.

Galanter, M.: *Competing Equalities: Law and the Backward Classes in India*, Berkeley, University of California Press, 1984.

Gargan, J.: *Handbook of Local Government Administration*, New York, Marcel Dekker, 1997.

Ghose, S.K.: *Politics of Violence: Dawn of a Dangerous Era*, Springfield, Nataraj, 1992.

Hans J. : *Politics Among Nations: The Struggle for Power and Peace*, New York, Knopf, 1960.

Hazard, H.J.: *The Soviet System of Government,* Chicago, University of Chicago Press, 1960.

Heimanson, Rudolph: *Dictionary of Political Science and Law,* N.Y.: Oceana Publications, 1967.

Howard, McIlwain: *Constitutionalism: Ancient and Modern,* N.Y., Cornell University Press, 1958.

Jack Peltason: *Federal Courts in the Political Process,* New York, Random House, 1955.

Jain, C.K.: *Rajiv Gandhi and Parliament,* New Delhi, CBS, 1992.

Jalal, A.: *Nationalism, Democracy, and Development: State and Politics in India,* Delhi; New York: Oxford University Press, 1997.

Jannuzi, F. : *India's Persistent Dilemma: The Political Economy of Agrarian Reform,* Boulder, Colorado: Westview Press, 1994.

Jenkins, Rob: *Democratic Politics and Economic Reform in India,* New York, Cambridge University Press, 1999.

Jones, W.H.: *The Government and Politics of India,* London, Hutchinson, 1971.

Joshi, B.: *A Democracy in Search of Equality: Untouchables, Politics and Indian Social Change,* New Delhi, Hindustan, 1982.

Joshi, Vijay: *India: Macroeconomics and Political Economy, 1964-1991,* Washington, World Bank, 1994.

Kashyap, C.: *National Policy Studies,* New Delhi, Tata McGraw-Hill for the Lok Sabha Secretariat, 1990.

Leslie, J.: *Toward Empowerment: Women and Politics in India,* Colorado, Westview Press, 1992.

Little, I.M.D.: *India: Macroeconomics and Political Economy, 1964-1991,* Washington, World Bank, 1994.

Mary, W.: *Asian Power and Politics: the Cultural Dimensions of Authority,* Cambridge, Belknap Press, 1985.

Max, Beloff: *Foreign Policy and the Democratic Process,* Baltimore, Johns Hopkins University Press, 1955.

Michael, B.: *The Politics of Succession in India,* Connecticut, Greenwood, 1976.

Morris, W.H.: *The Government and Politics of India*, London, Hutchinson, 1971.

Mukerji, S.K.: *Science in India: A Changing Profile*, New Delhi, Indian National Science Academy, 1984.

Nevitte, Neil, and Charles H. Kennedy: *Ethnic Preference and Public Policy in Developing States*, Boulder, Lynne Rienner Publishers, 1986.

Paul, H.: *Policy and Administration*, Birmingham, AL: University of Alabama Press, 1949.

Prahlad, K.: *Governance and Public Administration for Poverty Reduction*, Salvador, Brazil, 1997.

Prasad, S. : *Dr. Ambedkar. Social Justice and Political Safeguards for Depressed Classes*, New Delhi, Shree, 1991.

Pye, Lucian W. and Mary W.: *Asian Power and Politics: the Cultural Dimensions of Authority*, Cambridge, Mass, Belknap Press, 1985.

Robert, W.: *Public Bureaucracy and the Incentive Problem*, Washington, D.C., World Bank, 1994.

Schmidhauser, R.: *Supreme Court: Its Politics, Personalities and Procedures*, New York, Holt, 1960.

Sharman, R.: *Aspects of Political Ideas and Institutions in Ancient India* Delhi, Motilal Banarsidass, 1968.

Singh, D.R.: *Rural Leadership among Scheduled Castes*, Allahabad, Chugh, 1985.

Sondhi, Sunil: *Science, Technology, and India's Foreign Policy*, Delhi, Anamika Prakashan, 1994.

Srivastava, R.C.: *Judicial System in India*, Lucknow, Print House (India), 1992.

Subbarayappa, B.V.: *Science in India: A Changing Profile*, New Delhi, Indian National Science Academy, 1984.

Subhash, C.: *National Policy Studies*, New Delhi, Tata McGraw-Hill for the Lok Sabha Secretariat, 1990.

Sullivan, Ezra N.: *Bureaucrats and Policy Making*, New York, Holmes & Meier, 1984.

Victor G. : *Law as a Political Instrument*, New York, Random House, 1955.

Index

A

Administration, 52, 58, 83, 95, 98, 177, 180, 224.
Agriculture, 61, 107.
Alan Musgrave, 255, 256.
Ambassadors, 32, 33, 35.
Ancient Period, 45.
Architecture, 236.
Aristocracy, 45, 46, 88, 89, 194.
Aristotle, 1, 2, 21, 46, 52, 174, 175, 190, 194, 195, 257.
Art, 4, 30, 174, 233.
Arthur Collier, 246.
Ashoka, 263.
Assembly, 38, 40, 41, 42, 88, 92, 119, 122, 131, 135, 150, 188, 196, 197, 230, 260.

B

Bertrand Russell, 253.
British Idealism, 249.
British Rule, 216, 265.
Buddhism, 242, 263.
Buddhist, 1, 20, 191, 242, 257.
Bureaucracy, 56.
Bureaucratic Politics, 18, 55.

C

Challenges, 14, 19, 239.
Civil Liberties, 38, 65, 87, 91, 95, 96.
Civil Rights, 8, 43, 95, 96, 185, 198, 263, 265.
Civil Service, 58, 182.
Classical Realism, 232, 234, 235, 237.
Commission, 17, 41, 97, 160, 181, 262.
Committee, 93, 185, 262.
Communist Party, 66, 223.
Comparison, 34, 67, 87, 100, 136, 259.
Constitutional Courts, 184, 188, 189.
Constitutional Structure, 218, 224.
Contemporary Studies, 2.
Corporation, 70.
Corruption, 206, 214.
Critical Theory, 13.
Criticisms, 13, 51, 213, 217.
Cube Rule, 160, 161, 164.
Currency, 49.

D

David Stove, 251, 253, 254.
Demand Schedule, 73.
Department, 3, 9, 33, 58, 187.
Diplomacy, 8, 12, 15, 16, 30, 31, 32, 33, 34, 35, 36, 37, 180, 235.

E

Economic Growth, 199, 214, 215, 216, 238.
Economic Policy, 224.
Employment, 31.
Energy, 78, 79, 209, 258.
Entrenchment, 185, 186.

Evaluations, 78.
Executives, 90, 102, 104, 128, 162.

F

Federation, 218, 219, 220, 221, 222, 223, 224, 225, 226, 228, 229.
Friedrich Nietzsche, 251.

G

George Berkeley, 242, 245.
Governance, 2, 46, 54, 86, 185, 223, 234, 240.
Governmental Constitutions, 182.
Governmental Operations, 180.

H

High Commissioner, 262.
Historiography, 22, 24, 25, 26, 27, 28, 29.
Human Rights, 8, 9, 17, 38, 42, 44, 185, 188, 189, 211, 229, 240, 241, 259, 260, 261, 262, 263, 264, 265.

I

Identity, 51, 141, 158, 258, 265.
Incentive, 34, 57, 59, 60, 121, 176.
Independence, 54, 264.
Industry, 94, 98, 194.
Influential Power, 102, 105, 107, 108, 109.
Informal Diplomacy, 37.
Institution, 9, 19, 78, 131, 240.
Insurance, 65, 70 91.
International Relations, 1, 3, 8, 9, 10, 11, 12, 13, 14, 15, 16, 17, 18, 19, 20, 22, 23, 30, 232, 233, 237, 238, 239, 240.
International Trade, 216.

J

John Searle, 255.
Jonathan Edwards, 246.
Judge, 4, 176, 189, 211.
Judgement, 192.
Judicial Activism, 85.
Justice, 3, 45, 46, 50, 54, 55, 180, 189, 222, 261, 265.

L

Languages, 33.
Leader, 93, 94.
Legacy, 43.
Liberal Realism, 235.
Local Government, 41.

M

Majoritarian Elections, 114, 115, 121, 124, 127, 133, 159, 164.
Malebranche, 244, 245.
Management, 34, 89, 95, 152, 196.
Measurement, 78.
Military, 10, 36, 37, 180, 200, 213, 223, 232, 233, 234, 235, 237, 238.
Mission, 31, 35.
Monarchs, 7, 203, 204.
Motivation, 55, 236, 258.

N

Natural Resources, 14.
Natural Rights, 179, 180, 259, 264.
Neorealism, 11, 15, 235, 236, 237, 239.

O

Operation, 21, 68, 96, 120, 128, 213, 243.
Ownership, 65, 66, 69, 70, 84, 94, 98, 209, 260.

P

Parliamentary Constitutions, 114, 145, 156, 158, 159, 164.
Party Discipline, 108, 122, 123, 127, 131, 132, 133, 149, 167.
Party Executives, 162.
Payments, 97.
Plato, 1, 21, 46, 52, 175, 242, 243, 248, 254.
Political Economy, 1, 20, 45.
Political Freedom, 38, 214, 215.
Political History, 22, 24, 26, 191.
Political Ideologies, 4, 93, 176, 180.
Political Party, 40, 92, 91, 107, 111, 112, 170.
Political Power, 4, 5, 6, 77, 87, 88, 89, 91, 176, 177, 178, 229, 230, 231.
Political Stability, 58, 212, 214.
Poverty, 39, 179, 202, 215, 217, 240, 260.
Power Debate, 6.
Presidency, 170, 171.
Private Property Rights, 70, 97.
Profits, 65, 69, 72, 76, 77.
Proportional Elections, 114, 116, 121, 124, 133, 145, 156, 158, 165, 167, 168, 169.

R

Regional Legislation, 262.
Regulation, 63, 94, 96, 97.
Relations Theory, 9, 13, 240.
Resolution, 38.
Risks, 212.
Roman Empire, 21, 30, 191, 221.

S

Sanskrit, 20.
Single Party Executives, 162.
Social Changes, 49, 265.
Social Constructivism, 12, 13.
Social Contract, 48, 52, 53, 55, 175, 179, 192.
Social Justice, 54.
Social Welfare, 84, 97, 180.
Søren Kierkegaard, 251.
Stock Exchange, 67.
Strategy, 34, 138, 153, 234.
Structural Realism, 11, 235, 237.
Substitution, 76.
Supply Curve, 72, 74, 83.
Supply Schedule, 74.

T

Technology, 18, 74, 95, 205.
Territories, 182, 199, 219, 221, 225, 260.
Terrorism, 8, 41, 214.
Trades, 80, 84.
Transport, 180.
Tribal Democracy, 195.

U

University, 1, 2, 3, 9, 20, 34, 246, 249.

V

Vedas, 264.
Vedic Sanskrit, 20.

W

Welfare, 1, 20, 78, 84, 89, 97, 98, 100, 101, 140, 180, 199, 260.
World Bank, 214.
World Government, 181, 232.

❑❑❑